FOREIGN EXCHANGE MANAGEMENT

T. W. McRae
Management Centre, University of Bradford

and

D. P. Walker
Morgan Guaranty Trust Company, London

Prentice/Hall PHI International

ENGLEWOOD CLIFFS, NEW JERSEY   LONDON   NEW DELHI
SINGAPORE   SYDNEY   TOKYO   TORONTO   WELLINGTON

658.15
m 174

Library of Congress Cataloging in Publication Data

McRAE, THOMAS W
    Foreign exchange management.

    Bibliography: p.
    Includes index
    1. Foreign exchange   2. International business
enterprises — Finance. I. WALKER, DAVID P., joint
author. II. Title.
HG3851.M25   658.1'5   79-25099
ISBN 0-13-325357-0

British Library Cataloguing in Publication Data

McRAE, THOMAS WATSON
    Foreign exchange management.
    1. Foreign exchange administration
    2. Risk management
    I. Title   II. WALKER, DAVID P
    332.4'5   HG3853.R/

    ISBN 0-13-325357-0

ISBN 0-13-325357-0

PRENTICE-HALL INTERNATIONAL, INC.,
PRENTICE-HALL OF AUSTRALIA PTY., LTD., *Sydney*
PRENTICE-HALL OF CANADA LTD., *Toronto*
PRENTICE-HALL OF INDIA PRIVATE LIMITED, *New Delhi*
PRENTICE-HALL OF JAPAN, INC., *Tokyo*
PRENTICE-HALL OF SOUTHEAST ASIA PTE., LTD., *Singapore*
PRENTICE-HALL, INC., *Englewood Cliffs, New Jersey*
WHITEHALL BOOKS LIMITED, *Wellington, New Zealand*

Printed in the United States of America

80 81 82 83 84 5 4 3 2 1

To Catherine, our Parents and Pip

Contents

List of Figures and Tables

FIGURES

TABLES

Preface & Acknowledgments

PREFACE

This book is intended as a practical guide to foreign exchange exposure management. It is not an academic treatise, although recent findings by academic researchers, including those of the authors, are the foundations on which we have constructed our recommended procedures.

From 1946 until the late sixties little interest was shown in foreign exchange exposure. The Bretton Woods agreement of 1946 fixed the exchange rates between currencies within narrow limits and set down clear rules for altering these rates. The agreement was astonishingly successful. Possibly the most successful international agreement of all time. Most countries, and certainly all major countries, stuck by the rules. The fluctuation of foreign exchange rates was not a major problem of international trade.

Bretton Woods was built upon the US dollar, a strong currency, guaranteed by the world's most powerful trading nation. When, in the late sixties the US dollar fell sick, the Bretton Woods agreement collapsed. In 1971 an attempt was made to construct a new Bretton Woods at the Smithsonian Institute in Washington. The Smithsonian agreement failed and it was left to the free markets of the world to determine the exchange value of currencies.

The oil crisis sent the world's international money markets into turmoil. The rate of exchange between various currencies altered by as much as 5% in one day. The Smithsonian trade weighted index of the US dollar fell by 7% in 1979 alone. Sterling fell from 90% of the 1971 trade weighted index in January 1973 to 58% in November 1976 and then recovered to 73% by May 1980.

Such violent fluctuations affect almost every decision taken by a corporation which trades outside its own borders. The profits on contracts, the performance of foreign subsidiaries, the value of foreign assets and loans, the international tax liability, and the methods of international cash management are all strongly affected by changes in the rate of exchange between currencies.

All managers operating on the international market, not just international treasurers, need to understand (a) the mechanism of exchange fluctuations, (b) how to measure foreign exchange exposure and (c) how to hedge against exposure risk.

This book attempts to provide a strategic framework for measuring and hedging foreign exchange exposure risk: Part I provides the economic and institutional background, Part II the meat of the argument, and Part III the parameters and constraints on devising a foreign exchange exposure strategy.

There are some national or linguistic variations in the spellings of certain currencies. For consistency we have followed the style of *The Financial Times*.

ACKNOWLEDGMENTS

We are grateful to the many individuals and organizations for their assistance in the completion of this book. In particular, we would like to thank the treasury staff of the multinational companies who cooperated in our survey of foreign exchange management — without the time and information they so freely provided this book would not have been possible.

Part II of this book has also greatly benefited from the guidance given by Gunter Dufey of the University of Michigan, Dean Paxson of the Manchester Business School, and by Walter A. Gubert, John B. Haseltine, Alastair Hunter-Henderson, Peter J. Muller, Oliver W. Wesson and Michael B. Portington, all members of the International Money Management Group of Morgan Guaranty Trust Company of New York. It should be emphasised, however, that each Section of this book represents the views of the author. Remaining errors, of course, are entirely our own.

The following journals and organizations kindly gave us permission to publish material originally published by them: *The Economist, Financial Executive, Euromoney, Accounting Review, Business Horizons, Columbia Journal of World Business,* International Monetary Fund and the Institute of Chartered Accountants in England and Wales.

Finally, our thanks to Christina French, Pat Howard, Susan Solari, Christine Duncanson and Barbara Parry for their efficient handling of the manuscript.

T.W.M.
D.P.W.

May 1980

PART I

Background

T. W. McRAE

CHAPTER 1

Introduction

WHY IS FOREIGN EXCHANGE RISK SO IMPORTANT?

Ten years ago foreign exchange risk was seldom discussed. Things have changed. Now it is rare to read a corporation's annual report, or a discussion in the financial press about a corporation's performance, without some reference being made to the impact of foreign exchange risk. International business journals rarely make an issue which does not contain an article explaining some sophisticated technique of exposure management. A seemingly endless stream of seminars are advertised aimed at educating financial management in the complexities of foreign exchange risk. Why is foreign exchange risk so important today? We suggest three reasons:

the growth in international trade and financing
the increased magnitude of exchange rate fluctuations
the increasing visibility of the 'foreign exchange gain/loss' item in
    corporate financial statements.

The first two factors are the source of the foreign exchange risk problem; the third factor helps to explain why this problem is becoming increasingly important for corporate financial managers.

Table 1.1   The increase in the value of international trade 1948–1978

	1938	1948	1958	1968	1978*
Annual exports					
($ billion)	23	58	109	240	1450
Index	100	252	456	1008	6304
Periodic increase	1.00	2.52	1.81	2.21	6.25
(in money terms)					

*GATT Report January 1980

Source: United Nations Statistical Year Book, 1976. (Table 149, p. 424.)

The Growth in International Trade and Financing

The post-World War II period has witnessed a dramatic increase in international trading, as indicated in Table 1.1. The value of world trade has increased by a factor of 63 over the period 1938–1978. Part of this increase is due to inflation of course. After adjusting for inflation at 5% per annum (the average rate for advanced industrial countries over the period) we find that the volume of international trade increased sixfold between 1938 and 1975. Much of this increase has been due to the rapid growth of multinational companies over the period. We define 'multinationals' here in the broadest sense, to include all companies which have operating units located in more than one country. During the period 1950–1970 the sales of such companies increased tenfold in real terms.

Another important economic development over the last 20 years has been the substantial increase in international financing. The Euro-dollar market, for instance, has increased 20-fold in the last ten years to an estimated US $400 billion in 1978. The increase in the size of the Eurobond market, if less spectacular than its short-term counterpart, has also been substantial: at the end of 1977 the total value of Eurobonds was estimated at $74 billion. Clearly, corporate treasurers now look to world financial markets to raise funds.

The Increased Incidence of Exchange Rate Fluctuations

The huge increase in international trade and financing has resulted in enormous sums of money being transmitted across international frontiers. This immediately raises a problem. All the countries of the world do not use the same currency. The United States uses the dollar, the United Kingdom the pound sterling, and Guatemala the

quetzal, for instance. At the beginning of 1979
currencies were in circulation. If funds are to be tra
currency frontier then a swap between two currenci
effected. Here lies the root of the problem. How
currency *x* are equal to a unit of currency *y* — or m
how many units of *x will be* equal to a unit of *y*?

If all of the countries of the world fixed the value of .... currencies
inflexibly to a single commodity (e.g. gold) or a single major currency
(e.g. the US dollar), then little attention would be paid to exposure
management. Foreign exchange gains and losses would only arise as
and when these inflexible arrangements were altered, which would be
an uncommon and fairly predictable event. However, when most of
the world's major currencies are floating — with occasional and much
less predictable intervention from their central banks — then exposure
management becomes a major problem of international business.

Such a shift, from a relatively fixed to a very flexible exchange
rate regime, occurred in the early 1970s. The background to this
change is explained in the following chapter. As Figure 1.1 indicates,
it has created a situation where large currency movements have taken
place. Moreover, such movements can occur over a very short time
horizon. During the last two or three years, for instance, the US dollar
and the UK pound have altered several times by as much as 5% against
each other in a single day. Let us recall a single incident which
illustrates what can happen in a floating exchange rate system.

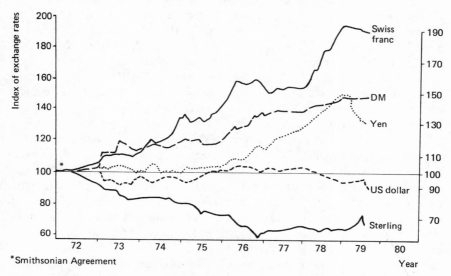

*Smithsonian Agreement

Figure 1.1 Index of Trade-weighted Values of Major Currencies since the
Smithsonian Agreement

August 1976 the UK pound stood at around $1.78. In early September the Bank of England ceased its abortive attempt to keep up sterling's value and it quickly fell to $1.66. The pound traded around this level until an article appeared in *The Sunday Times* on 24 October 1976 suggesting that one of the key conditions of the IMF loan then being negotiated was that the pound be allowed to fall to a 'defensible' level of $1.50. The truth of this report was immediately denied in official quarters but the next day the pound suffered its largest fall ever, dropping 11 cents or 7% against the US dollar in one day to $1.55. Subsequently, these losses were recovered — from November 1976 to November 1978, for instance, the pound appreciated by 35% against the dollar.

Clearly, changes of these magnitudes can have a dramatic effect on the performance of a company. A currency movement of a few percentage points can wipe out or double the profit on an international contract. A loan denominated in a foreign currency can, overnight, become a crushing financial burden because of the collapse of the company's 'home' currency. No international company can ignore the problem of foreign exchange risk in today's flexible exchange rate system.

The Increased Visibility of Foreign Exchange Gains and Losses

A third and very important reason for the significance of foreign exchange risk today is that the resulting gains and losses are now much more 'visible' because of stricter accounting rules. We are referring here, of course, to the impact that Financial Accounting Standard No. 8 (FASB 8) has had in the USA. By requiring that all (realized *and* unrealized) foreign exchange gains and losses be taken directly into each period's income statement, FASB 8 has generated greater swings in reported profits for US companies (and those foreign companies with a New York Stock Exchange listing).[1]

This increased visibility has clearly had a behavioral impact on US corporations who are now much more concerned with their accounting exposures. By contrast, European foreign currency accounting regulations are more flexible. In many countries the consolidation of foreign subsidiaries' financial statements is not required, and elsewhere the use of deferral or reserve accounting has reduced the visibility of certain kinds of foreign exchange loss. As Chapter 4 will demonstrate, this difference in accounting regulations has created parallel differences in the way US and European companies define and manage their exposures. Given the dominance of US multinational corporations in international business, however, the general point remains valid: the increased visibility of foreign exchange gains/losses in US financial statements has increased the behavioral significance of the foreign exchange risk problem.

In sum, then, foreign exchange risk has now become a major problem of international business. This book addresses the question of how this problem should be handled by international companies.

STRUCTURE OF THE BOOK

This book is organized into three sections, as follows.

Part I provides the economic and institutional background. In Chapter 2 the historical development of the international monetary system is analyzed and the prospects for future changes are assessed. Chapter 3 describes the mechanics of the foreign exchange markets, explaining the arithmetic of the transactions and the organization of the market.

Part II is the core of the book. It analyzes the development of a corporate exposure management program in a logical and systematic manner. The starting point for the formulation of such a program must be to decide exactly what the company controls which is exposed to foreign exchange risk. Chapter 4 categorizes and analyzes alternative exposure definitions and proposes a methodology for measuring these exposure types on a group and after-tax basis.

Chapter 5 then outlines a two-part exposure information system. The exposure identification system enables the company to calculate its exposures for each of the exposure types developed in the previous chapter. The management information system provides details of the decision parameters and constraints to be considered in deciding what exposure management action is required. Each part provides examples of the kind of exposure reports which are necessary.

Once group exposures are defined and measured, the company must decide how these are to be managed. Exposure management strategies are analyzed in Chapter 6. Aggressive and defensive risk/ return approaches are analyzed with reference to the currency forecasting debate. Defensive strategies are then evaluated and policy recommendations made for each of three prototype firms: the occasional exporter/importer, the significant exporter/importer and the multinational company.

Alternative tactics for the implementation of these strategies are evaluated in Chapters 7 and 8. Chapter 7 provides a classification of exposure management techniques into those which are 'internal' to the firm (netting, matching, leading and lagging, pricing policies and asset and liability management) and those which are 'external' (forward contracts, short-term borrowing, discounting, factoring and government exchange risk guarantees). Internal and external techniques are then examined in Chapter 7 and 8 respectively, in the context of both translation and cash flow exposure management where appropriate.

Finally, Chapter 9 evaluates and makes recommendations on how the corporate exposure management function should be organized. Organizational alternatives are analyzed for companies at various stages of international development. Six case studies are presented, illustrating the costs and benefits of such organizational approaches as export finance companies and reinvoicing vehicles.

Part III discusses the environmental factors and constraints within which the corporate exposure management function must exist. Chapter 10 examines the critical subject of exchange rate forecasting and the current debate between academics and practitioners on the usefulness of such forecasts. The methodology of currency forecasting is discussed and the track record of some forecasters is presented and evaluated.

Tax and exchange control constraints on exposure management are described and evaluated in Chapters 11 and 12.

NOTES

1. The FASB 8 requirement is currently being examined with a view to making it less onerous. It seems likely that a variation of the all-current rate method will be introduced in 1981, as explained in Chapter 4.

CHAPTER 2

The Development of the International Monetary System

THE ROLE OF MONEY

The completion of a business contract implies that each party has obtained a value at least equal to the value it has surrendered, otherwise the deal would not have been completed. Before the introduction of the common currency of money a deal was completed by swapping goods or services of at least equivalent value. The introduction of money introduced a small complication into the bargaining process since one party to the deal received money instead of goods. The money would be held for a period of time before being exchanged for goods of equivalent value. The small complication arose because the party who received money had to be convinced that the money was a genuine store of value which would hold its value through time so that it could be exchanged for goods of equivalent value at a later date.

The earliest form of money solved the store-of-value problem by using relatively scarce metals such as gold, silver or copper. These metals had a market value per unit of weight and so the current exchange value of the money could be found by simply weighing the coins. The value of the money was determined by the market value of the metals. A Venetian trader could swap cloth for gold coins in China as long as he had confidence in the purity of the gold in the coin, his confidence in the government issuing the coin was irrelevant. There was no essential difference between a French merchant selling wine in France or Egypt or Mexico, so long as he was paid in money coined in a precious metal since he was, in effect, swapping commodities as in a system of barter. He swapped so much wine for so much gold. Later he swapped the gold for some other commodity in some other part of the world.

An international payments system based on precious metals was by no means a perfect system. For example, the purity of the gold could be diluted with other metals making it difficult for a trader to assay the precise amount of gold in the coin. Precious metals are heavy and so difficult to transport. The volume of precious metals is limited and a sudden scarcity might provide insufficient funds to finance the desired rate of trade, and so on. The 19th century economic literature on international finance is almost exclusively devoted to a discussion of these deficiencies, but such a system has one outstanding advantage, namely that the value of a unit of international money, i.e. gold, is underpinned by the market value of the metal. It is not determined by international confidence in the government stamping out the gold coins.

We noted above that the volume of precious metal available might be insufficient to finance the desired volume of trade. An early and most important development in the history of credit occurred when governments overcame the scarcity by issuing coins with a face value far in excess of the value of the metal contained in the coin. This type of money is called *fiat* money. Its value is determined by the declaration of the issuing authority. In some cases fiat money can be converted into a precious metal such as gold at a given rate of exchange, but in many more cases this option is not available. The value of fiat money is thus certainly dependent on the confidence of the holders in the integrity of the issuing authority. If the issuing authority, for example the central bank, should decide to print a great deal more fiat money, without any corresponding increase in the real income of the community, then the value of fiat money will fall in the hands of the holders. Confidence in fiat money depends upon confidence in the issuing authority, which is usually the government.[1]

Another problem created by using fiat money in international trade is that each country issues its own fiat money. In the case of gold, the gold market can handle supply and demand for a single homogeneous community. In the case of fiat money, a foreign exchange market is needed to swap the dozens of different currencies that are supplied and demanded. A foreign exchange market is a much more complicated market than a gold market – some currencies are not wanted or not available, the depth of the market varies between currencies, some currencies have a forward market, others do not, and so on. We will discuss the mechanism of the foreign exchange market in the next chapter. The major events in the history of the development of international monetary systems are shown in Figure 2.1.

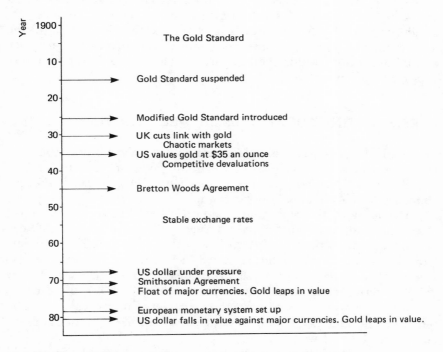

Figure 2.1 Major Events affecting Exchange Rate Systems 1900–1980

THE GOLD STANDARD

During most of the 19th and the early part of the 20th century international trading was conducted using a system called the gold standard. The principles on which this system was built were very simple. The pound (£) sterling, for example, a principal trading currency, was declared to be worth a certain weight of gold. Most international deals were denominated in sterling. Once the deal was completed the party receiving money, i.e. sterling, could either use this money to buy goods or services or, if he wished, take the sterling to the Bank of England and swap it for an equivalent amount of gold. So long as the Bank of England maintained a fixed ratio between its store of gold and the amount of fiat money issued, the pound sterling was 'as good as gold'. The international trader could have complete confidence in sterling as a store of value (if he had confidence in gold).

Note that the essential conditions for maintaining the gold standard are (a) the value of the fiat currency is fixed by reference to a certain weight of gold, (b) the currency is freely convertible into gold, (c) the international community have complete confidence in the integrity of the institution issuing the fiat currency, and (d) gold can be freely exported and imported.

FREE FLOATING CURRENCIES BETWEEN THE WARS

The gold standard was suspended during World War I but in 1925 the United Kingdom reintroduced convertibility in an attempt to stabilize world trade. The attempt was unsuccessful and in 1931 the UK abandoned the gold standard for good.

The ending of the pure gold standard ushered in one of the most chaotic periods in the history of international finance. Gold had been removed as the ultimate arbiter of the value of international money. How much was a US dollar, a Swedish Krone, or a Spanish peseta worth? How much would it be worth in three months time? In one year? International trade was severely disturbed by the lack of confidence in the value of foreign currencies. Currencies were competitively devalued in a desperate attempt to increase the devaluing countries' share of world trade.

A further consequence of the breakdown of the gold standard in 1931–1936 was the extraordinary growth of exchange controls. Each government set up a labyrinthine maze of legal impediments to prevent the export of its currency. These exchange control systems reached their zenith, or perhaps one should say nadir, in the 1950s.

The value of exchange controls in supporting the external value of the currency is highly dubious, but they have provided a lucrative income to lawyers and accountants. The exchange control system set up in the United Kingdom was one of the most complex of all. In Chapter 12 we will discuss the conventional procedures of exchange control.

The United States adopted the modified gold standard in 1935. This system differs from the pure gold standard run by the Bank of England in that (a) the US Treasury would buy and sell gold for foreign currency only to another government agency and (b) the export and import of gold was prohibited. However the price of gold was fixed at $35 an ounce, and the US Government guaranteed that it would control the price at this level. Rather surprisingly, despite inflation, it did maintain this price for 36 years until 1971!

The heavy unemployment and serious disruption of world trade experienced between 1931 and 1938 has been blamed on the breakdown in the international currency system during this period. It seems likely that the real causes lay much deeper.

BRETTON WOODS

Towards the end of World War II the governments of the leading trading nations of the free world decided that the chaotic financial conditions of the inter-war period could not be tolerated after the war had ended. The leading monetary experts came together at Bretton Woods in the USA in 1945 to hammer out an international currency system which would stabilize the external value of the world's main currencies. This conference replaced the pure gold standard with a dollar—gold standard and established the International Monetary Fund (IMF) to administer the system.

The Bretton Woods agreement turned out to be brilliantly successful. Once sterling had been devalued from $4 to a more realistic $2.80 in 1948 the external values of the currencies of the world's leading trading nations remained remarkably stable against one another for 18 years from 1949 to 1967.

In effect the Bretton Woods agreement replaced gold with the US dollar as the common measure of value and tied the value of the US dollar to a fixed weight of gold. Every one of the 43 countries setting up the IMF agreed a fixed exchange rate between their currency and the US dollar. They also agreed to control the fluctuations in value between their currency unit and the dollar to within 1% of the agreed rate. If the government of a beleaguered currency felt that it was no longer able to maintain its currency value within the agreed ±1% band then it could negotiate an adjustment with the IMF. The IMF would agree the adjustment *in advance* with the other members of the fund. Thus retaliatory devaluations were avoided.

The US Government agreed to maintain the value of gold at its 1935 price of $35 an ounce. The other members of the fund agreed to maintain the value of their currency within 1% of the agreed fixed exchange rate with the dollar.[2]

The onus of making the system work was placed squarely on the back of the authorities supervising the non US currencies. The monetary authority in each of these countries was required to monitor the dollar exchange rate and take action if the rate approached either the upper or lower bound. Each monetary authority maintains a stock of foreign currency and gold. If the exchange rate approaches the lower bound, the authority buys its own currency by using up this stock, if the rate approaches the upper bound it sells its own currency for foreign currency and so drives the value of its currency down, this results in the stock of its foreign currency rising.

If the stock of foreign exchange and gold is not sufficient to hold up the external value of the currency, other tools of economic control such as raising the interest rate or cutting government expenditure are available. (We will return to this point later.) If all else fails the government can negotiate a new fixed exchange rate with the IMF.

Note that if all the other countries in the scheme do their duty the dollar is automatically maintained within its limit with other currencies. The US Government need not intervene in the world's currency markets to control the value of the dollar. It is difficult to control the external value of a single currency without the cooperation of other governments.

THE LINK WITH GOLD IS BROKEN

The Bretton Woods agreement began to break down between 1968 and 1971. One by one the major currencies of the world broke away from the limits set by the agreement. In 1971 the United States Treasury decided to break the link between the dollar and gold. The United States was no longer prepared to sell gold for dollars at a fixed rate of exchange. The gold-backed dollar standard was at an end.

The end of the Bretton Woods agreement marked the end of the most successful era of stable international money since the gold standard was suspended in 1915. The basic unit of value, an ounce of gold, was no longer immutable at $35. The value leapt to $40, then $100 and by January 1980 had reached the incredible figure of $800 an ounce. By the end of 1973 international money had lost its basic unit of value. Even the US dollar, for so long the accepted unit of account, began to lose credibility as a constant store of value as inflation reached substantial levels in the United States.

The imminent collapse of international monetary stability threatened the growth of international trade. On 17 and 18 December 1971 the major trading nations of the world met at the Smithsonian Institution in Washington and hammered out a new agreement on international money. The key decisions of this conference were as follows:

1. Currency values were realigned in terms of the US dollar. The dollar was devalued by around 7% against other major currencies.
2. The margins within which a currency was allowed to fluctuate in value were widened to 2¼% either way from the central rate.
3. Gold was upvalued from an official rate of $35 an ounce to $38 an ounce.

THE FREE FLOATING ERA

Unfortunately, the 1971 Smithsonian agreement enjoyed only a limited success. The year 1973 ushered in the era of free floating currencies. One by one the major international currencies – the US dollar, the pound sterling and the Japanese yen floated freely on the world's money markets. Huge devaluations and revaluations became the order of the day. The dollar, in particular, declined steadily in value against many other major currencies. The oil crises of 1974 and 1979 destabilized the world's money markets as the exporters of oil built up immense short-term currency holdings in US dollars, and many other countries ran up equally immense balance of trade deficits.

The several attempts which were made during the late 1970s to underpin the world's international monetary structure ended in spectacular failure. Individual countries began to despair of a world solution and various groups of countries tried to design mechanisms within which they could float their joint currencies as a *block float* against the dollar (see Table 2.1).

The best known example of this partial solution to the international money problem was the 'snake' set up by the European Economic Community (EEC). This was followed by the rather more ambitious European Monetary System (EMS). The last section of this chapter is devoted to a discussion of these two systems.

CURRENCY AREAS

The Bretton Woods dollar/gold system virtually set up the whole non-communist world as a US dollar area, but within this area there still existed substantial sub-systems based on the value of other major currencies.

Many small countries, and even some large ones, preferred to tie the value of their currency to a major currency, usually the currency of a country with which they had close trading links. The job of external currency management was, in effect, delegated to a 'big

Table 2.1 Currency areas. The table shows those major currencies to which other countries have pegged their own currencies. Many of the independent floaters kept their currencies closely in line with the US dollar, although the link was informal.

(a) *Independent Floaters*	(c) *US Dollar Peggers*	(d) *French Franc Peggers*
Japan	Bahrain	Cameroon
Philippines	Barbados	Central African Empire
Spain	Bolivia	Gabon
UK	Ghana	Ivory Coast
USA	Guatemala	Madagascar
Yugoslavia	Haiti	Niger
Canada	Indonesia	Togo
Greece	Pakistan	Upper Volta
Mexico	Paraguay	
Nigeria	Rwanda	(e) *S.D.R.* † *Peggers*
Saudi Arabia	Ethiopia	Tanzania
Iceland	Costa Rica	Malawi
Portugal	El Salvador	Iran
Norway/Sweden	Jamaica	Uganda
	Libya	Zambia
(b) *EMS*participants*	Trinidad & Tobago	Jordan
Belgium	Venezuela	Kenya
Denmark	Dominica	
W.Germany	Egypt	(f) *'Other' Basket Peggers*
Netherlands	Guyana	Tunisia
France	Honduras	Austria
Italy	Iraq	Cyprus
Ireland	Korea	Fiji
Luxembourg	Syria	Finland
	Thailand	Malaysia
	S. Africa	Malta
		Morocco
		Sri Lanka

*   EMS   – European Monetary System
†   SDR   – Special Drawing Rights, see p. 17.

Adapted from: Heller, H.R., 'Choosing an Exchange Rate System", *Finance and Development,* June 1977.

brother'. The external value of the currency of the smaller country was protected from the large oscillations which a currency of tiny volume can be subject to if left to itself.

The largest currency area, outside the US dollar area, was the sterling area which was created in 1931 when the UK cut the link with gold. In the early days it encompassed most of the British

Empire, Africa and South East Asia. The setting up of rigid exchange controls during World War II and after, reduced the area considerably. One by one its members opted out, usually into the dollar area. When sterling was floated on 23 June 1972 the sterling area was, in effect, abolished. By 1979 the sterling area consisted of little more than the UK, the Channel Islands, the Gambia and Gibraltar. Despite this fact, over 10% of world trade is still denominated in sterling.

Several other currencies are used as international trading currencies outside their own country. The French franc is the external currency of the franc area based on the old French Empire mainly in West Africa. The Russian rouble is used as the currency of the Comecon countries in Eastern Europe, and we should not forget that the Deutsche Mark is the currency of invoice of rather more of world trade than the pound sterling. Some currencies are tied to the value of the Special Drawing Rights (SDRs) issued by the IMF — the Malawian kwacha for example. Ambitious plans have been floated to create a new currency, called the Europa, which will be used as the common currency of the EEC. This leads us into a discussion of international currencies not based on the currencies of nation states.

INSTITUTIONAL CURRENCIES

All of the international currencies discussed previously were based on the external use of the internal currency of a nation state — the US dollar, the pound sterling, the Russian rouble or the French franc. Only gold, which is a commodity not a currency, was not based on the confidence attached to the government of a nation state.

The problem in using the internal currency of a nation state as an international currency is that the relative value of the currency tends to become entangled in the internal politics of the nation state. For example, an approaching election might tempt the government of the state to expand the money supply (to encourage economic growth) and this may well cause internal inflation and external devaluation of the currency. Only in those few countries like the United States and Germany, where the monetary authorities are relatively independent of government control, would this not be true. Even in the United States, benign neglect of the falling external value of the dollar from 1976 to November 1978 was essentially a tactic determined by the internal political setup.

Over the years many schemes have been suggested for creating a truly international currency issued by a *supranational* organization. Maynard Keynes, the English economist, suggested the use of an international currency called Bancor which would be issued by an international central bank, a bank of banks. The key idea behind the scheme is to persuade nation states not to run continuing deficits or surpluses on their balance of payments and so destabilize the world economy.

The Bretton Woods agreement established the International Monetary Fund as a kind of world central bank to fulfil this role and in 1969 the IMF created a form of international currency called Special Drawing Rights (SDRs). This currency could be used to supplement gold and foreign (national) currencies in a nation state's foreign reserves. SDRs were created to supplement the world's stock of international liquidity, there being a theory, popular in the late 1960s, that the expansion of world trade was being held back by a shortage of international liquidity. The volume of SDRs could be allowed to expand to meet the needs of international trade.

In fact international liquidity expanded too rapidly in the 1970s and the need for SDRs abated. The facility, however, is still available. SDRs are held by many countries as part of their foreign exchange reserves and the quantity of SDRs can be expanded by the IMF if the need for them arises.

THE WERNER REPORT

The European Economic Community was set up in 1958 to coordinate the economies of several of the major countries of Western Europe. From its inception it was suggested that monetary union must be an essential precondition of ultimate economic union. In 1968 a working party was set up by the Council of Ministers to suggest a series of stages leading to economic and monetary union. This commission under the chairmanship of Pierre Werner of Luxembourg, is popularly known as the Werner Commission and its report as the Werner Report.[3]

The Commission's objectives were threefold: (a) total convertibility of currencies, (b) the elimination of fluctuations in exchange rates, (c) the fixing of irrevocable parity rates. In order to achieve these within the EEC it made the following recommendations:

1. monetary and economic policy should be coordinated,
2. the budgets of governments should be harmonized in accordance with EEC policy,
3. taxation systems and policies should be harmonized,
4. the capital markets of the EEC should be integrated.

These heroic objectives were supposed to be realized by 1980, but the disparate economic performance of the various economies in the EEC has prevented this.

One consequence of the Werner Report was the implementation of the EEC currency 'snake'. The government responsible for controlling each currency agreed to keep the value of their currency within 2% of an agreed norm. The snake has proved of limited success in stabilizing currency values since not all the EEC countries, the UK and France for example, remained in the snake for long.

The failure of the snake encouraged discussion of a common currency for the EEC. The idea had been around since 1958 but in 1975[4] and 1978[5] major pressure groups pushed the idea to the fore. The adoption of a common currency by all of the countries within the EEC would be introduced in two stages. During the first the national currency would run in parallel with a common EEC currency called the Europa. The exchange rate between the national currency and the Europa would be based on a weighted average of the participating currencies. The contribution of a national currency to the weighted average of the Europa would rise by the rate of inflation of its consumer price index. Thus strong pressure would be imposed on each national government to avoid inflation. A high relative inflation rate would entail a government paying over a great deal of money to the European Central Bank. This money would presumably be raised from local taxation. In effect, the Europa system would reduce inflation rate differences between EEC currencies by taxing the inflation differential.[6]

The individual persons or companies in each EEC country could hold either Europas or their national currency as liquid assets. Since the Europas would be partly inflation-indexed they would presumably gradually replace the local currencies. This would lead to the second stage when a single currency, the Europa, would be adopted as the currency of the EEC. All currency controls within the EEC would be abolished automatically by this step.

We have spent some time discussing the problems of setting up a common currency within the EEC because it seems likely that this move may be the harbinger of a series of attempts to create composite currency areas in various parts of the world such as the Andean Pact countries, Comecon countries and the Middle East. The removal of currency fluctuations between a group of countries brings useful benefits by encouraging trade and investment, but a common currency also entails a common or harmonized monetary policy. This, in turn, entails a surrender of a certain portion of national sovereignty to the supranational monetary authority.

In the long run the imposition of monetary discipline on a country by the supranational authority will benefit the citizens of that country. The trouble is that in the short run the supranational authority becomes a tempting target for politicians who are afraid to tell the constituents who voted them into power the naked truth about the economic consequences of their own lack of discipline. Monetary cooperation implies economic and political cooperation. Without this a supranational currency has no chance of success.

THE EUROPEAN MONETARY SYSTEM

The introduction of a common currency for the EEC is still a distant objective (in 1980) but a step in this direction was taken in 1979 with the introduction of the European Monetary System (EMS). This block float of member countries against external currencies is intended to stabilize internal trading values within the EEC and so encourage internal trade by reducing currency risk.

Seven countries within the EEC have linked the value of their currencies in such a way that the maximum difference between their values is restricted within given bounds. The system is unusual in that *two* mechanisms have been set up to link currency values. The first is a conventional parity grid. A central rate is agreed for each currency and the monetary authority controlling this currency agrees to maintain the value of its currency within 2¼% of this central rate against other currencies (Italy is allowed ±6%) (see Table 2.2).

The second mechanism of control involves the ECU, the newly created European Unit of Account. The ECU is a composite currency unit made up of a basket of European currencies. The relative weight each currency contributes to the value of the ECU depends upon the income and trade of the country concerned. The Deutsche Mark makes up about one third of the total value of the ECU since Germany accounts for about one third of the total income of the participants in the scheme.

Each currency has a central parity rate against the ECU and a percentage margin beyond which it must not vary without permission. The percentage margin varies with each currency. If a currency contributes a great deal of the ECU's value the margin is narrow. If the currency contributes only a small part of the ECU's value, the margin is wide. Thus, currencies in the EMS operate within two margins, the parity grid margin and the ECU margin. The ECU margin is said to be tighter than the parity grid margin for most currencies. The ECU itself is not stable but floats as the currencies of which it is composed float up or down against external currencies. Also, the ECU cannot under the scheme be traded like other national currencies.

Table 2.2 The bounds on currency values within the European Monetary System. A possible grid.

ECU central rates	The fixed points for EMS: Parity grid: upper and lower limits					
1 ECU	1 DM	1 FFr	1 G	100 BFr	100 lire	100 Kr.
Irish £ 0.663	0.270	0.117	0.249	1.718	0.613	0.956
	0.258	0.112	0.238	1.642	0.544	0.914
DKr 7.086	2.887	1.250	2.664	18.36	6.553	
	2.760	1.195	2.546	17.55	5.812	
Lire 1148	485.6	210.3	448.1	3090		
	430.7	186.5	397.4	2740		
Belg/Lux Fr 39.46	16.07	6.958	14.83			
	15.37	6.652	14.18			
Guilder 2.721	0.944	0.480				
	0.902	0.459				
FFr 5.798	2.362					
	2.258					
DM 2.511						

Source: The Economist, 17 March 1979, p. 74.

What happens if a currency within the EMS bumps up against its lower or upper bound? Various lines of credit, both short-term and long-term, have been made available to assist central banks in keeping their rates within the agreed margins. Full EMS members can borrow unlimited funds for up to six weeks, short-term funds for up to nine months via central bank swaps are available and inter-government credits for several years can be arranged. These credits will be used to cover a temporary payments imbalance. A permanent imbalance of trade would require an agreed alteration in the central exchange rate of the currency. It is hoped that sometime in the future these temporary arrangements can be replaced by a fully fledged European Monetary Fund to administer the system.

SUMMARY

When money replaced barter in international trading the initial solution was to choose a single commodity, gold, as the international currency. The value of gold was determined by supply and demand for the commodity, not by confidence in the government issuing the gold coins.

When paper 'fiat' money was introduced on a large scale for (internal) payment of debts in the 19th century it set a problem for traders operating in foreign countries. The pound sterling was not legal tender in Germany nor the US dollar in the United Kingdom. A market in foreign exchange developed in each country. The value of this fiat currency depended on confidence in the integrity of the government issuing the currency.

This problem was solved by introducing the pure gold standard whereby the monetary authority in each major country agreed to a fixed rate of exchange between a unit of its currency and a specific weight of gold. So long as various other conditions were fulfilled, such as the free export and import of gold, the value of a unit of foreign currency was 'as good as gold.'

The pure gold standard collapsed after World War I and a period of free floating exchange rates ensued. The uncertainty attached to the value of foreign currencies during this period inflicted serious damage on international trade and investment.

In 1935 the United States government agreed to try to maintain the price of gold at $35 an ounce. This ushered in the modified gold standard.

In 1945 the Bretton Woods agreement laid firm foundations to the modified gold standard by setting up the International Monetary Fund as a kind of World central bank. Each subscriber to the IMF agreed to maintain the external value of its currency within 1% of an agreed fixed rate with the US dollar. The United States Government, for its part, agreed to maintain the value of gold at $35 an ounce, and to freely buy or sell gold for dollars to other governments at this rate. The system proved to be durable so long as the world had confidence in the US dollar.

The long series of balance of payments deficits starting in the early 1960s weakened the free world's confidence in the US dollar. In August 1971 the US Treasury ceased to buy or sell gold for dollars at a fixed rate and the modified gold standard came to an end. Within eight years the free gold price leaped from $40 an ounce to over $800 an ounce. This reflected a general lack of confidence in paper currency as a store of value.

The floating currency value regime initiated in 1971 resulted in massive and sudden changes in the relative values of currencies. Frantic efforts were made to stabilize currency values by giving additional powers to the IMF to police manipulation of exchange rates. Various currency snakes were set up to limit the relative change in value of currencies. These control measures have achieved a very limited success.

Large fluctuations in the foreign exchange market can only be achieved by coordinating the economic management of the free world's economies. This, we believe, will take some time to achieve.

REVIEW QUESTIONS

1. What is the main advantage of using a precious metal as an international currency compared to, say, the US dollar?
2. Suggest some of the disadvantages of using gold as the international currency.
3. What is fiat money? What are its main advantages and disadvantages?
4. State the essential conditions for maintaining a gold standard for international payments.
5. If gold is removed as the ultimate arbiter of the external value of a currency, how can the currency be valued, i.e. against what?
6. Describe the modified gold standard adopted by the US in 1935. How did it differ from the classical gold standard used in the 19th century?
7. Describe the international currency system worked out at Bretton Woods in 1945. Why was it so successful? Why did it break down in 1971?
8. 'The onus of making the Bretton Woods agreement work was placed squarely on the back of the authorities supervising the non-US currencies.' Do you agree? Why?
9. What is the mechanism by which a central bank or treasury can control the external value of its currency?
10. What is the immediately observable cause of a weak currency?
11. Suggest two popular remedies for reviving a weak currency.
12. Describe the mechanism by which a fall in the external value of a currency can be halted by raising the level of internal interest rates.
13. Describe three currency areas. What is the advantage to a currency of small volume in tying itself to a major international currency? Can you think of any disadvantages?
14. What is an SDR? Why has it proved to be an inadequate substitute for gold?
15. What were the objectives of the Werner Report? What were its four recommendations?
16. Why is it proving so difficult to set up a common currency, the Europa, within the EEC?

17. Describe the mechanism of the 'block float' of EEC currencies within the European Monetary System (EMS).
18. What is the difference between the ECU and the US dollar as the basis for a multinational currency system?

NOTES

1. The Bank of England in the UK was an independent organization until it was nationalized in 1946. The US Federal Reserve is not directly controlled by the US Treasury. The German Bundesbank is not controlled by the government.
2. Actually several major contributors agreed a band width of 0.75% each side of the fixed rate, i.e. UK, France, Sweden.
3. See Interim Report on the establishment by stages of economic and monetary union (in the EEC). Supplement to Bulletin 7 – 1970 EEC Commission.

> 'On the realization by stages of economic and monetary union in the Community.'

> Presented to Council of Ministers. 8 October 1970. EEC Commission.

4. An influential group of economists advocated a common currency in 1975. See 'A Currency for Europe'. *The Economist* 1 November 1975.
5. In 1978 the Chairman of the EEC Commission advocated the speeding up of the process towards a common currency. The German Chancellor, Herr Schmidt and the French President Monsieur Giscard D'Estaing made sympathetic noises. The UK government opposed the idea.
6. See *The Banker* January 1978 pp. 22–25 for a useful discussion of the subject.

BIBLIOGRAPHY

Coombes C.A. (1976), *The Arena of International Finance*, New York, John Wiley.
Grubel H.G. (1969), *The International Monetary System*, Penguin Modern Economics, Harmondsworth, Penguin.
Hirsch F. (1967), *Money International*, Harmondsworth, Penguin.
Magnifico G. (1973), *European Monetary Unification*, London, Macmillan.
Triffin R. (1966), *The World Money Maze*, New Haven, Conn., Yale University Press.

CHAPTER 3

The Mechanics of Foreign Exchange

TYPES OF FOREIGN EXCHANGE MARKETS AND TRANSACTIONS

There are two types of foreign exchange market. The *interbank* market where banks exchange foreign currency between themselves, and the *commercial* market where corporations and individuals buy and sell currency.

There are three types of foreign exchange transaction. The *spot* trade, the *forward* trade and the *swap*. The spot trade is at the *current* rate of exchange offered between one currency and another. The forward trade represents a trade offered between one currency and another at *some future date*. The swap is a simultaneous sale and purchase of an amount of foreign currency for two different dates.

The payment date or value date on a spot transaction is usually two *business* days after the spot transaction is agreed. These two days allow the two parties to the deal to complete the debit and credit in their respective bank accounts in say New York and London. Occasionally, spot trades are made for *next day value*, i.e., US/Canadian dollar deals, and same day trades for cash are possible but unusual.

A forward transaction is set up when a deal is agreed to buy or sell currency at a fixed rate at a specific date in the future. No currency is received or sent until the future date arrives. However, the amount of money to be received or sent in the future in both currencies has now been fixed.

When banks trade between themselves in the interbank market or when they deal with large multinational corporations they usually use swap transactions. The swap is a useful device for investing idle cash balances and balancing out the maturity profile of a foreign exchange portfolio. The mechanism of swapping has become quite sophisticated with various types of swap available such as spot—forward and forward—forward swaps.

QUOTING FOREIGN EXCHANGE RATES

Foreign exchange rates can be quoted in one of two ways. The first way, the indirect quote, is to quote one unit of the local currency as equal to n units of the foreign currency. The second way, the direct quote, is to quote n units of the local currency as equal to one unit or 100 units of the foreign currency.

London invariably uses the first method of quotation; New York sometimes uses the second method,[1] for example:

In London (indirect quote)

> £1 is worth 1.7172 US dollars
> £1 is worth 4.23 Dutch guilders
> £1 is worth 477 Japanese yen

In New York (direct quote)

> 100 Deutsche Marks are worth 41.95 US dollars
> 100 Indian rupees are worth 11.35 US dollars
> 100 Japanese yen are worth 0.3245 US dollars

Care must be taken when reading off exchange rates to see which method is being employed.

A foreign exchange dealer may quote two rates (Table 3.1) to a potential customer — a *bid* rate and an *offer* rate. The dealer is willing to buy at the bid rate and sell at the offer rate. When he makes the quotation, he does not know whether his customer is a buyer or a seller of currency. For instance, in the example quoted in Table 3.1 the FE dealer is quoting a spread of DM 1.8222 to DM 1.8232 to the US dollar. This means that he is prepared to sell Deutsche Marks at 1.8222 to the dollar and buy them at DM 1.8232 to the dollar. Conversely, he will buy dollars at DM 1.8222 to the dollar and sell dollars at DM 1.8232 to the dollar.

Table 3.1 Quotation rates by foreign currency dealer in New York

A dealer in New York quotes the following rates to a customer. He does not know if the customer is a buyer or a seller.

US$1	1.8222	1.8232	DM
US$1	1.6175	1.6205	Sw.Fr.
US$1	194.70	194.90	Yen

Note: This assumes that the dealer is quoting using the indirect system, i.e. in units of foreign currency per US dollar.

THE SPREAD

The bank does not charge a large fee to a trading customer, it makes most of its profit from the *spread* between the bid price and the offer price. It charges a small commission in many countries. The spread is conventionally very narrow in stable currencies with a high volume of trading. However, in unstable, infrequently traded currencies, it can become a good deal wider. It widens with uncertainty — the spread on international trading currencies such as the pound, the US dollar or the Deutsche Mark will widen if the international money markets are in turmoil.

By convention, a currency is quoted to four decimal places or four significant figures. The units of quotation are called *points* or *pips*. For example, a quotation of DM 3.9825 to DM 3.9845 has a spread of 20 points or 20 pips. Among themselves, foreign exchange dealers often quote only the junior pips in a transaction. For example, in the above case they would quote '25 to 45'.

The value of a currency is often expressed as a single figure, i.e. £1 is worth DM 3.9835, rather than being quoted as both a bid and offer rate. This single rate is the *middle rate* arrived at by adding the bid and offer rate together and dividing by two. In the example given the dollar bid rate is 3.9825 and the dollar offer rate 3.9845, so the middle rate is $(3.9825 + 3.9845)/2 = 3.9835$.

The foreign exchange dealer need not quote the same rate to every customer. Large regular customers may be quoted rather better rates than small irregular customers. Large deals may receive better quotes than small deals since transaction costs vary little with the size of the deal. The dealer's existing book of deals will also affect the rate offered. If a transaction will balance his book he is more likely to quote a favorable rate. This applies particularly to forward rate quotes where the volume of trading is lower. It is worth shopping around!

If the transaction is too large to be handled all at once the dealer may offer an *at best* deal. This means that he will try to sell or buy the currency over a period of time – hours or days. The customer pays the average rate over all deals.

Finally, a customer in the United States may tell the dealer to buy or sell currency if the exchange rate reaches a specified figure. This can protect a company treasurer against sudden changes in currency values. This type of instruction is called a *stop out*.

OFFICIAL AND FREE MARKET RATES

Many currencies have an *official* rate at which they are supposed to trade against other currencies. This rate is usually stipulated by the government of the given country. The value of the currency is supposed to fluctuate within a narrow band around the official rate of exchange. Before 1972 most of the major international trading nations had agreed fixed exchange rates with the International Monetary Fund (IMF) and they helped each other to keep their currencies within this intercurrency 'snake'. In 1972 a number of important currencies including sterling opted out of the fixed parity system and allowed their currencies to *float*.

A special category of currencies are those which have an official rate, stipulated by government, which differs widely from the free market rate. For example, on 18 March 1977 the following official and free market rates per US dollar (banknotes) were quoted by the Foreign Commerce Bank in Zurich, Switzerland:

	Currency unit	Free market rate	Official rate
Ghana	New Cedi	8.000	1.150
Japan	Yen	280.0	308.0
Nigeria	Naira	.9000	.6535
Israel	Pound	9.500	8.780
Uganda	Shilling	20.00	8.160

Where the free market rate is very different from the official rate, the free market rate is usually the relevant rate in calculating the value of a contract.[2]

CROSS RATES

The *cross rate* between currencies is the ratio of two external currencies both expressed in the local currency. For example, if the spot rate between the pound and Italian lire is 1 : 1518 and that between the pound and French franc is 1 : 8.4936, the cross rate between the lire and the franc is 1518/8.4936 = 178.72. A table of cross rates is printed daily in the financial press.

THE FORWARD MARKETS

A forward exchange contract covers the purchase or sale of a fixed value of foreign currency into local currency at some future date. The most common period is three months ahead but contracts for one month, six months, nine months or even a year ahead are not uncommon. 'Odd day' transactions outside these conventional periods can also be arranged.

Only a few forward markets are *deep*, in the sense that a large volume of business is transacted in them. The deep markets are between the US dollar and sterling, the West German Deutsche Mark and the Swiss franc. Outside these currency channels the market tends to be shallow, particularly in times of economic instability.

Many currencies have no forward market. Several have forward markets at times of financial stability which dry up immediately economic conditions threaten to become unstable. Certain banks and individuals are known to keep forward books on individual currencies in stable times (see Appendix 3A on pages 41—42). The movement out of fixed parities in 1973 dried up many of the forward markets, and generally disorganized this sector of the FE market, although activity is now increasing. International financial stability is an essential condition of cheap, deep, and long forward exchange markets. It seems unlikely that these conditions will prevail during the last quarter of the present century.

The trouble with shallow FE markets, whether spot or forward, is that a single large transaction can move the market price by a substantial amount. Thus the market is only able to absorb large transactions by spreading them over a period of time.

The forward market in sterling and US dollars handles a volume of business which is about 10% that of the spot market, but interest in using the forward market seems to be increasing among traders in the advanced industrial nations. Forward rate premiums and discounts do not vary as much as spot rates since they are ultimately determined by relative interest rates in the two countries concerned, unless exchange control regulations intervene. However, forward margins, premiums or discounts, increase in times of financial uncertainty as the demand and supply for future currencies affects the demand for funds and so the rate of interest.

Participation in the forward market is often strictly controlled by exchange control regulations. In France, for example, a forward contract in foreign exchange is only permitted on a firm contractual commitment in a foreign currency. However, in the USA, UK, West Germany and Switzerland dealings on the forward exchange market are less restricted and this provides traders in these countries with more flexibility in their use of the forward markets.

QUOTING FORWARD RATES

Forward rates are quoted as being at either a *premium* or a *discount* on the spot rate. For example if the spot rate for sterling to dollars is 1 : 1.6314 and the three months forward rate is 1 : 1.6009, the dollar is standing at a premium of 305 points to the pound.

Notice that when the method of quotation is *n* units of foreign currency to one unit of the local currency (as it is with sterling) then the premium is subtracted from the spot rate and the discount is *added* to arrive at the forward rate. When *n* units of local currency are expressed as one unit of the foreign currency then the reverse rule applies: the premium is added and the discount subtracted to arrive at the forward rate.

This calculation is a common source of error in the arithmetic of foreign exchange. Always remember that when more units of currency A are required in the future to buy the same number of units of currency B, then currency A is falling in value relative to B and will, therefore, stand at a discount to currency B. When one currency stands at a discount to another it means that its forward exchange value is below the spot exchange value. When a currency is at a premium it means that the forward exchange value is above the spot exchange value. This is illustrated in the following examples.

A London dealer quotes the following rates between sterling and the French franc:

Spot: £1 = FFr 8.50
Forward — 3 months — 3.5 centimes discount

The three months forward rate is therefore 8.5000 + 0.0350 = FFr 8.5350 to the pound sterling.

A Dutch dealer quotes the following rates between the Dutch guilder and the US dollar:

Spot: $1 = DG 2.4552 (Dutch guilders)
Forward — one month — 1.5 points (DG) premium

The one month forward rate is therefore 2.4552 + 0.0150 = DG 2.4702 to the US dollar. Note that since we are quoting in one unit of the foreign currency we add the premium. It is the US dollar which is at a premium relative to the Dutch guilder, not vice versa.

These examples have quoted the forward exchange rate as a single price. Usually, rates are quoted on both a bid and offer price, as the following example indicates.

A London dealer quotes the following rates between sterling and the Swiss franc:

Spot: £1 = 4.31 — 4.33 Swiss francs
Forward — three months: 5.5 — 4.5 centimes premium.

	Bid SwFr	*Offer* SwFr
Spot sterling rate	4.310	4.330
Less: three months premium	0.055	0.045
Forward exchange rate — 3 months	4.255	4.285

If the customer offers the dealer £100,000 to be delivered in three months time, he will be offered, in return, SwFr425,500 to be delivered in three months. If the customer offers the dealer SwFr100,000 in three months time, he will be offered, in return, 100,000/4.285 = £23,337 to be delivered in three months.

CONVERSION TO ANNUAL RATE OF INTEREST

In Chapter 10 we will see that the forward premium or discount on one currency, relative to another, is closely related to the rate of interest available on external currency deposits denominated in the currencies of the two countries. For this reason, we will have occasion to convert the premium or discount into an annual rate of interest. A simple method of doing this calculation which is accurate enough for most purposes, is as follows:

$$\frac{\text{Annual rate}}{\text{of interest}} = \frac{\text{Spot rate} - \text{forward rate}}{\text{Forward rate}} \times \frac{12}{\text{Period (in months)}} \times \frac{100}{1}$$

For example, a London dealer quotes the following rates between sterling and the US dollar:

Spot: £1 = 2.2420
Forward – three months – 1.25 cents premium

Calculate annual rate of interest.

$$\text{Annual rate of interest} = \frac{2.2420 - 2.2295}{2.2295} \times \frac{12}{3} \times \frac{100}{1}$$

$$= 0.00561 \times 4 \times 100$$

$$= 2.24\% \text{ (approx)}$$

INVESTING FOR HIGHEST RETURN

So long as exchange control regulations permit, a company treasurer will wish to place his surplus funds in that currency market which provides the highest return. However, the rate of return will be affected by the probability of a devaluation or revaluation of the currency in which the loan is denominated. The treasurer can cover himself against this risk by selling the loan proceeds forward in the foreign exchange market. The true rate of return, therefore, must take the nominal rate of interest on the loan and adjust it for the cost of forward exchange cover. For example:

	Percentage rate	
	Bid	Offer
Euro-sterling market	8.75	9.25
Euro-dollar market	5.83	6.03
Spot rate: £1 =	1.7170	1.7180
Forward – 3 months premium	1.25c	1.15c
Forward rate – 3 months	1.7045	1.7065

A company treasurer has $1 million to invest for three months. He can obtain 8.75% (annual rate) on the Euro-sterling market. Does it pay him to convert the US dollars to sterling and loan the money for three months on the Euro-sterling market at 8.75% (annual rate)?

First convert the dollar premium to an annual rate:

$$r = \frac{0.0125}{1.7045} \times \frac{12}{3} \times \frac{100}{1} = 2.93\%$$

	(%)
Euro-sterling rate – 3 months money	8.75
Less: annualized dollar premium (%)	2.93
	5.82

The Euro-dollar market rate, at 5.83, is marginally higher than the covered Euro-sterling rate over the three-month period. Therefore, he invests the money in the Euro-dollar market.

THE ORGANIZATION OF THE FOREIGN EXCHANGE MARKET

There are up to four participants in the foreign exchange market. The foreign exchange dealers or brokers, the commercial banks, the customers, and usually, the exchange control agency. The United States does not have an exchange control agency, although the Federal Reserve Board has responsibility for this function.

Foreign Exchange Dealers in the UK

The foreign exchange dealers stand at the heart of the FE market in the UK where there are 13 accredited dealers operating. They are 'accredited' in the sense that they have been given permission to operate as FE brokers by the Bank of England.

An FE dealer in the UK is a money *wholesaler*. He only deals in very large amounts of currency. He normally deals with the FE department of a commercial bank although certain large organizations such as multinationals deal with him directly. The Bank of England has tried to organize the foreign exchange market so that the commercial banks operate between the commercial customers and the FE dealers. In the UK dealers do not use their own funds to stabilize the price of currencies.

Since FE dealers pitch their prices to match the daily supply and demand conditions in the market, they do not attempt to predict the future value of currencies. The forward rates on foreign exchange simply reflect the *current* supply and demand conditions for currencies in the future and in the long term are *not* a good predictor of FE rates. As we shall see later, they reflect interest rate differentials in the two countries.

In the USA and UK there is no central building, such as the Stock Exchange, within which foreign currency contracts are exchanged. The dealers in the FE market are connected to one another by telephone and electronic visual display units. Contracts are initially oral contracts which are typed out later, batched by computer at the end of each day, and sent out to the other contracting party. Dealers' offices vary in size from a mere dozen operators to as many as 150 handling the transactions.

The FE market is now an international market that never closes. Somewhere in the world, night and day, someone is buying and selling currency. The larger banks deal continuously for 24 hours a day handing on 'open' transactions in London to be closed in some far off market by an associate company. The dealers have agreed a set of generally accepted 'ground rules' as to how FE transactions are conducted and they have also developed an international jargon to facilitate accurate transmission of information. These developments have greatly assisted the efficiency of FE market operations.

Foreign exchange brokers in the USA

Commercial banks in the United States normally operate their foreign currency transactions through foreign exchange brokers. For example, the eight foreign exchange brokers working in New York receive hundreds of bids and offers for foreign currency each day from banks and the treasury departments of the very large multinational corporations.

The broker acts as an intermediary, putting the bidding banks in contact with banks offering the same currency. He arranges transactions but does not himself buy or sell currency. He charges a small commission on each deal he arranges, at around one hundredth of one per cent (0.01%) of the selling price of the deal. This commission is shared equally between the buyer and seller of the currency. Deals are usually expressed in so many units of foreign currency per US dollar. There is no official agency in the United States to regulate the activity of foreign exchange brokers, but brokers police their own operations very efficiently. Errors or misunderstandings are invariably settled amicably.

The commercial banks

In the UK all the commercial banks operate foreign exchange dealing rooms. In the United States a few large banks in New York transact most of the foreign exchange business on behalf of the myriad of smaller banks throughout the country. These smaller banks operate their deals through correspondents in the New York money market. A large number of foreign banks operate foreign exchange departments in New York and London.

The large banks in New York and London tend to specialize in certain currencies and so act to create an efficient market in these currencies. They will buy and sell, at a price, and this ensures the existence of a market. The banks, however, will normally be trying to balance their books in each currency. This market in foreign exchange between the large banks is, as we noted above, called the *interbank* market. It is the pressures of demand and supply in this market which usually determines the exchange value of a currency, except in those cases where the central bank intervenes to manipulate the currency value.

Organisation of a bank's FE department

The FE department of a bank generally resides within the treasury division which is controlled by the bank's international treasurer. A chief dealer reports to this individual and has general responsibility for currency dealing including individual control limits on currency traders.

Various currency traders, sitting at the end of telephones, handle specific currencies. The traders link the bank's customers with the dealers or brokers, making quotations and arranging deals. They must be aware of the bank's changing portfolio of deals and have a good ear for coming changes in the market. Since they commit the bank to specific deals and can make substantial profits and losses in the fine margins operating in foreign exchange deals, FE traders hold a very responsible position calling for cool nerves and very quick thinking.

Foreign exchange trading results in real profit or loss plus opportunity profit or loss. The calculation of total profit or loss for a trading period is thus quite a difficult accounting operation. Kubarych (1978) discusses the problem in some detail.

Settlement of foreign exchange transactions

Foreign exchange transactions are normally arranged by word of mouth over the telephone. The dealer or broker fills in a trading slip or trade ticket with the key details of dates, customer, currency, rate and amount. The trading slips are numbered in sequence in advance for the purpose of control. The sequence is audited later for missing tickets. The slips are passed to the accounting office where the formal foreign exchange contract is completed. This includes, at least, the date of the transaction, the name and address of the customer, the value date for completion, the exchange rate agreed, the amounts of both currencies involved and the various instructions regarding payment.

The payment instructions can be quite complex. They will include the name and address of the foreign bank involved in the transaction, that is the bank which will send or receive the foreign currency, the account number of the customer in this bank, and the address and account number of the bank handling the other side of the deal.

Several copies of the formal contract are produced. One copy is sent to the customer to confirm the transaction, a second copy is sent to the correspondent bank in the foreign country, informing him as to the amount and value date, a third copy will be sent back to the dealer who originated the transaction for checking purposes, and a fourth will be retained by the accounting department.

The communication with the foreign correspondent bank is normally done by cable transfer but recently the SWIFT[3] system for handling FE transactions by computer has been introduced and most leading European and US banks have entered this system. The SWIFT system is claimed to be cheaper, faster and more accurate than the cable transfer system.

One important technical point regarding the availability of FE funds is that funds settled in a bank outside the USA are usually available to the recipient on that day, but funds settled in a New York bank through the New York Clearing House Association are not available until the next business day following the value date of the contract. A small exchange rate adjustment may be made to compensate for this delay.

The Chicago International Money Market

An international money market (IMM) for trading in currency futures was set up in Chicago in 1972. This futures market operates in much the same way as markets in commodity futures which exist in several countries. It deals in forward contracts for relatively small standard amounts of money (yen: 12.5 million; sterling: £25,000). The time period permitted on forward contracts is also limited to four payment days per year, in mid-March, June, September and December.

Trading is organized in the form of an auction in which registered brokers bid in accordance with the instructions received from their clients. An upper and lower bound is set for each day, beyond which the individual exchange rates are not allowed to fluctuate. When an exchange rate hits the floor or ceiling, dealings may be suspended. Customers pay a brokerage fee to the broker dealing on their behalf. The fee is very low, but the fact that each customer must put down a deposit on each contract is a more limiting feature of the contract since this increases the transaction cost.

The IMM provides a device for individuals or companies to hedge Trading Commission. Total turnover is relatively small representing, at $50 billion in 1979, perhaps 2% of foreign exchange dealings by the major US banks. Turnover is, however, expanding rapidly.

The IMM provides a device for individuals or companies to hedge or speculate in currencies where local exchange control regulations may prohibit trading. The IMM is not suitable for *large* deals or for deals where precise timing is a crucial factor, but it provides a further degree of flexibility for treasurers operating in the international money markets.

What currencies are traded?

A relatively few currencies account for most of the foreign exchange traded in both New York and London. In London the US dollar and sterling predominate although the Deutsche Mark is becoming stronger. The figures for New York are known in more detail since the FE turnover of 44 large US banks was tabulated in April 1977. The figures are provided in Table 3.2. Note the high proportion of deals in Deutsche Marks and the relatively minor role of sterling.

Most dealers in the United States go through the US dollar market. That is to say if a US corporation wishes to sell yen for Deutsche Marks, it sells yen for US dollars and uses the dollars to buy Deutsche Marks rather than selling yen for Deutsche Marks. The reason for this indirect trading is the depth of the US dollar market in New York compared to the depth of the other currency markets. Direct deals selling one foreign currency for another are more common in London. Sterling is declining in importance as an international trading currency, being gradually replaced by the Deutsche Mark, the Swiss franc and the Japanese yen.

Table 3.2 The foreign exchange turnover of 44 banks in the United States. April 1977.

Distribution by Currency Expressed as a Percentage of Total Turnover

Deutsche Mark	27.3
Canadian dollar	19.2
Pound sterling	17.0
Swiss franc	13.8
French franc	6.3
Dutch guilder	5.7
Japanese yen	5.3
Belgian franc	1.5
Italian lire	1.1
All other	2.8
Total	100.0

Source: Kubarych (1978).

REVIEW QUESTIONS

1. The following table provides spot and forward currency quotations on three currencies. Use this information to answer the questions set out below.

Quotations in London (units of foreign currency per £1)

	Spot (1 June)		3 months forward (1 September)	
	Bid	*Offer*	*Bid*	*Offer*
US$	1.7125	1.7135	1.6750	1.6770
FFr	8.5600	8.5900	8.5925	8.6325
DM	4.0550	4.0650	4.0013	4.0213

(a)   The method of quotation used is to quote several foreign units of currency to one local unit. Supposing the alternative method of one hundred foreign units to n local units had been used, what would the spot bid rates have been?

(b)   Quote the spot cross rates (offer rates) of French francs against Deutsche Marks as at 1 June.

(c)   What is the spread on the three months forward rate on US dollars, Franch francs and Deutsche Marks?

(d)   If you wish to convert £100,000 into French francs on 1 June, how many francs would you get from the deal?

(e)   If you have DM 1,000,000 on 1 June and wish to convert them into sterling, how much would you get?

(f)   What is the middle rate on Deutsche Marks three months forward on 1 June?

(g)   Calculate the discount or premium on the three months (bid) forward rate on US dollars, French francs and Deutsche Marks against sterling.

(h)   If the six months (bid) forward rate on the US dollar is at a premium of 3.50 cents against the pound, calculate the actual six months forward rate.

(i)   A contract entered into on 1 June will provide an inflow of DM 500,000 on 1 September. If you sell these Deutsche Marks forward for sterling at 1 June, how many pounds will you receive on 1 September?

(j)   You buy a machine tool from France on 1 June for FFr 800,000. The payment is due in three months. You decide to buy FFr 800,000 three months forward with sterling. How much will this cost you?

(k)   Calculate the premium on Deutsche Marks three months forward (bid) as an annual percentage rate. Do the same for the discount on French francs.

(l)   If the interest rate on external funds in Germany is 5% and France 10%, would it pay to transfer £1 million of free sterling funds to France or Germany for three months? Assume that you cover the funds forward.

2. A forward contract is entered into on 1 July selling $1,000,000 three months forward against sterling at $1.65. The spot rate at 1 July was $1.68. During the three months to 1 October, there was a marked improvement in sterling against the dollar. The spot rate at 1 October was $1.72 to the pound. Calculate the profit or loss on the deal compared to not covering forward.

3. On 1 March a UK exporter contracts to sell a batch of furniture to a US importer on a 90-day term invoice. The contract is denominated in US dollars. The value of the contract is for $5 million. To cover against the risk of devaluation of dollars against sterling, the exporter arranges to borrow $5 million for three months at 11% from the Euro-dollar market. He sells these dollars immediately at the spot rate (£1 = $1.70) at 1 March and invests the proceeds in UK government bonds yielding 10% annually. On 1 June the exporter receives $5 million from the US importer and uses this money to repay the Euro-dollar loan. If the spot rate on 1 June was £1 = $1.72, calculate whether the exporter would have made a profit or loss if he had not covered the deal forward but borne the risk of devaluation himself.

4. An amount of $500,000 becomes available to you for six months. You can leave this amount on loan in the Euro-dollar market or transfer it to the Euro-sterling market. Assuming that you decide to cover the amount six months forward, which option would give you the highest rate of return (ignore tax)?

	Bid	Offer
Euro-sterling market — 6 months rate	$13\frac{1}{8}$	$13\frac{5}{8}$
Euro-dollar market — 6 months rate	$6\frac{3}{8}$	$6\frac{5}{8}$
Spot sterling rate	1.7185	1.7195
Forward cover — six months	1.6505	1.6520

NOTES

1. As from 1 September 1978 foreign currency brokers in New York decided to quote in indirect terms, that is, so many units of foreign currency per US dollar. The pound sterling and Canadian dollar are still in US terms, i.e. so many US dollars to one unit of sterling or one Canadian dollar.
2. Occasionally an international contract may be quoted at the *official* rate, particularly if the government of the developing country is involved. This can be advantageous if it allows official conversion of a weak currency at a rate well above the free market rate. This applied to some government contracts in Nigeria in the late 1970s, see Pick's Currency Year Book for a list of black market rates.
3. The SWIFT system was initiated in September 1977. It is based on Brussels and over 600 banks have joined the Society. The acronym SWIFT stands for 'Society for Worldwide Interbank Financial Telecommunications'.

BIBLIOGRAPHY

Evitt H.E. (1971), *A Manual of Foreign Exchanges (in the UK)*, London, Pitman.
Holmes A. and Schott F.H. (1965), *The New York Foreign Exchange Market*, New York, Federal Reserve Bank.
Kubarych R.M. (1978), *Foreign Exchange Markets in the United States*, New York, Federal Reserve Bank.
Rodriguez R.M. and Carter E.E. (1976), *International Financial Management*, Englewood Cliffs, N.J., Prentice-Hall.
Swiss Bank Corporation (1976), *Foreign Exchange and Money Market Operations*.

APPENDIX 3A

Market Availability for Spot and Forward Transactions

	Currency unit	London spot market	London forward market	Local forward market
Australia	Australian dollar	A	A	A
Algeria	dinar	NA	NA	NA
Argentina	new peso	Sellers only	NA	NA
Austria	schilling	A	A	A
Bahrain	dinar	A	A	A
Bangladesh	taka	Sellers only	NA	NA
Belgium	Belgian franc	A	A	A
Bermuda	Bermudan dollar	A	NA	NA
Brazil	cruzeiro	Sellers only	NA	NA
Burma	kyat	A	NA	NA
Burundi	Burundi franc	NA	NA	NA
Colombia	peso	Sellers only	NA	NA
Canada	Canadian dollar	A	A	A
Chile	peso	NA	NA	NA
China	Ranminbi yuan	A	A	A
Denmark	Danish krone	A	A	A
Egypt	Egyptian pound	NA	NA	NA
Finland	markka	A	A	A
France	franc	A	A	A
French Africa	CFA franc	A	A	A
Germany	Deutsche Mark	A	A	A
Ghana	cedi	A	NA	NA
Greece	drachma	A	NA	A
Hong Kong	Hong Kong dollar	A	A	A
India	rupee	A	NA	NA
Indonesia	new rupiah	Sellers only	NA	NA
Italy	lira	A	A	A
Japan	yen	A	A	A
Kenya	Kenyan shilling	A	A	A
Kuwait	dina	A	A	A
Malawi	kwacha	A	A	A
Malaysia	ringgit	A	A	A
Mexico	peso	A	A	NA
Morocco	dirham	A	NA	NA

Netherlands	guilder	A	A	A
Netherlands Antilles	guilder	A	NA	NA
New Zealand	NZ dollar	A	A	A
Nigeria	naira	A	NA	NA
Norway	Norwegian krone	A	A	A
Oman	rial Omani	A	NA	NA
Pakistan	rupee	A	NA	NA
Peru	sol	NA	NA	NA
Philippines	peso	Sellers only	NA	NA
Portugal	escudo	A	A	A
Qatar	Qatar ryal	A	A	A
Rhodesia	Rhodesian dollar	NA	NA	NA
Rwanda	Rwanda franc	NA	NA	NA
Salvador	colon	Sellers only	NA	NA
Saudi Arabia	ryal	A	A	A
Singapore	Singapore dollar	A	A	A
Sierra Leone	leone	A	NA	NA
South Africa	rand	A	A	A
Spain	peseta	A	A	A
Surinam	Surinam guilder	Sellers only	NA	NA
Sri Lanka	rupee	A	NA	NA
Sweden	Swedish krona	A	A	A
Switzerland	Swiss franc	A	A	A
Taiwan	New Taiwan dollar	NA	NA	NA
Tanzania	Tanzanian shilling	A	NA	NA
Thailand	baht	Sellers only	NA	NA
Trinidad & Tobago	T.T. dollar	A	NA	NA
Tunisia	dinar	Sellers only	NA	NA
Turkey	T. lira	NA	NA	NA
Uganda	Ugandan shilling	A	NA	NA
United Arab Emirates	UAE dirham	A		A
United Kingdom	pound sterling	A	A	A
Uruguay	new peso	Sellers only	NA	NA
USA	US dollar	A	A	A
Zaire	zaire	NA	NA	NA
Zambia	kwacha	A	NA	NA

Key: A = Available
       NA = Not available

PART II

Corporate Exposure Management

D. P. WALKER

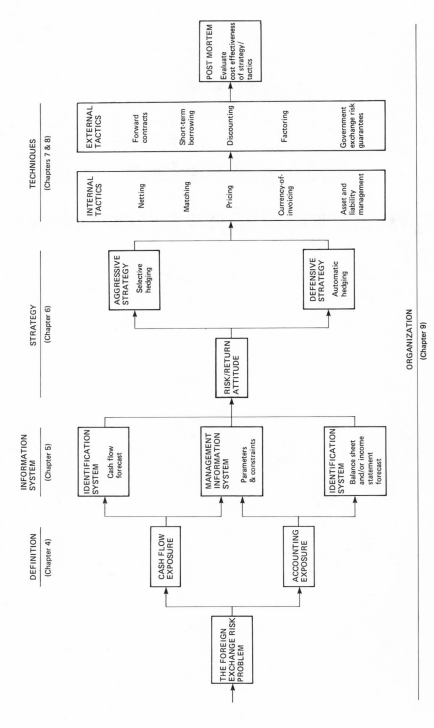

Figure II.1 Exposure Management System – an Outline

PART II

Introduction

Corporate exposure management is now a very complex problem. It is complex largely because of (a) the increasing size and variety of exposures which companies incur as they develop internationally, and (b) the increased volatility of the foreign exchange markets. Given this complexity, a logical and structured approach is needed to manage foreign exchange risk. The kind of framework needed, as illustrated in Figure II.1, can be categorized into the following five elements:

1. **Define** *exposure — what does it mean in the context of our company? The key distinction here is between 'cash flow' and 'accounting' exposure.*

2. *Set up the* information system *required to monitor exposure, as we have defined it. The two main components here are the exposure identification system and the exposure management information system.*

3. *Develop a* strategy *for managing the exposures we have identified. A company can take either an aggressive or a defensive approach, depending on its willingness to try to outpredict the forward rate.*

4. *Select and employ exposure management* techniques, *to implement the strategy in a cost-effective way. The focus should be on tactics which are internal to the company, as well as external (market-related) techniques.*

5. *Finally, and perhaps most importantly, each company must* organize *the exposure management function so that these other elements can be carried out effectively within the existing organizational structure. We should emphasize here that each company has its own organizational and other peculiarites, and so no single exposure management system is right in all situations.*

The elements of this framework are analyzed in Chapters 4 to 9.

BIBLIOGRAPHY

Aliber R.Z. (1978), *Exchange Risk and Corporate International Finance*. London, Macmillan.

Dufey G. and Giddy I.H. (1978), *The International Money Market*. Englewood Cliffs, NJ, Prentice-Hall.

Eiteman D.K. and Stonehill A.I. (1978), *Multinational Business Finance*. New York, Addison-Wesley.

Jacque L.L. (1978), *Management of Foreign Exchange Risk*. Toronto, Lexington Books.

McRae T.W. and Walker D.P. (1978), *Readings in Foreign Exchange Risk Management*. Bradford, MCB Publications.

Rodriguez R.M. and Carter E.E. (1976), *International Financial Management*. Englewood Cliffs, NJ, Prentice-Hall.

Shapiro A.C. (1978), *Foreign Exchange Risk Management*. New York, American Management Association.

Shapiro A.C. (forthcoming), *International Financial Management*. Boston, Allyn and Bacon.

CHAPTER 4

Alternative Definitions of Foreign Exchange Risk

The starting point for the formulation of a company's foreign exchange risk management program must be to decide exactly what the company has which is at risk. Quite simply, an asset, liability or income-stream is said to be 'exposed' to exchange risk when a currency movement will change, for better or for worse, its parent or home currency value. Exposure is therefore a neutral concept. It merely signifies that a company has assets, liabilities or income-streams denominated in currencies other than its own. The 'risk' element is that the currency movement will produce adverse results, which will not necessarily be the case.

All foreign-currency-denominated assets, liabilities, and income-streams are therefore exposed to exchange risk. Basically, this exposure is of two types. First, there is the exposure inherent in foreign currency transactions, known as 'transactions' exposure'. This consists of both trading items (foreign-currency-invoiced trade receivables and payables) and capital items (foreign currency dividend and loan payments). Second, there is the exposure associated with the ownership of foreign-currency-denominated assets and liabilities.

Transactions' exposure is usually clear and well-defined. If a US company invoices an export customer for, say, FFr 1 million, then for the period between the contract date and the date the receivable is settled the exporter has an exposure of FFr 1 million. If the French

47

franc were to depreciate by 5% against the US dollar during this period then a realized loss of 5% of the exposure will have been incurred.

An essential element of transactions' exposure, then, is that it may result in an actual cash loss (or gain) to the company. It may also affect a company's tax position, since such realized gains and losses are taxable or allowable against tax. This kind of exposure is now fully recognized by almost all participants in international business. Hence there is no need here to discuss it further.

The exposure inherent in ongoing foreign operations is, however, a much more problematical issue. Confusion has arisen from the fact that accounting practice and economic logic give two very different pictures of the way in which currency fluctuations affect the value of foreign operations. Briefly, the accounting approach is concerned essentially about translation adjustments in a company's consolidated accounts whereas economic or cash flow exposure is concerned with the effect of currency movements on the future cash flows produced by foreign operations. The first type of effect gives rise to unrealized adjustments, whilst the latter leads to gains and losses which will actually be realized. Let us now analyze these two interpretations of exposure.

ACCOUNTING EXPOSURE

Accounting ('translation') exposure arises on the consolidation of foreign subsidiaries' accounts into the parent-currency-denominated group financial statements. This process requires the application of a rate or rates of exchange to foreign subsidiaries' accounts, so that they can be translated into the parent currency. Since both balance sheets and income statements must be consolidated, then they both generate translation exposures. However, primary emphasis here will be on balance sheet translation since this is the source of the fundamental conceptual problems. The measurement of income statement exposure will be analyzed subsequently.

Certain items in a foreign subsidiary's balance sheet may be translated at their historical exchange rates (the rate prevailing at the date of acquisition or at the date of any subsequent revaluation). Hence their parent-currency-translated value cannot be altered by currency movements – such assets and liabilities cannot be exposed in the accounting sense.

Other items, however, are translated at current or 'closing' exchange rates (the rate prevailing at the balance sheet date). Even when the value of such items is fixed in terms of the foreign subsidiary's currency, the parent-currency-translated value will alter from year to year if the exchange rate of the foreign subsidiary's host country changes *vis-à-vis* the parent currency. Therefore all foreign currency items which are consolidated at current rates are exposed in the accounting sense.

To sum up, then, accounting exposure indicates the possibility that those foreign-currency-denominated items which are consolidated into a company's published financial statements at current rates will show a translation loss (or gain) as a result of currency movements since the previous financial reporting date. Unfortunately, however, this kind of exposure gives only an arbitrary indication of the real effects of currency fluctuations on a company's foreign operations. One important reason here is that companies use a variety of translation methods in the consolidation of foreign subsidiaries, so that the identification of accounting exposure elements is an arbitrary process. (Indeed, many multinational companies outside North America and the UK do not even consolidate their foreign subsidiaries for financial reporting purposes, so that accounting exposure becomes a non-sequitur. For an examination of this form of diversity of accounting practice, see Walker, 1978.)

Translation Methods — A Worldwide View

Since only those currency items translated at current rates are (in the accounting sense) exposed to exchange risk, then the question of which items should be translated at which rate is a vital one in determining a company's accounting exposure. Unfortunately there is worldwide disagreement on this question. As a result there are three basic translation methods in use, each with its own assumptions as to the applicability of historical or current rates to various balance sheet items. These three methods are the 'current/non-current' (traditional or working capital) method, the 'all-current' (closing) rate method and the 'monetary/non-monetary' method. Table 4.1 summarizes the translation rules of each of these three methods.

Current/Non-Current Method

This is based on the conventional accounting distinction between current and long-term items. Current items are translated at current rates and long-term items at historical rates. The accounting exposure inherent in each foreign subsidiary, as measured by this method, therefore consists of its net current assets.

Table 4.1: Translation Rules Used In Current/Non-Current, All-Current Rate and Monetary/Non-Monetary Methods

	Current/non-current method		All-current rate method		Monetary/non-monetary method	
	Closing rate	Historical rate	Closing rate	Historical rate	Closing rate	Historical rate
Assets:						
Cash/securities	+		+		+	
Receivables †	+		+		+	
Inventory	+		+			+
Fixed assets		+	+			+
Liabilities:						
Current payables	+		+		+	
Long-term debt		+	+		+	
Equity*	residual		residual		residual	

*Adjusted for the translation gain or loss
† Any long-term receivables (settlement date beyond one year) would be translated at the *historical* rate, under the current/non-current method.

The current/non-current method was the first and, until the 1960s, the most widely used translation method in both the UK and the USA. During the last 20 years, however, it has been the subject of increasing criticism from within the accounting profession, particularly with regard to the inherent assumptions that inventory is exposed to exchange risk while long-term debt is not. Accordingly there has been a shift away from the current/non-current method, although the USA and the UK have moved in different directions. The Financial Accounting Standards Board (FASB) currently requires that all US companies must use the 'temporal' method of translation (FASB, 1975), which is basically the same as the monetary/non-monetary method when applied to traditional, historical-cost-based accounts. In the UK, where all three translation methods are still acceptable at the present time, it is the 'all-current' rate method which now predominates.

Thus the current/non-current method can no longer be applied in the USA, and it is now used by only a dwindling minority of UK companies. Moreover, it may soon be totally abandoned in the UK, following the publication of Exposure Draft 21 (ASC, 1977). Elsewhere, the use of the current/non-current method is also declining and, as Table 4.2 indicates, it is now the least commonly used method.

Table 4.2: Translation Methods Used in 64 Countries

	Majority of companies use:				No method predominates
Current/non-current method	All-current rate method	Monetary/non-monetary method	Temporal method		
El Salvador	Australia	Bahamas	Argentina	Belgium	
Germany	Botswana	Costa Rica	Austria	Brazil	
Iran	Colombia	Guatemala	Bermuda	Italy	
Malawi	Denmark	Honduras	Bolivia	Mexico	
New Zealand	Fiji	Korea	Canada	Morocco	
Pakistan	France	Nicaragua	Chile	Nigeria	
South Africa	Greece	Philippines	Dominican	Portugal	
Zambia	Hong Kong	Sweden	Republic	Spain	
	India	Taiwan	Ecuador	Zaire	
	Rep. of Ireland		Jamaica		
	Ivory Coast		Panama		
	Japan		Peru		
	Jersey, C.I.		U.S.A.		
	Kenya		Venezuela		
	Malaysia				
	Netherlands				
	Norway				
	Paraguay				
	Senegal				
	Singapore				
	Switzerland				
	Trinidad & Tobago				
	U.K.				
	Uruguay				
	Zimbabwe				
Total number of countries 8	25	9	13	9	64

Source: Adapted from Price Waterhouse International, *International Survey of Accounting Principles and Reporting Practices.* London, Price Waterhouse International, 1979, pp. 249–52.

All-Current Rate Method

According to this method all foreign-currency-denominated items are translated at the closing rate of exchange. Therefore all foreign assets and liabilities are assumed to be equally at risk, and the accounting exposure inherent in each foreign subsidiary's balance sheet is simply its net equity.

The all-current (or 'closing') rate method is the one now chosen by the vast majority of UK companies. The English Institute's recent surveys of published accounts showed that it is used by more than 90% of the companies which disclosed their translation method. The all-current rate method is also the most widely used approach on the Continent. As shown in Table 4.2 for instance, it is used by the majority of those French, Dutch, and Swiss companies which consolidate their foreign subsidiaries. In striking contrast with most of the rest of the world, however, the closing rate method is not currently recognized as acceptable by the Financial Accounting Standards Board in the US. This may change, however, since the Board is now reconsidering its position.[1]

Monetary/Non-Monetary Method

Non-monetary assets (both short-term and long-term) are translated at their historical exchange rates; monetary items are translated at current rates. The accounting exposure inherent in each foreign subsidiary, as measured by this method, is therefore defined as its net monetary assets.

As Table 4.2 shows, the monetary/non-monetary method is the most prevalent translation method used in a number of Central and South American countries. The monetary/non-monetary method does not, however, predominate in any Continental European country, although its adoption has been advocated by the French Conseil National de la Comptabilité (1976).

In the USA this method was first sanctioned by the American Institute of Certified Public Accountants (AICPA) in 1965 (Accounting Principles Board, 1965), and this led to an increasing switch by US companies from the traditional (current/non-current) method to the monetary/non-monetary approach. However, in 1975 the Financial Accounting Standards Board, concerned about the the lack of uniformity in US practice, went further by requiring that for fiscal years beginning on or after 1 January 1976, all US companies must follow the 'temporal' convention. Many South American countries have subsequently shifted towards the US approach, as shown in Table 4.2.

Temporal Method

The key argument underlying the temporal approach is that the translation rate adopted must preserve the accounting principles used to value assets and liabilities in the original financial statements. The translation rate for each asset or liability will therefore depend on the measurement basis used in the foreign subsidiary's accounts. Hence the temporal convention requires that the historic rate should be used for items stated at historic cost and the closing rate for items stated at replacement cost, market value or expected future value.

When applied to traditional, historical-cost-based accounts the temporal and monetary/non-monetary methods give basically the same results.[2] In effect, then, US companies are currently required to adhere to the monetary/non-monetary approach. Yet it should be emphasized that the temporal and monetary/non-monetary methods are not synonymous. If applied to inflation-adjusted-accounts, for instance, the temporal convention would give the same result as the closing rate method.

Clearly, then, companies throughout the world are using a variety of translation methods in the consolidation of their foreign subsidiaries. National differences are illustrated in Table 4.2 which gives a country-by-country breakdown of the translation methods used in 64 countries. Of the 55 countries where one method can be identified as predominating, eight used the current/non-current method, 25 used the all-current rate method, 9 used the monetary/non-monetary method, and 13 used the temporal method.

The overall world picture is summarized in Table 4.3 which again illustrates both inter- and intra-country differences. Only the USA is internally consistent; elsewhere, all three translation methods are used. Even more striking is the difference between the USA and the rest of the world, with the FASB — between 1976 and 1980, at least — not even allowing the use of the translation methods most commonly used in Europe and many Commonwealth countries.

Given this diversity it is disturbing to realize that the choice of translation method can have a significant effect on parent-currency accounting results. Indeed, identical firms could show different translation gains or losses merely because they used different methods of translating their foreign subsidiaries' accounts. This can be clearly demonstrated by the use of a simple example.

Table 4.3: Translation Methods: A Worldwide View

	All-current rate method	Current/non-current method	Monetary/non-monetary method
Britain	B	D	D
USA	E	E	A*
Commonwealth	C	C	C
Continental Europe	B	C	C

A. Sole method used
B. Predominant method used
C. Occasionally used
D. Rarely used
E. Not acceptable

*Temporal convention (which is basically the same as the monetary/non-monetary method when applied to historical cost-based accounts).

Source: Adapted from Flower J.F., 'Coping with currency fluctuations in company accounts', Euromoney, June 1974, Table 3.

Table 4.4: Effects of the Use of Different Translation Methods on the Consolidation of Foreign Subsidiaries – An example

	Subsidiary balance sheets at 1 January & 31 March 1979	Subsidiary's £-translated balance sheet at 1 January 1979	Subsidiary's £-translated balance sheet at 31 March 1979		
			All-current rate method	Current/ non-current method	Monetary/ non-monetary method
	DM '000	£ '000	£ '000	£ '000	£ '000
Cash	1,500	300	375	375	375
Inventory	4,000	800	1,000	1,000	800
Fixed assets	5,500	1,100	1,375	1,100	1,100
Total assets:	11,000	2,200	2,750	2,475	2,275
Short-term payables	1,500	300	375	375	375
Long-term debt	3,000	600	750	600	750
Total liabilities:	4,500	900	1,125	975	1,125
Net worth	6,500	1,300	1,625	1,500	1,150
Accounting exposure: positive or (negative)			1,625	1,000	(750)
Translation gain or (loss) (20% of accounting exposure)			325	200	(150)

Source: Walker, D.P., 'An Economic Analysis of Foreign Exchange Risk', London, Institute of Certified Accountants in England and Wales. Occasional Paper No. 14, 1978, p. 25.

A UK company has set up a subsidiary in West Germany on 1 January 1979. The underlying transactions were booked by the parent at the prevailing exchange rate of £1 = DM 5. The opening Deutsche Mark balance sheet and its sterling equivalent are shown in columns (1) and (2) of Table 4.4.

The German subsidiary did not begin operations in the first quarter of 1979, so that at year end (31 March 1979) the Deutsche Mark balance sheet was exactly the same as at 1 January 1979. However, during this quarter sterling depreciated by 20% against the Deutsche Mark so that the closing rate of exchange was £1 = DM 4. This rate was therefore applied in the consolidation of some or all of the subsidiary's items, depending on which translation method was used. The results, as measured by each of the three methods, are shown in columns (3)–(5) of Table 4.4.

This demonstrates the significance of the use of different translation methods, with results ranging from exchange gains of £325,000 (all-current rate method) and £200,000 (current/non-current method), to a loss of £150,000 (monetary/non-monetary method). Since these various methods are recognized by the accounting professions in most parts of the world, then the identification of accounting exposure and the concomitant balance sheet translation gains and losses is surely an arbitrary process. The fundamental point is that none of the outcomes shown in Table 4.4 have very much to do with the economic or cash flow effects of currency movements on a company's foreign operations.

CASH FLOW (ECONOMIC) EXPOSURE

A generally accepted method of valuing an asset is to discount the future net cash flows (after-tax) which the asset is expected to produce. This is known as the net present value (NPV) of future cash flows. In the valuation of foreign assets the only additional step required is that the NPV of cash flows (including indirect cash flows generated by the subsidiary but arising elsewhere in the corporate group, such as trading profits, management fees, and royalties) must then be translated into the parent currency at some rate of exchange.[3] The NPV of a foreign subsidiary should therefore be defined as follows:

$$NPV_0 = \sum_{t=0}^{n} \frac{(CIF_t - COF_t)\, ER_t}{(1+d)^t}$$

Where

NPV	=	net present value (parent currency equivalent).
CIF	=	cash inflows (denominated in foreign subsidiary's local currency).
COF	=	cash outflows (denominated in foreign subsidiary's local currency), including tax payments.
ER	=	exchange rate (parent currency value of one unit of foreign currency).
d	=	discount rate (the rate of return required by the parent company for its investment in the foreign subsidiary).
t	=	period t.
n	=	the last period in which cash flows are expected.

Clearly, it is in the economic or cash flow valuation of the foreign subsidiary where the real impact of currency movements occurs. The economic evaluation of exchange risk should therefore be defined as the possibility that the parent-company-denominated NPV of the foreign subsidiary's future cash flows will be adversely affected by exchange rate movements. In other words, exposure is that component of a firm's value (future cash flows) which is related to the future exchange rate scenario.

This exchange rate impact will comprise two different kinds of effects, analogous to the price and quantity effects of basic economic theory. A change in the foreign subsidiary's exchange rate will not only have the automatic effect of altering the 'price' at which future local currency (LC) cash flows are transformed into the parent currency (ER in the above equation), but it may also change the quantity (CIF − COF) and timing (t) of these cash flows. Hence the economic analysis of exchange risk is concerned with estimating the effects of currency movements on foreign operations' future LC cash inflows (sales revenues) and cash outflows ('physical' input and financing costs). A conceptual framework will now be outlined for economic exposure analysis, using the simple case of a devaluation of a foreign subsidiary's host currency (hereafter referred to as 'the devaluation'). This framework is expressed diagrammatically in Figure 4.1.

Cash Inflows : Sales Revenues

A change in the subsidiary's host country exchange rate (irrespective of whether it moves in relation to the parent currency) can have two types of effect on the subsidiary's sales revenues. It can alter the size of the market in which the subsidiary sells its output ('market size' effect) and/or it may alter the share of this market which the subsidiary

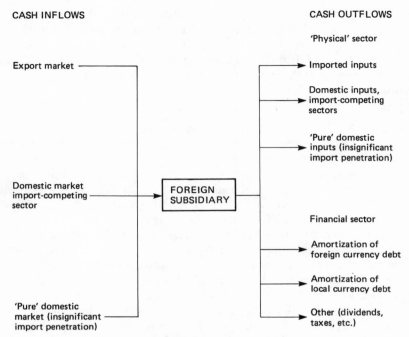

Figure 4.1 A Framework for the Analysis of Cash Flow Exposure

holds ('market share' effect). The direction and incidence of these effects will vary according to the market characteristics of the subsidiary. These market characteristics can be categorized into three market types: the export sector; the import competing sector of the domestic market; and the 'pure' domestic market (i.e. zero or insignificant import penetration). We will now examine the devaluation (market size and share) effects for each of these three market categories.

Export Sector

Whilst a devaluation will have little or no effect on the total size of the export market it will have a favorable market share effect. Hence the LC revenues produced by the foreign subsidiary's exports should be increased. The export oriented subsidiary may reduce its foreign (that is, 'foreign' to the subsidiary's host currency) currency selling price by the devaluation percentage (maintaining the LC equivalent), which will presumably lead to a higher sales volume. Alternatively, it can maintain its foreign currency prices (raising the LC equivalent), thereby increasing by the devaluation percentage the LC revenue per unit of an unchanged sales volume. In other words, devaluation should produce increased sales and/or higher profit margins — either way, LC export revenues should benefit from the devaluation. They may not benefit by the full devaluation percentage, however, since foreign markets may be the subject of increased competition from other exporters.

Domestic Market, Import-Competing Sector

As in the export sector, the market share effect will be favorable because it will increase the competitiveness of local *vis-à-vis* foreign goods. Hence subsidiaries selling goods which compete with imports in the domestic market should also produce increased revenues, unless overseas exporters are willing and able to suffer a fall in revenue denominated in their own currencies. Typically, then, a devaluation will lead to an increase in the LC price of imported goods, in the short term at least. The long-run outcome may be that foreign suppliers move their production facilities to devaluation-prone markets. (Volkswagen, for instance, operate profitable assembly plants in Brazil, Mexico and the USA. Other European and Japanese car producers may well follow Volkswagen's initiative.) Foreign subsidiaries located in the devaluing country and operating in the import-competing sector of the domestic market will therefore benefit, again in the form of increased sales volume and/or higher profit margins.

Devaluation will also have a positive effect on nominal domestic income because of the foreign trade multiplier. However, the rising price of imports and import competing goods in the devaluing country may reduce real income. More importantly, domestic demand is likely to be dampened by the government deflationary measures which usually accompany devaluations. The favorable market share effects of a devaluation may therefore be partly offset by adverse effects on the total size of the domestic market.

Pure Domestic Market

Foreign subsidiaries operating in this market category are most likely to lose from a devaluation, since there will be no favorable market share effects to offset the probable adverse domestic income effect.

Cash Outflows

For analytical purposes it is useful to make the distinction between 'physical' input (labor, raw material, and plant) costs and 'financing' (working capital and borrowing) costs.

Physical Sector

Devaluation will increase the LC cost of physical inputs for most firms operating in the devaluing country. The extent of input price increases will depend on such macroeconomic factors as the pre-devaluation employment situation, the effectiveness of the government deflationary program and the speed with which inputs can be shifted between different sectors of the economy. Within this general pattern, Shapiro (1975) has proposed a threefold classification of the production function into imported, traded domestic, and non-traded domestic inputs. Clearly, those companies which import a large proportion of their inputs will be hardest hit by a devaluation. Their costs may not rise by the full devaluation percentage, however, if competition from domestic producers forces overseas suppliers to absorb part of the cost increase. Even firms using mainly domestic inputs will be subject to rising costs, since expansion in the export and import competing sectors will force up factor prices. This will, of course, affect traded rather than non-traded input costs, which will be least affected by the devaluation.

Financial Sector

Devaluation will have a twofold impact on financing costs, since it will alter companies' working capital requirements as well as the cost of borrowing. In terms of working capital requirements, it has been argued above that a devaluation may lead to increased sales revenues and rising input costs. If this is the case then larger cash and inventory balances will be required and customers' credit needs will be larger, resulting in additional working capital requirements.

The effect on borrowing costs will depend on the currency denomination of the company's liability structure. The obvious impact on the cost of foreign (that is, 'foreign' to the subsidiary's host currency) currency-denominated loans, as most companies are now fully aware, is that the effective interest rate will be increased. Not so obvious, however, is the effect on domestic interest rates. These usually rise when a currency comes under pressure and a devaluation is expected. Also, interest rates will remain high after a devaluation if continuing inflationary pressures are expected. Hence, the interest cost of almost all loans is likely to rise as a result of devaluation — the only exception is a company's existing fixed-rate domestic debt.

After adjusting expected future LC cash inflows and outflows for the 'quantity' effect of a devaluation, the cash flow analysis must finally take account of the 'price' effect. The adjusted net LC cash flow which the subsidiary is now expected to produce is therefore translated into the parent currency at the new rate of exchange, giving the parent-currency-denominated net cash flow.[4] If the loss on translation at the new rate (the 'price' effect) is more than offset by an improvement in LC cash flows (the 'quantity' effect), then the parent company will benefit from the devaluation since the value of its foreign subsidiary is increased. If the reverse is true then the parent company should consider neutralizing the exposure by, for instance, changing the financing, sourcing, and marketing structure of its subsidiary.

Clearly, however, such an analysis of future cash flows is a very difficult and complex task. It requires the estimation of such variables as the devaluation reactions of competitors (price elasticity of supply), consumers (price elasticity of demand) and the local government (will price controls be introduced?). Nevertheless, it is essential that each firm try to measure its currency exposures. How can this be done in practice?

AN EXPOSURE MEASUREMENT METHODOLOGY

So far we have discussed accounting and cash flow exposures in broad, conceptual, and pre-tax terms. In practice, however, these broad principles must be transformed into a usable method for calculating each kind of exposure on an after-tax basis. Before analyzing exposure measurement in detail, two important points should be made.

Firstly, when discussing a firm's exposure, one must specify (a) the *viewpoint* (parent company, division or subsidiary) which is being taken and (b) the *time frame* under consideration. The significance of these two parameters to the exposure measurement process should be clear from the analysis below. All that need be stated here is that the size and direction of a firm's exposures can be very different, depending on the viewpoint and time frame chosen.

The second point is that *quantification* is a key feature of the definitional process. To be of practical value the exposure concept must ultimately provide a quantification of the impacts of currency movements on a company. As a management tool, then, exposure in a specific currency should be that number which, when multiplied by an exchange rate change, produces the gain or loss incurred by the company:

$$\text{Exposure} \quad \times \quad \frac{\text{Percentage exchange}}{\text{rate change}} \quad = \quad \frac{\text{Foreign exchange}}{\text{gain or loss}}$$

This formula is the basis for the measurement process: for each method by which foreign exchange gains/losses can be calculated there is a corresponding definition of exposure.

From the viewpoint of the parent company, the international treasurer will want to measure the possible impacts of currency movements on the group's (a) consolidated balance sheet, both current and future; (b) consolidated income statement for the future period; and (c) future cash flows. Hence there are three measures of exposure, the first two of which (current balance sheet and the following period's income statement) comprise the firm's accounting exposure. The calculation of all three exposure elements in each currency should be an essential part of each firm's definitional process. This applies even to the firm which has focused its exposure concerns on a single element. For instance, a corporation may give primary emphasis to the cash flow definition but may also want to manage accounting exposures where the impact could be significant ('significance' is often defined as a threshold acceptance level, such as a projected percentage impact on future earnings per share). For the company focusing on accounting exposures, the reverse logic may apply.

A methodology for quantifying each of the three exposure elements will now be presented. To facilitate the explanation, this model will be described in the context of a simple example. Specifically, we will show how to measure the sterling exposure of a US company which has a UK subsidiary.

Balance Sheet Exposure

Foreign exchange gains/losses here derive from the process of translating each unit's foreign-currency-denominated balance sheet items into its local currency and then (for foreign units) translating the local currency balance sheet into the parent currency.[5] This exposure consists of three elements:

1. All balance sheet accounts of the foreign (UK) subsidiary which are denominated in the subsidiary's local currency (sterling) and which are to be translated into the parent currency at the closing exchange rate.

2. The foreign (UK) subsidiary's local currency (sterling) tax-related exposures arising from the foreign (non-sterling) currency receivables/payables — third party and intercompany — on the foreign (UK) subsidiary's balance sheet. For example, if the UK subsidiary has a DM 100 receivable outstanding at balance sheet reporting date, then this represents a sterling asset exposure equivalent to (DM 100 $\times$ t_{UK} /100), where t = the percentage tax rate. This arises because an appreciation of sterling against the Deutsche

Mark means that the Deutsche Mark receivable is worth less in sterling terms. Since the resulting foreign exchange loss in the UK is tax deductible, the appreciation of sterling has generated a sterling cash inflow (local tax credit). The corollary of this is that the UK subsidiary has an after tax Deutsche Mark asset exposure of $[DM\,100\,(100 - t_{UK})/100]$.

3. The after-tax sterling exposures arising from the sterling receivables/payables — third party *and* intercompany — on other (non-UK) subsidiaries' balance sheets. For example, if a French subsidiary has a £100 payable then this represents a sterling liability exposure equivalent to $[£100\,(100 - t_F)/100]$. An appreciation of sterling against the franc means that the sterling payable increases in value in French franc terms. Part of this exposure (i.e. £100 $\times\,t_F/100$) is absorbed by the French tax authorities. The balance represents a sterling liability exposure to the French company.

The measurement of balance sheet exposure is a relatively straight-forward process. To calculate the three elements the subsidiaries' projected balance sheets must be disaggregated by currency and the effective marginal tax rates must be ascertained and applied. The sum of these three parts gives the balance sheet exposure which will generate the foreign exchange gain/loss at the next reporting date.

Income Statement Exposure

Foreign exchange gains/losses here derive from the process of translating each unit's income statement into the parent-currency-consolidated statement. As with balance sheet translation, this is a two-step process. The foreign currency items on each unit's income statement must first be translated into its local currency and then (for foreign units) this local currency income statement must be translated into the parent currency.

Income statement exposure measures the possible impacts of currency movements on each unit's projected local currency and foreign currency revenues and expenses, as measured in parent currency terms. In effect, then, exposure here consists of the parent currency value of each unit's net income. Contrary to balance sheet exposure, however, the gains/losses which income statement exposure generates do not explicitly appear as foreign exchange gains/losses on the company's financial statements.

To illustrate the kind of impacts which income statement exposure generates, consider the case of a UK subsidiary (US parent) which sources entirely from Spain in pesetas and sells entirely in the local market. How would the consolidated income statement be exposed to currency movements?

Projected cost of goods sold (less inventory on hand assuming FIFO inventory accounting) represents a short peseta exposure — if the peseta depreciates against the US dollar then group consolidated expenses are reduced. Just as with balance sheet exposure, however, this short position must be tax-effected. Hence the projected exposure consists of both a peseta exposure (projected peseta expense multiplied by a factor of $(100 - t_{UK})$ and a sterling exposure (projected expense multiplied by (t_{UK}), where t_{UK} is the percentage effective tax rate). On the revenue side, projected sterling sales represent a long sterling exposure to the parent. There are no tax effects here since there can be no realized foreign exchange gains/losses.

The measurement of income statement exposure requires the application of this kind of analysis to each unit's projected income statement, categorized by currency. Quantification is achieved by applying alternative exchange rate assumptions to the basic formula:

$$\text{Exposure} \quad \times \quad \frac{\text{Percentage exchange}}{\text{rate change}} \quad = \quad \frac{\text{Foreign exchange}}{\text{gain/loss}}$$

One of the key variables of the income statement measurement process is the exposure period. This will reflect the company's operating characteristics and, specifically, should incorporate the concept of a price adjustment lag. This lag is defined as the length of time it will take to raise selling prices in order to offset the adverse impact of a currency movement on operations as measured in parent currency terms. The assumption here is that prices can be increased so that projected net income measured in parent currency terms can be protected. If this is not possible then the loss becomes a permanent one. Hence the price adjustment lag is a key determinant of the exposure period.

Income statement exposure is much more difficult to measure than its balance sheet counterpart. Certainly, many US corporations — by simply adding back inventory to the FASB 8 balance sheet exposure number — are estimating income statement and hence total accounting exposure incorrectly. This 'inventory add-back' method is inadequate on three counts: it focuses on the cost of inventory, not the gross revenues generated by it; it assumes the inventory on hand is purchased and sold in the subsidiary's local market, ignoring imports/exports and foreign currency expenses and revenues; and it assumes the inventory turnover period is the exposure period when in fact the exposure term will be the price adjustment period, which can be very different. Hence, even inventory not yet purchased can be exposed.

Cash Flow Exposure

This is the most difficult of the three exposure types to measure. Indeed, the concept itself is very difficult to translate into a quantifiable form. There are three approaches:

The narrow approach, limited solely to the *actual* cash flows which are to be transferred between the foreign subsidiary and the parent company over the exposure period, is the most commonly used. This consists of intercompany trade payments, dividends, and quasi-dividend flows (e.g. management fees, royalties) and intercompany debt servicing. The main strength of this approach is that it is easy to calculate. However, it is very limited. In essence, the 'actual' approach is the transactions' exposure existing between the parent company and foreign subsidiary. It excludes foreign subsidiary cash flows which are generated but not repatriated during the exposure period.

The second approach focuses on the parent currency value of the *available* net cash flow (surplus *or* deficit) produced by each unit. Availability here refers to the extent to which the local net cash flow can be utilized or funded by the parent. Utilization takes such forms as dividend and quasi-dividend remittances (management fees, royalties) intercompany debt servicing and intercompany trade flows. Parent company funding of deficit units normally takes the form of a loan or equity injection. Local exchange controls and local borrowing capacity are key determinants of availability.

The third and broadest approach includes the *total* net cash flow produced by the foreign subsidiary over the exposure period, regardless of whether this is planned to be remitted or is 'available' for remittance. It should be added, of course, that once funds are repatriated then they are no longer exposed.

Whatever the focus, the measurement of cash flow exposure requires an evaluation of how the parent currency value of each unit's projected cash flows (broken out by currency) will be affected by currency movements. To illustrate, consider the case of a subsidiary currency (sterling) appreciation. The following sterling cash flows will increase in parent currency (US dollar) terms:

  local (UK) sales receipts and sterling-invoiced export receipts;
  local payments for inventory and sterling-invoiced import payments;
  local payments for selling, general, administrative, and financial costs;
  local tax payments, adjusted for the foreign exchange loss on foreign currency (non-sterling) cash inflows and the foreign exchange gain on foreign currency cash outflows.

Once these projected flows have been isolated and quantified for the exposure (price adjustment plus receivables collection/payables turnover) period, cash flow exposure can be calculated by again applying alternative exchange rate scenarios to the basic formula.

DOES FOREIGN EXCHANGE RISK MATTER?

Currency depreciation is almost always associated with a relatively high rate of inflation, especially in a floating rate system. In our earlier conceptual analysis of the devaluation case the effects of inflation were ignored. Yet inflation will have an important influence on a subsidiary's LC cash flows and, as Shapiro (1975, pp. 487–492) has shown, its effects will generally be opposite to those of devaluation.

For example, inflation will have an adverse market-share effect on sales revenues in the export- and import-competing sectors, whilst it will have a favorable (nominal) income effect on domestic demand. It will drive up the cost of physical inputs in domestically sourced production functions, whilst not affecting imported inputs. Indeed, it is only in the financial sector that the impact of devaluation and inflation will be similar: both can be expected to increase working capital and borrowing costs.

In sum, then, devaluation will tend to favor companies in the export- and import-competing sectors and those which are domestically sourced and financed. Inflation will tend to have the opposite effects. It should also be added, of course, that inflation and currency depreciation are experienced simultaneously. Indeed, this interaction between the opposing processes of inflation and currency depreciation poses the question of whether exchange risk really exists at all. If the adverse (beneficial) effects of LC depreciation are simultaneously and exactly offset by the beneficial (adverse) effects of LC inflation, then does exchange risk exist? This is the essence of a view which is gaining increasing influence in the academic world (Aliber and Stickney, 1975 and Aliber 1974).

The rationale of the new view is based on two economic theorems: the purchasing power parity (PPP) theory and the interest rate theory of exchange rate expectations (the Fisher effect). The rationale of both theorems is based on arbitrage: commodity arbitrage in the first case and covered interest arbitrage in the second. These theories are analyzed in detail in Chapter 10, but a brief description is required here.

The PPP theory states that the difference between the inflation rates of two countries tends over time to equal the rate of change of the exchange rate between their two currencies. The implication is that 'if gains and losses from exchange rate changes tend over time to be offset by differences in relative inflation rates, it matters little in which currency the firm buys its inputs or sells its products, since any devaluation (revaluation) of a foreign currency will sooner or later be offset by a correspondingly higher (lower) rate of inflation in that currency' (Giddy, 1977).

According to the Fisher effect, the difference between the interest rates of two currencies should equal the expected rate of change of the exchange rate during the appropriate maturity period. Hence, 'it would not matter in which currency the firm borrowed or loaned funds, given a sufficiently long time horizon, since any exchange loss (gain) would eventually be offset by an interest rate advantage (disadvantage)' (Giddy, 1977).

The question 'does exchange risk matter?' now becomes an empirical one. If these two theories hold then it will not matter in which currencies a firm buys/sells or borrows/lends, since the effects of currency movements will be offset by countervailing changes in inflation and interest rates. There is a lot of evidence which suggests that these theories *do* hold in the long run, i.e. over three years or more (see Chapter 10). In the long run, then, the rate of return on the asset side and the cost of capital on the liability side both adjust to offset the effects of currency movements. In the long run, exchange risk does not exist.

Unfortunately, however, both the PPP theorem and the Fisher effect fail a crucial real-life test — they do not hold in the short run. When the theorems are tested on an annual basis there are significant deviations from the projected exchange rate path, and the correlations are much worse for quarterly tests. In other words, whilst the long-term trend is accurately reflected in the PPP and Fisher paths, in the short run actual exchange rates will deviate around these paths. Hence, exchange risk stems from deviations from the expected rate (indicated by the forward rate or interest rate differential). These unexpected exchange rate changes cause a variability in cash flow, and it is this which constitutes the firm's exchange risk. In short, exchange risk stems from unexpected changes in exchange.

SUMMARY AND CONCLUSIONS

Two kinds of exposure to exchange risk are distinguished: the exposure inherent in foreign-currency-denominated transactions and the exposure associated with the ownership of ongoing foreign-currency-denominated assets and liabilities. It is the second kind of exposure which is the problematical area. There are two opposing viewpoints here: the 'accounting' (translation) approach and the 'cash flow' (economic) approach.

Accounting exposure indicates the possibility that those foreign-currency-denominated items (balance sheet and income statement) which are consolidated into a company's published financial statements at current exchange rates will show a translation loss (or gain) as a result of currency movements since the previous reporting date. This is an arbitrary indication of the real effect of an exchange rate change on the value of a company's foreign operations. It is arbitrary for two reasons. First, different countries, and different firms within individual countries, use a variety of methods to value their foreign assets and liabilities and hence to calculate translation gains and losses. Thus two otherwise identical firms could show different levels of exposure and different translation gains and/or losses merely because of differences in their foreign currency translation procedures. The second and fundamental weakness of accounting exposure is that it ignores the future effects of currency movements on cash flows.

In contrast, cash flow exposure is concerned with the effects of an exchange rate change on the parent currency value of the future cash flows generated by a company's foreign operations. The cash flow impact consists of both 'price' effects (the effect on the price at which future local currency cash flows are transformed into the parent currency) and 'quantity' effects (the effect on the quantity and timing of these local currency cash flows). The cash flow analysis therefore recognizes that a devaluation of a foreign subsidiary's host currency vis-à-vis the parent currency will not automatically reduce the parent currency value of the foreign subsidiary's 'exposed' net assets or liabilities, as suggested by the accounting approach.

The choice of exposure definition (accounting, cash flow or both) can only be made by each company's policy makers. This choice becomes crucial when the accounting and cash flow approaches give very different pictures of a company's exposure — indeed, a company can be 'long' according to one definition and 'short' according to another. In this situation senior management must decide where its priorities lie. Irrespective of this choice, however, both exposure types should be monitored. Many companies place primary emphasis on cash flow exposure, for example, but also monitor accounting exposures so that management action can be taken if the expected impact on financial reports reaches an unacceptable threshold level. The starting point for exposure management, then, is exposure measurement. Whilst both accounting (balance sheet and income statement) exposure and cash flow exposure are difficult to measure, reasonably firm quantification is possible. This requires a sophisticated firm-specific analysis of financing, sourcing and selling patterns, tax effects, and price adjustment lags.

The effects of inflation on a foreign subsidiary's local currency cash flows are generally opposite to those of devaluation. The interaction of these two opposing processes has led to the view that, in the long run, exchange risk does not exist. This view is based on the long-run acceptance of the PPP theorem (relative inflation rates equal the rate of change of the exchange rate) and the Fisher effect (interest rate differentials equal the expected rate of change of the exchange rate). In the short run, however, these two theorems do not hold. Hence we are left with the view that exchange risk stems from the short-run deviations of an exchange rate from its expected long-run path.

REVIEW QUESTIONS

1. You are the treasurer of a multinational manufacturing company and your finance director has asked you to prepare a paper on exposure definition. Outline the accounting and cash flow approaches and make your recommendations.

2. Calculate the balance sheet translation gain/loss, using the all-current, current/non-current, monetary/non-monetary and temporal methods, for the following:

> US parent company
> UK subsidiary
> US dollar depreciates from $2 to $2.25 against sterling
> UK balance sheet is as follows:

	£' Millions
Cash	2
Marketable securities (valued at cost)	4
Inventory (written down to current market value)	10
Fixed assets	14
Total assets	30
Short-term payables	8
Long-term debt	12
Total liabilities	20
Net worth	10

3. The European operations of a US-based car manufacturer consist of an engine production factory in France and assembly plants in Germany and Belgium. The French subsidiary buys all its inputs and was financed domestically, and sells its entire output to its German and Belgian affiliates. A significant 'across-the-board' depreciation of the French franc is expected. Discuss how the company might react, at the local and parent level, to the cash flow and accounting impacts of a French franc depreciation.

4. Discuss, in the context of Figure 4.1, what would be the most appropriate sectoral structure for a subsidiary located in a strong currency country.

5. What are the major determinants of a company's price adjustment lag?

6. Evaluate alternative approaches to measuring cash flow exposure.

7. Does foreign exchange risk matter? Discuss whether multinational companies need to manage their exposures. Examine both the economic fundamentals and the behavioral considerations of the corporate treasurer.

NOTES

1. An FASB exposure draft on foreign currency accounting is expected in mid-1980. It is highly likely that a radically different translation standard will subsequently be adopted in the USA, probably in 1981. At the present time the basis of the planned exposure draft is as follows:

Translation method: The temporal method is to be replaced by the all-current rate method. Hence firms that have 'short' balance sheet positions under FASB—8 will generally find themselves 'long' under the new standard.

Two additional refinements to the all-current rate method are also being considered:

  (a) special overseas operation, such as foreign sales, shipping or financial vehicles, are to be accounted for in 'functional' currencies (for example, the US dollar for an oil marketing operation). All balance sheet accounts not denominated in the functional currency are first to be restated into the functional currency using the monetary/non-monetary method, and then translated into the parent currency using the all-current rate method.

  (b) operations in extremely high inflation countries (exceeding, say, 30—40% per annum for two or three consecutive years) can revalue their non-monetary balance sheet items using a local inflation index, before translating them at the current exchange rate.

Disposition of Foreign Exchange Gains/Losses: The basic distinction is drawn between transactional gains/losses (generated by foreign currency exports, imports and loans) and translation gains/losses (arising from the consolidation of foreign subsidiaries' balance sheets). Transactional adjustments, both realised and unrealised, are to be taken direct to the income statement; translation gains/losses are to be taken to a reserve account in shareholders' equity.

Exceptions to this basic distinction are also envisaged:

(a) if an operation is substantially and/or permanently impaired, translation adjustments should be taken to the income statement.

(b) foreign exchange adjustments or intercompany transactions involving the parent and on transactions that hedge a net foreign investment are to be taken direct to shareholders' equity.

It should be added, however, that there is still much debate and disagreement in the US financial community on the advisability of these proposals. Hence the shape of the forthcoming exposure draft and, more particularly, of the resulting accounting standard are still unknown.

2. The two main differences between the temporal and monetary/non-monetary methods are as follows:

(a) *Inventory:* where inventory is stated in the original accounts at market value (i.e. where market value is less than historical cost) the temporal method requires that this should be translated at closing rates. According to the monetary/non-monetary method, however, inventory is always translated at the historical rate of exchange.

(b) *Investments:* where investments are stated in the original accounts at historical cost the temporal method requires that they should be translated at the historical exchange rate. According to the monetary/non-monetary method, however, investments should always be translated at the closing rate.

In contrast to the monetary/non-monetary method, then, in certain circumstances the temporal method treats inventory as an 'exposed' item and investments as 'non-exposed' items.

3. For simplicity we abstract here from the question of the remittability of the foreign subsidiary's cash flows, which is a very real problem in some environments. The foreign operation may generate significant cash flows and profits, which can mean an impressive consolidated cash flow and income statement and capital base, but if excess funds cannot be remitted to the parent then the subsidiary's value is clearly reduced.

4. It should be added, of course, that the negative price effect associated with the devaluation of a foreign subsidiary's host currency will only be applicable to that part of the subsidiary's net cash flow which is to be repatriated to the parent company. Retained cash flows, which often represent a significant proportion of total earnings, will therefore *not* be subject to the negative price effect.

5. 'Foreign' here means foreign to the currency of the country of each unit, i.e. in our example, for the German subsidiary this means all currencies other than the Deutsche Mark; 'parent currency' refers to the currency of the parent company.

BIBLIOGRAPHY

Accounting Principles Board (1965), Opinion No. 6, *Status of Accounting Research Bulletins.* New York, American Institute of Certified Public Accountants, para. 18.

Accounting Standards Committee (1977), Exposure Draft 21, *Accounting for Foreign Currency Transactions*. London, Institute of Chartered Accountants in England and Wales.

Aliber R.Z. (1974), 'The short guide to corporate international finance', University of Chicago, unpublished paper.

Aliber R.Z. and Stickney C.P. (1975), 'Accounting measures of foreign exchange exposure: the long and short of it', *Accounting Review*, January.

Burns J.M. (1976), *Accounting Standards and International Finance*. Washington DC, American Enterprise Institute for Public Policy Research.

Conseil National de la Compatabilité (1976), Document de travail: Groupe Consolidation, *Report sur la Consolidation des Bilans et des Resultats*. Paris.

Dufey G. (1972), 'Corporate finance and exchange rate variations', *Financial Management*, Summer.

Dukes R. (1978), *An Empirical Investigation of the Effects of Statement of Financial Accounting Standards No. 8 on Security Return Behavior*. Stamford, Conn., Financial Accounting Standards Board.

Evans T.G., Folks W.R. Jr, and Jilling M. (1979), *The Impact of Statement of Financial Accounting Standards No. 8 on the Foreign Exchange Risk Management Practices of American Multinationals: an Economic Impact Study*. Stamford, Conn., Financial Accounting Standards Board.

Financial Accounting Standards Board (1975), *Statement of Financial Accounting Standards No. 8: Accounting for the Translation of Foreign Currency Transactions and Foreign Currency Financial Statements*. Stamford, Conn.

Giddy I.H. (1977), 'Exchange risk: whose view?'. *Financial Management*, Summer.

Harrigan P. (1976), 'The double sand-bag in foreign exchange accounting', *Euromoney*, June.

Shank J.K., Dillard J.F., and Murdock R.J. (1979), *Assessing the Economic Impact of FASB 8*. New York, Financial Executives Research Foundation.

Shapiro A.C. (1975), 'Exchange rate changes, inflation and the value of the multinational corporation'. *Journal of Finance*, May.

Walker D.P. (1978), 'An economic analysis of foreign exchange risk', Occasional Paper No. 14. London, Institute of Chartered Accountants in England and Wales.

Watt G.C., Hammer R.M., and Burge M. (1977), *Accounting for the Multinational Corporation*. New York, Financial Executives Research Foundation.

CHAPTER 5

The Exposure
Information System

GENERAL REPORTING PRINCIPLES

Just as with other areas of corporate exposure management, no single exposure information system will be right for all companies. The appropriate system must be firm-specific: it must take account of the size of the company and its constituent units, the exposure objectives and strategy of the company, its operating and organizational characteristics, personnel strengths, and so on. There are, however, five basic elements which should be present in all exposure information systems:

1. *The information should be anticipatory.* Since the objective is to make decisions about how to handle future events then the focus should be on forecast data. Historical information *per se* is of limited value.

2. *Reporting frequency must be adequate.* In practice, quarterly reporting from major operating units is usually too infrequent for treasury management purposes, given that significant operational and exchange rate changes can take place in the interim. Hence infrequent reporting can mean that exposure decision making is overtaken by actual events.

3. *The information flow should be direct to the treasury.* The channeling of treasury information flows via controller/ accounting departments causes delays and weakens the link between operating and group treasury management. This can also impede exposure identification if such information is aggregated by division or into a single currency.

4. *The rationale of the information requirement must be understandable.* For motivational purposes it is essential that the data gatherers (operating units) understand how their information is to be used, and its importance. The onus of communication here lies with corporate and/or regional treasury.

5. *The degree of information required should be subsidiary-specific.* While the typical problem is that exposure reports are insufficiently detailed it is also a mistake to ask all operating units, big and small alike, to adhere to the same reporting requirements. A 20-line monthly balance sheet exposure report from a subsidiary with $250 million annual sales may be worthwhile; if the same report is requested from the $5 million units then management time and motivation are needlessly wasted.

These are the general reporting principles which should be the basis of all exposure information systems. For analytical purposes these systems can be categorized into two functional components: *the exposure identification system,* which supplies information on the accounting and/or cash flow exposures generated by group companies; and the *exposure management information system,* which provides details of the decision parameters and constraints to be considered in deciding what exposure management action is required. These two components are analyzed separately below.

THE EXPOSURE IDENTIFICATION SYSTEM

The structure of the exposure identification system follows the exposure classification used in the last chapter: a set of exposure reports is required for each of balance sheet translation, income statement translation, and cash flow exposures. The scope and frequency of these reports should be a function of the size and exposure characteristics of each operating unit — the larger and more unstable are the exposures, the more frequent should be the exposure reporting system. An outline of a comprehensive exposure information system is given in Table 5.1.

Table 5.1: Outline of Exposure Identification System

Reporting Unit: / Reporting Frequency	Major units	Minor units
Annual	Pro-forma balance sheet Pro-forma income statement Pro-forma flow of funds Review of credit facilities and investment opportunities	Pro-forma balance sheet Pro-forma income statement Pro-forma flow of funds Review of credit facilities and investment opportunities
Quarterly	Balance sheet exposure forecast: long-form Income statement exposure forecast	Balance sheet exposure forecast: short-form Transactional exposure forecast
Monthly	Balance sheet exposure forecast: short-form Transactional exposure forecast	
Intra-monthly	Ad hoc notification of material changes in exposures	Ad hoc notification of material changes in exposures

The annual reports simply consist of financial statement projections and an outline of available credit facilities and investment opportunities. Most of these reports should already be prepared for general planning purposes. Hence their inclusion in the exposure identification system does not represent a significant additional reporting burden for either major or minor units. The objective here is to give the treasury department a broad picture of the future activities of each of the units.

Quarterly reporting should be oriented much more towards exposure measurement and management. The basic accounting exposure information is provided in the balance sheet exposure report (long-form for major units, short-form for minor units) and income statement exposure forecast (major units only) — specimen copies are provided in Figures 5.1, 5.2, and 5.3 respectively. A key characteristic of these reports is that they should be broken out by currency and by unit and country of operation — otherwise tax effects are hidden, since each unit may have a different marginal tax rate. Group balance sheet and income statement exposures can then be calculated by tax-adjusting

UNIT _____   PREPARED BY _____
UNIT CODE NO. _____   DATE PREPARED _____
LOCATION _____   BALANCE SHEET REPORTING DATE _____
LOCAL CURRENCY _____

All amounts in $ '000 equivalents, using budget exchange rates issued by Corporate Treasury

Balance sheet line	Balance sheet account	Items translated at current exchange rates			Items translated at historical exchange rates	TOTAL
		Parent currency (US $)	Local currency	Foreign* currency		
	ASSETS:					
1	Cash					
2	Short-term investments					
	Trade receivables:					
3	intercompany					
4	third party					
5	Short-term intercompany loans					
6	Inventory					
7	Prepaid expenses					
8	Other current assets					
9	TOTAL CURRENT ASSETS:					
	Long-term receivables					
10	intercompany					
11	third party					
	Long-term investments:					
12	intercompany					
13	third party					
14	Net fixed assets					
15	Other long-term assets					
16	TOTAL LONG—TERM ASSETS					
17	TOTAL ASSETS					
	LIABILITIES					
	Short-term debt:					
18	intercompany					
19	third party					
	Trade payables:					
20	intercompany					
21	third party					
22	Current tax payable					
23	Deferred income					
24	Other current liabilities					
25	TOTAL CURRENT LIABILITIES:					
	Long-term payables:					
26	intercompany					
27	third party					
28	Long-term debt					
29	Other long-term liabilities					
30	TOTAL LONG—TERM LIABILITIES:					
31	TOTAL LIABILITIES					
32	Minority interest					
33	Capital					
34	Retained earnings					
35	TOTAL EQUITY					
36	TOTAL LIABILITIES AND EQUITY					
37	NET EXPOSED ASSETS/ (LIABILITIES), PRE—TAX					
38	FORWARD CURRENCY SALES (PURCHASES)					
39	UNCOVERED NET EXPOSED ASSETS (LIABILITIES), PRE—TAX					
40	MARGINAL TAX RATE = %					

*Specify foreign currencies

Figure 5.1 Balance Sheet Exposure Forecast — Long Form

UNIT _____ UNIT LOCATION _____ PREPARED BY _____ FORECAST DATE _____
UNIT CODE NO. _____ LOCAL CURRENCY _____ DATE PREPARED _____ REPORTING DATE _____

(All amounts in $'000 equivalents, using budget exchange rates issued by corporate treasury)

Balance sheet account	1 Current exchange rate per $	2 Cash and securities	3 Receivables Inter-company	4 Receivables Third party	5 Other assets carried at current rates	6 Inventory	7 Short-term debt	8 Payables Inter-company	9 Payables Third party	10 Long-term debt	11 Other liabilities carried at current rates	12 Net exposed assets (liabilities)	13 Forward currency purchases (sales) *	14 Uncovered asset (liability) exposure
												PRE-TAX SUMMARY		
Currency														
Parent currency (US $)	1													
Local currency														
£														
DM														
FFr														
etc.														
TOTAL														
MARGINAL TAX RATE =	%													

*Specify maturities

Figure 5.2 Balance Sheet Exposure Forecast – Short form

UNIT_____   PREPARED BY_____
UNIT CODE NO._____   DATE PREPARED_____
LOCATION_____   FORECAST DATE: QUARTER ENDING_____
LOCAL CURRENCY_____

	All amounts in $'000 equivalents, using budget exchange rates issued by corporate treasury					
Income statement line	Income statement item	Items translated at average exchange rates			Items translated at historical exchange rates	TOTAL
		Parent currency (US $)	Local currency	Foreign * currency		
	Revenues:					
1	Domestic					
2	Intercompany export					
3	Third party export					
4	Total sales					
	Less Cost of sales:					
5	Domestic					
6	Intercompany import					
7	Third party import					
8	Total cost of sales					
9	Gross profit					
	Less Expenses:					
10	Selling, general, administrative					
11	Depreciation					
12	Other					
13	EBIT†					
14	Interest expenses					
15	EBT††					
16	Tax expense					
17	NET INCOME					

*Specify foreign currencies
† EBIT — Earnings Before Interest and Tax
†† EBT — Earnings Before Tax

Figure 5.3 Quarterly Income Statement Exposure Forecast

each exposed line item and summarizing the after-tax exposures by currency.

The minimum reporting frequency for transactional exposure information should be monthly for major units and quarterly for minor units. This report is simply a foreign currency cash flow forecast broken out by currency and by maturity, as illustrated in Figure 5.4. It should differentiate between the following: (a) intercompany versus third-party flows — relevant for the exposure management (e.g. lead/lag) decision; (b) capital (e.g. loan amortization, dividends, royalties) versus trading flows — relevant for the exposure management decision because of exchange controls (e.g. restrictions on the netting of financial with commercial flows and on the forward purchase or sale of foreign currency); (c) planned versus firm contractual flows — again relevant for exposure management purposes because of exchange controls on, for instance, forward cover and foreign currency borrowing; and (d) the transactional exposure report should also

UNIT: USA Inc.   CURRENCY FORECAST: £   PREPARED BY: D.P.W.
COUNTRY: USA   FORECAST PERIOD: 6 months ending 30 June 1980   DATE PREPARED: 28 Dec. 1979

$/£ RATES at 28 December 1979
SPOT 2.2100
1 MONTH 2.1900
3 MONTH 2.1600

£'000	JANUARY	FEBRUARY	MARCH	APRIL	MAY	JUNE	SIX MONTHS TOTALS
RECEIPTS							
Third party UK Ltd	3,000	3,000	4,000	4,000	4,000	4,000	22,000
Intercompany, unit UK Ltd	5,000	5,000	6,000	6,000	6,000	8,000	36,000
Intercompany, unit							
Intercompany, unit							
TOTAL RECEIPTS	8,000	8,000	10,000	10,000	10,000	12,000	58,000
PAYMENTS							
Third party UK Ltd	2,000	3,000	3,000	4,000	4,000	5,000	21,000
Intercompany, unit UK Ltd	1,000	1,000	1,000	1,000	1,000	1,000	6,000
Intercompany, unit							
Intercompany, unit							
TOTAL PAYMENTS	3,000	4,000	4,000	5,000	5,000	6,000	27,000
NET RECEIPT (PAYMENT)	5,000	4,000	6,000	5,000	5,000	6,000	31,000
FORWARD COVER – Receipts	4,000	3,000	5,000	1,000			13,000
FORWARD COVER – Payments							
NET EXPOSURE	1,000	1,000	1,000	4,000	5,000	6,000	18,000

FORWARD CONTRACT DETAILS

Contract date	30.7.79	20.10.79	20.10.79	28.10.79	15.11.79	2.12.79	14.12.79
Settlement date	JAN.	JAN.	FEB.	FEB.	MARCH	MARCH	APRIL
Rate	2.2000	2.1500	2.1400	2.1200	2.1300	2.0900	2.0800
Amount	2000	2000	2000	1000	2000	3000	1000

13,000

Figure 5.4 Transactional Exposure Forecast

PREPARED BY _____   DATE PREPARED _____

Exposure type / Currency	Balance sheet exposure as at: _____	Income statement exposure period: _____	Cash flow exposure period: _____	Forward purchases (sales) period: _____
FORWARD MARKETS:				
Belgian franc Canadian dollar Dutch guilder French franc German mark Italian lira Swedish krona Swiss franc UK pound etc.				
TOTAL COVERABLE				
NO FORWARD MARKET				
Argentinian peso Brazilian cruzeiro Colombian peso Greek drachma Venezuelan bolivar etc.				
TOTAL NON-COVERABLE				

Figure 5.5 Group Exposure Projection — Summary   ($ millions)

include details of forward contracts. Apart from identifying the net uncovered position, this also enables corporate and/or regional treasury to monitor the forward cover activities of local operating units.

In addition to periodic exposure reports, all units should submit ad hoc telex reports of material changes in exposures (accounting or cash flow) immediately the changes are anticipated or take place. Materiality should be set at a specific threshold level, defined in terms of significance to the corporate group rather than to each entity — hence it would be very unlikely that such reports would emanate from minor units. This ad hoc reporting ensures a quick management response to significant exposure developments.

The final component of the exposure identification system is a report summarizing group exposures by currency and by exposure type. This should be prepared periodically (monthly or quarterly) by corporate treasury. A sample of such a report is given in Figure 5.5. Two important points to note are, firstly, that currencies are categorized according to the availability of forward cover. This distinction is useful since, if forward cover is not available, the pricing flexibility of the local operation becomes critical. Secondly, long and short positions in the various currencies should not be netted since the summary number would be meaningless. A net zero position across a number of currencies can hide significant exposures — for example, if a company is 'long' in Brazilian cruzeiros and simultaneously is equally 'short' in Deutsche Marks, it is certainly not in a neutral exposure position.

THE EXPOSURE MANAGEMENT INFORMATION SYSTEM

Once a company has calculated its exposures on a group basis there remains the problem of deciding what management action should be taken. For most companies the first and fundamental step in this decision process is to form a view of how exchange rates are likely to change over the exposure period. This involves the collection and summation of both internal information (from international treasury, the corporate economists department, local unit personnel) and external information (major banks or currency forecasting groups).

Two common weaknesses here are that the summation process is done informally and the resulting forecast takes the form of a single point estimate. The histogramming technique is a useful means of correcting these two weaknesses. The approach is a simple one. Each forecasting participant assigns probabilities to a range of future exchange rates, rather than a single point estimate. These ranges are then summarized, using weights assigned to each participant based (for instance) on previous forecasting accuracy. The participants' weighted probability range, expressed in histogram form, can then be compared with the appropriate forward rate for decision-making purposes (see Kabus (1976), pp. 95—105). Hence subjective and implicit 'gut feelings' are systematically quantified and made explicit. Histogramming formats for the individual and summary exchange rate forecasts are shown in Figures 5.6 and 5.7.

The local input into the group currency forecast, which is often neglected, is particularly important. To the extent that local management are making decisions which implicitly or explicitly are based on judgments about future exchange rates then there should be a regular two-way flow of information between local treasury, purchasing and sales personnel and corporate treasury. Local units' currency reports can also be used to update corporate and/or regional treasury's records on local exchange control and tax constraints on such exposure management techniques as leading and lagging, forward cover and foreign currency borrowing/investing.

Once the currency probability ranges have been formed, these can then be applied to group exposures to produce range estimates of

INDIVIDUAL HISTOGRAM – £/$

Forecaster __Assistant Treasurer International__

Currency _____£_____ against US $

Forecast period _____THREE_____ months

Current spot rate ____$2.2000 = £1____

Appropriate forward rate _$2.1800 = £1 (£ discount)_

Date _____13 December 1979_____

Forecast

A	B	C	D
Expected values	Confidence level: probability of expected value occurring*	Forecaster weighting†	Weighted probability (B x C)
2.1200 – 2.1499 (mid-point = 2.1350)	0.05	0.25	0.0125
2.1500 – 2.1799 (2.1650)	0.2	0.25	0.05
2.1800 – 2.2099 (2.1950)	0.3	0.25	0.075
2.2100 – 2.2399 (2.2250)	0.35	0.25	0.0875
2.2400 – 2.2699 (2.2550)	0.1	0.25	0.025
	1.00		0.25

* The probabilities assigned to the expected values must add up to 1.00
(i.e. 100%) for each forecaster

† Each forecaster is assigned an accuracy weighting. The weightings for
all the forecasting participants must add up to 1.00 (i.e. 100%)

Figure 5.6 Exchange Rate Histogramming – Individual Forecast

expected foreign exchange gains and losses. Figure 5.8 provides a sample format for the kind of gain/loss projection which should be made for each exposure type. This format focuses on the expected case and the projected best and worst cases, which may then be compared with the costs of eliminating the exposures. This is sensitivity analysis at its simplest but it does serve to indicate the fallibility of single point estimates. A broader range of possible outcomes can be analyzed if required.

Exposure management actions can then be taken based on a comparison of projected costs and benefits. It is important that the effectiveness of these decisions and actions are monitored. The simplest

SUMMARY HISTOGRAM – £/$

Tabulated summary forecast

Expected values / Participants weighted probabilities*	2.1200 – 2.1499 (2.1350)	2.1500 – 2.1799 (2.1650)	2.1800 – 2.2099 (2.1950)	2.2100 – 2.2399 (2.2250)	2.2400 – 2.2699 (2.2550)
Assistant Treasurer International	0.0125	0.05	0.075	0.0875	0.025
International Economist	0.0225	0.06	0.0525	0.0150	0
International Purchasing Manager	0	0	0.06	0.09	0
Regional Treasurer	0.015	0.045	0.045	0.0375	0.0075
UK Financial Manager	0.003	0.015	0.045	0.06	0.027
Banker/ Consultant	0.0075	0.0525	0.0525	0.03	0.0075
Total	0.0605	0.2225	0.33	0.32	0.067

* Column D of Histogramming – exercise 1 for each participant

Graphical summary forecast

Confidence level %: 50 40 30 20 10

6% | 22% | 33% | 32% | 7%

Expected values

Figure 5.7 Exchange Rate Histogramming – Summary Forecast

case is the analysis of the forward cover decision. Opportunity gains/losses can be estimated by comparing the forward currency receipts (payments) with those which would have been received (paid) by taking the settlement date spot rate. The selective hedging strategy should also be evaluated against a 'hedge everything' as well as a 'do nothing' approach. This kind of 'post-mortem' analysis is useful both for performance evaluation purposes and as an input into subsequent forward cover decision making. Similar audits can be applied to other exposure management actions.

PREPARED BY _____

DATE PREPARED _____

EXPOSURE TYPE _____

EXPOSURE TIME HORIZON _____

A	B	C	D	E	F	G	H	I	J Net benefit (cost) of forward		
Currency	Exposure $'000	Expected rate change %	Expected gain (loss) $'000	Best rate change %	Best case gain (loss) $'000	Worst rate change %	Worst case gain (loss) $'000	Forward premium (discount) %	Expected case	Best case	Worst case
TOTAL											

Figure 5.8 Foreign Exchange Gain/Loss Projection

CONCLUSION

We have outlined the kind of exposure identification and management reports which, in general terms, should be a useful element of the multinational company's exposure management system. It should be re-emphasized, however, that the precise form of each company's exposure information system must be tailored to its specific operating and organizational characteristics and its exposure management objectives. No single system can possibly be right for all companies.

REVIEW QUESTIONS

1. Construct a simple numerical example which shows that exposure reports (either balance sheet, income statement or cash flow) should be broken out by entity and country of operation if exposures are to be identified on an after-tax basis.

2. Devise a six-month transactional exposure forecast for the Italian subsidiary of a French company. Plug in some numbers for the Italian subsidiary's imports (on three months terms), dividend remittances and forward exchange contracts. Note that Italy and France have extensive exchange controls.

3. Devise a monthly telex report, to be completed by foreign subsidiaries, showing the parameters and constraints which would be useful for global treasury (exposure and liquidity) management decision making.

4. Form groups of five or six and carry out a histogramming exercise for the dollar/sterling rate one month out. Then decide whether to cover a £1 million receivable due in one month. Finally, after one month, carry out a 'post-mortem' on your forward cover decision.

BIBLIOGRAPHY

Kabus I. (1976), 'You can bank on uncertainty', *Harvard Business Review*, May–June.

Lietaer B.A. (1971), *Financial Management of Foreign Exchange*. Cambridge, Mass., MIT Press.

Prindl A.R. (1976), 'Guidelines for MNC money managers', *Harvard Business Review*, January–February.

CHAPTER 6

Alternative Strategies for Exposure Management *

TWO FUNDAMENTAL STRATEGIC QUESTIONS

All corporate exposure management strategies must address two questions. Firstly, which definition(s) of exposure is our company concerned with? If the answer embodies more than one definition then priorities and the trade-off between the alternatives should be clearly defined — for example, how much cash are we willing to spend to protect against a given unrealized translation loss? Secondly, given our definition of exposure, what is our corporate attitude towards risk? Are we trying to maximize foreign exchange gains (as we have defined them) or minimize exchange losses? Also, what time frame are we considering — do we want to smooth short-term results at the expense of longer-term fundamentals, or vice-versa? (The time frame consideration is also relevant to the first strategy question, since short-term profit priorities will tend to induce companies to emphasize accounting rather than cash flow exposures.)

The alternative exposure definitions (cash flow versus accounting exposure) have been set out in Chapter 4, and so our concern now is

---

* This Chapter is based heavily on Dufey and Walker (1978). We are particularly indebted to Professor Dufey for his contribution here.

with corporate risk/return attitudes. A key factor here is senior management's weighting of opportunity foreign exchange losses. These do not appear in financial statements but nevertheless represent a reduction in the accounting or economic returns that the company could have made. For instance, if the treasury management decide to cover a foreign currency receivable in the forward markets and the eventual settlement date spot rate is more favorable than the forward rate previously taken, has the treasury made a bad decision? The answer will depend on how aggressive are the risk guidelines given to the treasury department by top management.

AGGRESSIVE AND DEFENSIVE STRATEGIES

Analytically, at least, two fundamental exchange risk management strategies can be distinguished which we will call 'aggressive' and 'defensive'. (In practice, of course, these fundamental strategies rarely exist – rather, companies will tend to lie somewhere on a spectrum of risk/return trade-offs between the two polar types.) The difference between these two approaches can be most easily demonstrated by reference to the case of a single and one-off export sale. The aggressive exporter would try to invoice the sale in what he expected to be a hard currency (relative to his own currency), and he would only cover the currency receivable when the forward rate of exchange was more favorable than the spot rate which he expected would prevail at the settlement date. Exchange forecasts therefore play a key role in the invoicing and forward-cover decisions. In contrast, the defensive firm would try to invoice the export sale in its home currency. Where this is not possible the exposed receivable would be automatically covered, irrespective of the view of future currency movements. Indeed, such firms would not be concerned with exchange rate forecasts since their cover policy is automatic.

These two strategies can also be applied to decisions of a more fundamental and long-term nature. As regards currency of financing, for instance, the aggressive firm would choose that currency-denomination of debt which would minimize expected effective interest costs (i.e. interest cost plus expected exchange gain/loss). In contrast, the defensive firm would match either the currency-denomination of assets with liabilities (minimizing translation exposure) or the currency-denomination of cash inflows with outflows (minimizing cash flow exposure), depending on how the firm defined exchange risk. Either way, a lower level of 'risk' is traded off against higher expected effective interest costs.

Now, which of these two ideal types should international companies lean towards as the basis for their exposure management strategies? A key factor here will clearly be the company's ability to forecast exchange rates and, in particular, its ability to 'beat' the forward rate. This subject is examined in detail in Chapter 10, but some brief comments are necessary here.

THE FORECASTING DEBATE

Dufey and Giddy (1978) have distinguished three situations within our present flexible exchange rate system which have an important bearing here.

Situation 1: Foreign Exchange Market Biases. These occur because such market imperfections as government controls and intervention cause the forward rate to deviate in a systematic way from the market's actual expectation of future spot rates. This is the kind of bias which is illustrated, *ex post*, by the finding (Kettell, 1978) that the forward buying rate of US dollars and Deutsche Marks consistently underestimated actual future dollar/sterling and Deutsche Mark/sterling rates in 1975 and 1976. When treasury management is aware of such situations then a selective forward-cover policy, for example, is worthwhile. Hence in 1975—76 a company selling dollars or Deutsche Marks for sterling would have done consistently better by taking the spot rate at settlement date rather than the forward rate; conversely, the *buyer* of dollars or Deutsche Marks for sterling should have taken the forward rate.

Situation 2: Special Forecasting Abilities. This is similar to the first situation in that once again there are profitable opportunities to be gained from aggressive currency management, but this time the opportunities arise because the firm has an unusual forecasting ability. It should be stressed, however, that such forecasts are unlikely to be obtained from reading *The Financial Times* or the *Wall Street Journal* — this kind of information will already be embodied in the market's expected or forward rate (unless Situation 1 holds). The firm must have access to information not available to most other market participants, or access to some special expertise in interpreting generally available information, if it is to consistently 'beat' the forward rate.

Apart from the fact that both give rise to profit opportunities, these two situations have one other thing in common − they are much less likely to prevail in our present flexible rate system than in the Bretton Woods era. Under the Bretton Woods system, even in its deteriorating stages in the late sixties, the forecasting game consisted of the following three-step procedure:

1. from balance of payments trends one derived the pressures on a currency;
2. the level of central bank foreign exchange reserves (including borrowing facilities) gave an indication of when the situation became critical;
3. then came the crucial step of predicting which one of the rather limited policy options the nation's economic decision makers would resort to in a crisis: internal deflation, interventionism and exchange controls, or devaluation.

Clearly, the success or failure of forecasting depended largely on step (3) and there was no doubt that some participants did very well. Some US corporations, for example, spent considerable resources on analyzing both the power structure and the economic ideology of key decision makers in various countries (see, for example, Shulman, 1972). Moreover, since the downside risks of actions taken on the basis of these forecasts were quite limited, and also as more people caught on to this game, forecasting became more and more self-fulfilling.

Yet this situation has changed considerably. The actions of monetary authorities have become much less predictable, even under our 'dirty' or managed floating. Short-term pressures on currencies have both increased and are no longer uni-directional − sterling, for instance, has weakened in one day by as much as 5% only to strengthen in the next few days by about 3%. Clearly, foreign exchange risks are now much greater. Essentially these developments mean that currency forecasting has become much more difficult, both in terms of the likelihood of making the right decision and the costs associated with getting the forecast wrong. This brings us to the third and most likely situation which may now prevail.

Situation 3: Efficient Foreign Exchange Markets. Here, the foreign exchange markets are reasonably efficient and normally financial management knows of no systematic biases or constraints on market rates. Management's currency expectations are synonymous with those of the market, as generally embodied in forward rates. Unlike the first two situations, profit opportunities are rare, occurring only when there is discernable bias in the forward rate because of government intervention and exchange controls. In this situation the aim of international financial management should be to arrange the affairs of a company so that, whatever the exchange rate change may be, its detrimental effects on expected returns are minimized.

Before applying this general risk-minimizing principle to some practical situations we must first comment, albeit briefly, on the kind of 'detrimental' effects which can arise from currency fluctuations. The kind of exposure we are concerned with here is the potential effect of currency movements on the future cash flows produced by foreign operations. As outlined in Chapter 4, in the long run the effects of an exchange rate change on cash flows tend to be offset by countervailing movements in inflation and interest rates. The detrimental effects of currency movements — foreign exchange risk — therefore arises from the short-run deviations of an exchange rate around its long-run path.

DEFENSIVE STRATEGIES FOR THREE PROTOTYPE FIRMS

Rather than use an abstract microeconomic model of the firm we will introduce three prototypes, each of which exemplifies a particular kind of international operation. The aim here is to develop the sort of financial policies, appropriate for each of these three types, which will minimize the effects of a given exchange rate change. The types of operation we will discuss can be identified as follows: the capital equipment producer who *occasionally exports* one of his products; the producer of consumer goods who has developed a *significant export market*, and *the multinational company* with interrelated operations in many countries.

The Occasional Exporter

The occasional exporter is a paradoxical animal. This type of company hardly exists in reality, yet it seems that conventional exchange risk analysis is concerned exclusively with the problems faced by such a firm. The company usually produces for the domestic market but occasionally it obtains an order from abroad, and here it runs into a problem. If the export sale is invoiced in foreign currency then its receivable is subject to exchange risk. (The exporter could denominate the contract in his own currency, of course, but this simply throws the risk on to the overseas company).

Conventional wisdom suggests that the solution to this kind of exchange risk problem lies in using the forward exchange markets. During the negotiations our exporter checks the forward rates quoted for the time the payment is to be received. This exchange rate is then used to decide whether or not the receipt in terms of the exporter's home currency is attractive enough to go through with the export sale.

Simultaneously with the agreement of an export sale, the exporter enters into an offsetting forward exchange transaction. This takes the form of a promise by the export company to deliver at some date in the future a certain amount of foreign currency (the export receivable). In return its contracting party, usually a bank, would promise to pay the exporter at the time a fixed amount of domestic currency. This amount is, of course, determined by the forward exchange rate prevailing at the time when all commitments are made.

Should the spot rate at settlement date — or, indeed, any appropriate forward rate available during the credit period — be more favorable than the contracted (forward) rate, then our exporter will have incurred an opportunity loss. However, this is not really relevant. He has made the decision to sell on the basis of a certain receipt (abstracting from the credit risk) at which he found the export transaction to be profitable and worthwhile. Of course, with the covering transaction he has avoided the loss resulting from a possible depreciation of the foreign currency over the credit period; in doing so he has also forgone the possibility of a gain if the foreign currency appreciates. The rationalization for this is that the exporter is in the business of making and selling a product, and not in the foreign exchange business.

The important point to emphasize, however, is that this 'classical' covering operation will only work for a particular type of business. Should the amount that our exporter receives through the forward market be below his minimum selling price, he will simply sell his equipment in the domestic market — and this is precisely the problem. How many firms really do have this ready alternative? A far more frequent situation is the one represented by our second prototype.

The Significant Exporter

The distinguishing feature of the significant exporter is that he has permanently committed substantial resources to servicing the foreign market(s). A depreciation of the foreign currency will shrink not only the value of foreign receivables already booked, a one-time loss, but it will also affect future cash flows. The real problem, then, is the effect on the future stream of home currency revenues. What action can management take to alleviate this problem? One obvious option is for our exporter to raise foreign currency prices. The long-run validity of the purchasing power parity (PPP) theorem suggests that the cash flow effects of a currency movement will be offset by countervailing inflation rate changes. In the long run, then, foreign currency selling prices can be increased sufficiently to re-establish the home currency value of the export revenues to their former level. This assumes that the exporter can adjust his selling prices quickly in response to the relatively high inflation/currency depreciation rate in his export markets. However, lengthy price adjustment lags are often an important source of exchange risk to the individual firm. (Hence a company may take forward cover against the foreign currency receipts which it expects to collect during the price adjustment period).

This 'long-run' argument also assumes that the exchange rate is located on its long-run equilibrium path. In the short run, however, exchange rates deviate significantly from their expected long-run paths — hence the definition of foreign exchange risk in terms of *unexpected* exchange rate movements. Moreover, these deviations are sufficiently large to concern management: a 'temporary' adverse deviation of an exchange rate from its expected path for a few months could have a drastic effect on our exporter's cash position, rate of return on assets, and management performance reviews. For example, if the currency depreciation in the export market exceeds the compensating foreign currency price increases, the rate of return on export operations will obviously fall. It will be little comfort to the outgoing management that the exchange-rate/inflation-rate relationship will correct itself in the long run — management may not be able to afford to wait that long.

How could the classical hedging policy outlined above for the 'occasional exporter' help in such a situation? Let us assume our significant exporter makes regular (monthly) shipments and bills accordingly on 90-day terms. How would the situation look if he sold his expected foreign currency receipts forward at each shipment date, instead of waiting for the currency to be remitted and then exchanging these funds through the spot market? There are two possible conditions which might have a bearing on such action: the relative transaction costs and the relative stability of the spot and forward markets.

Foreign exchange transaction costs consist of two elements: foreign exchange commissions and the spread between buying and selling rates. If transaction costs are higher in one market than the other then this might influence the choice between spot and forward markets. This issue can be settled quickly: foreign exchange commissions on forward contracts are either the same or higher than those on spot deals, and spreads tend to be larger in the forward market. Hence transaction costs in the spot market tend to be smaller. More important for our analysis is the stability of spot versus forward rates, which can be measured by the expected deviation from the current rate (spot or forward) for a given future time period. If this deviation should be less in the forward market than in the spot market then it can be argued that exchange risk will be reduced by taking the forward rate.

To illustrate, assume that our exporter receives a regular (monthly) amount of foreign currency. This he must convert into his own currency, either through the spot market as he receives the foreign exchange or by selling the expected amount receivable on a 90-days forward basis (or whatever period is appropriate to his billing procedures). Assuming that we are now operating in the Situation 3 forecasting environment (Efficient Foreign Exchange Markets — see p. 88), where the firm is unable consistently to outpredict forward rates, his exchange rate expectations will not influence the 'spot versus forward' choice. Yet if he were to expect greater variability from one period (month) to the next in one market versus the other, he may prefer going through the market which has less variability since he would expect its scope for unpleasant surprises to be smaller.

During the Bretton Woods era, the spot rate was expected to fluctuate less than the forward rate because central banks (with a very few, albeit notable, exceptions) concentrated their stabilizing interventions in the spot market. This left forward rates free to fluctuate around the spot rates, as interest rate differentials and expectations about the future spot rates fluctuated. In the post-Bretton Woods era, however, the volume of official intervention in spot markets seems to have been considerably reduced for most currencies. (The major exceptions are the European Monetary System (EMS) currencies). A corollary of this is that the volatility of spot rates relative to forward rates of major currencies has increased. In testing three pairs of currencies (dollars/lira, dollars/sterling, and dollars/Deutsche Marks) for the floating years 1972–74, Dufey and Min (1975) found that the percentage deviations from one period to the next were virtually the same for the spot and forward rates of all three pairs.

Can our second type of exporter now use the forward market to protect profits from its export sales? We have seen that the major advantage of going through the forward market for our occasional exporter was that he was able to avoid an unprofitable transaction by taking account of the forward rates. Yet what about the exporter who has developed a significant export market and whose very existence depends on this market? If he does not like the promised rate received through the forward market he has very little choice, besides shutting down his operation. Therefore he must continue to sell in the export market, his only hope being that either the 'temporary' exchange-rate/inflation-rate imbalance will reverse itself in the not-too-distant future or that he may be able to take some policy action.

Only prayer might help our firm as regards the first possibility. The second option is of more interest. Our exporter can, of course, seek out opportunities for further raising his selling prices and lowering his costs. Yet we are assuming here that our exporter is already selling at the maximum price which his markets will bear. Similarly, the question must be asked whether the firm really needs a depreciation of the currency in its export market in order to look for opportunities for cost reduction. The only type of cost reduction we are concerned with here is that which is caused directly by the currency movement. Clearly, insofar as inputs denominated in the depreciating currency are being used or can be used in the production process, some relief will be obtained. Whether this is possible or not is largely a matter of the specific production process. Little can be said here except that treasury and operating management must routinely explore this opportunity after a change in the exchange-rate/inflation-rate relationship. The result of this exploration is a significant determinant of a firm's exchange risk.

The focus of attention here, however, is on the scope for financial management action, and specifically on the exposure implications of the currency-of-financing decision. Currency-of-financing policy is potentially a very powerful exposure management tool. If a company's operations generate exposed assets or cash inflows, these exposures can be neutralized by creating financial liabilities or cash outflows in the same currencies. The net asset or cash flow variability resulting from the deviations of an exchange rate from its expected path can thus be neutralized. In concrete terms this principle suggests that a company which has built a significant export market in foreign currencies should hold a portion of its liabilities in the currency(ies) of its export markets, so that it gets relief from the very event that degenerates its operating margins.

The Multinational Company

The term 'multinational company' is used here to refer to companies which have interrelated operations in many countries. Since the shift from a discussion of the case of the exporter to that of the multinational enterprise appears to be a mental giant-step we will deal here with the simplest case possible, viz. a company that has *one* foreign manufacturing subsidiary.

Again, the important question is how the currency movement will affect the benefits (future cash flows) derived by the parent from its foreign venture. Remember that the long-run validity of the PPP and Fisher theorems means that the cash flow effects of currency movements are offset, *in the long run*, by countervailing changes in relative inflation and interest rates. So what we are concerned with here is the impact of unexpected deviations of an exchange rate (either short-term oscillations or structural changes caused by, for instance, the discovery of oil) from its long-run path. This impact will consist of two kinds of effects, analagous to the price and quantity effects of basic economic theory.

The first and obvious result is that foreign currency revenues will be repatriated to the parent company at a different rate of exchange. What ultimately counts, of course, is the effect on profits in terms of the currency which the parent company uses as a base currency and, more importantly, in which the company's shareholders hold their wealth.

The second type of impact is that an exchange rate change will affect the quantity of future local currency (LC) cash flows generated by foreign operations. This is the focus of financial analysis: how will the LC cash flows produced by the subsidiary be affected by, say, a depreciation of the LC? The macroeconomic adjustment process provides us with the relevant variables for such an analysis, as explained in Chapter 4. As far as operating profit is concerned, three relevant market sectors can be distinguished in which the subsidiary buys its inputs and sells its output: the export market, the import competing sector of the domestic market, and the 'pure' domestic market (zero or negligible import penetration).

The analysis of the 'extreme case' is relatively simple. For instance, a subsidiary that sells its output in the export market and buys its inputs in the 'pure' domestic sector will undoubtedly experience a rise in LC operating profits, if the LC devaluation is greater than the compensating price-level change. This should be sufficient to convert into an increased flow of home currency (HC) units for the parent – the beneficial 'quantity' effect more than outweighs the adverse 'price' effect.

At the other extreme is the case of a subsidiary which sells its output in the 'pure' domestic market (where it faces strong competition from other local producers) while it obtains the bulk of its inputs from, say, its foreign parent. If the devaluation again overcompensates for higher LC inflation then in this case LC profitability will suffer, and the situation will look even worse in terms of the HC (i.e. 'quantity' as well as 'price' effects are adverse).

Many permutations lying between these two extremes are possible, as demonstrated in Chapter 4.[1] Yet the essential point has been made: the effect of an unexpected[2] exchange rate change on the profitability of foreign operations for the parent company depends entirely on the specific operating pattern of that subsidiary, and any management policy that does not take account of such differences is suboptimal. More particularly, the effects of a currency movement are determined by four factors: the origin of the subsidiary's inputs; the destination of its output; the degree of competition in input and output markets; and the degree of flexibility of the operation. Given the unpredictability of currency markets, the last factor is a key determinant of the susceptibility of a subsidiary to changes in exchange rates. To the extent that it can or cannot switch its sourcing and selling patterns between foreign and domestic markets and/or raise its prices, the exchange risk situation will be more or less serious.

This cash flow analysis now leads us to the question of changes in stock values. The starting point here is that the economic values of assets are determined by future cash flows: as expectations about such future flows change, so do assets values. For example, the plant and equipment of the subsidiary whose export revenues are favorably affected by a currency depreciation in relation to its cost stream will be worth more, regardless of whether or not this increased value is reported in our accounting methods. Yet what about current assets and liabilities?

Inventories are relatively easy to evaluate. If the currency movement has caused the unit LC price of our final product to increase, the LC value of inventories should rise proportionately. The resulting economic value for the parent should be computed by translating the increased LC value at the new exchange rate into HC units.

The analysis becomes more controversial as we proceed to LC-denominated monetary assets, especially cash, receivables and payables. Let us again consider the exporting subsidiary whose profits increased because of the depreciation. A certain level of LC cash is required to conduct operations. What will happen to the value of this LC cash as the LC depreciates *vis-à-vis* the HC? As regards its economic value the answer will depend on the function that this monetary asset performs for the subsidiary and, most importantly, whether this function changes because of the exchange rate change.

In the case where the subsidiary's export sales volume is unchanged but it is able to raise its LC selling price by the depreciation percentage (thus leaving the foreign currency price of its output unchanged), then the normal level of LC cash balance required to continue operations will very probably stay unchanged. Since it still performs the same service for the subsidiary, it seems to us that its economic value to both subsidiary and parent company is unchanged. In other words, its HC value is unchanged.

Alternatively, should the subsidiary increase its volume of operations because of the currency movement and therefore increase the necessary level of liquid funds, a loss would be incurred. The difference between the old and the new (higher) cash balance must come from funds that otherwise would have been transferred to the parent as profit. Instead, these funds are now tied 'forever' and become part of the investment base – in an ongoing firm they are committed forever. This change in the required cash balance should be included with the change in operating cash flows for that period in order to calculate the overall impact of a currency movement on the firm.

The same kind of analysis also holds for the subsidiary's receivables and payables. For example, an *increase* in LC payables would free LC funds and provide the parent company with additional HC cash. The analysis of payables is important, for all borrowings can be viewed as such after allowances are made for maturity.

All this will be anathema to those who tend to think about these matters in accounting terms. Just the thought of LC cash not decreasing in value in terms of the HC by the same percentage as the LC depreciation will cause considerable consternation. It may help to emphasize that the cash balance that concerns us here must be regarded as an integrated element of that bundle of assets and liabilities that make up an ongoing foreign subsidiary. It cannot be compared with a discretionary cash balance left in another country, which is obviously subject to exchange risk.

To sum up, then, the general rule governing economic loss or gain on current assets and liabilities is as follows: to the extent the exchange rate causes additional (or fewer) net current assets to be required, a one-time loss (or gain) is incurred. This loss (or gain) for the parent is equal to the additional HC funds forgone.

The Multinational's Risk-Minimizing Financing Policy

Now that we have analyzed the economic effects of currency movements on a firm's profitability we can turn to the problem of an appropriate currency-of-financing pattern. The rules we developed earlier for the 'Significant Exporter' can again be applied. If exposure neutralization is the company's objective, then its liability portfolio should be structured in such a way that the outflow on liabilities (effective interest costs) offsets as much as possible the change in the inflow on assets (operating profits).

The rationale of this approach is straightforward. Manufacturing companies expect to make a profit because of their ability to exploit certain specialized market opportunities — to make cars, chemicals or computers. The role of financial management is to protect this expected profit from unexpected changes in financial market (interest and exchange rate) conditions.[3] Protection can be achieved by manipulating operating and/or financial variables. The operating response consists of structural or business opportunities to create matched currency cash flow patterns. Operating actions, such as altering sourcing, product, plant location, market selection, credit, pricing and currency-of-invoicing policies, are examined in Chapter 7. However, the currency-denomination of operating variables is determined largely by intrinsic business conditions (production and marketing factors). Such constraints are far less important as regards financial variables, although even here credit availability is a problem in certain environments. Generally, then, adjustments to offset exchange risk will occur on the liability rather than the asset side.

How can this general principle be implemented? The basic step is to estimate how deviations around the expected exchange rate will affect the operating cash flows of the firm as a whole. This may not be an easy task. As indicated above, operating cash flows can be affected positively, negatively or not at all by a currency movement, depending on where the firm buys its inputs and sells its output and on the pricing and locational flexibility of these markets. Having established how net operating cash flows will be affected, it is then a straightforward task to choose the risk-minimizing liability structure. A unit should be financed in the currency(ies) against whose value its operating cash flows are positively correlated. Take the case of a French subsidiary exporting to Germany. Here the operating returns of the subsidiary are positively correlated with movements in the Deutsche Mark and so the subsidiary should be financed in Deutsche Marks. A depreciation of the Deutsche Mark would then reduce not only cash inflows (operating returns) but also cash outflows (effective interest costs). In this way the change in the net cash flow on the asset side can, to some extent at least, be offset by a change on the liability side. The firm's cash flow (economic) exposure to exchange risk is thereby reduced.

SUMMARY AND CONCLUSIONS

Two fundamental attitudes towards foreign exchange risk have been identified, which we have called 'aggressive' and 'defensive'. A key factor in a company's choice between these two strategies will be its ability to accurately forecast exchange rates – specifically its ability to outpredict the forward rate. In contrast to the Bretton Woods era, in the existing flexible exchange rate environment such forecasting is very difficult. Hence a generally defensive exposure management strategy is recommended: the aim should be to arrange the affairs of a company so that, whatever the exchange rate change may be, its detrimental impact is minimized. This general principle is then applied to three prototype international firms: the 'occasional' exporter, the 'significant' exporter, and the 'multinational' company.

For the occasional exporter the classical exposure management operation – cover all exposed transactions on the forward currency markets – is the obvious defensive approach. For the other two prototypes, however, this strategy is much less appropriate. For the significant exporter and the multinational company, economic exposure to exchange risk can only be minimized by structuring the group's liabilities in such a way that the change in cash inflows (operating revenues) induced by a currency movement is offset as much as possible by a countervailing change in cash outflows (effective interest costs).

REVIEW QUESTIONS

1. You are the treasurer of a multinational company and your finance director has asked you to prepare a paper on exposure management strategy. Outline the aggressive and defensive approaches and make your recommendations.

2. For a major exchange rate, tabulate and graph the three-month forward (mid) rate, against the spot (mid) rate at maturity, by month over a two-year period (i.e. 24 comparisons). Does this show the forward rate to be an inaccurate but unbiased predictor of future spot rates?

3. For the same exchange rate and period, calculate the buy–sell spreads and the stability (month-to-month percentage deviations) of spot versus forward rates. Discuss the exposure management implications.

4. Why should the occasional exporter's exposure management strategy differ from that of the significant exporter or multinational company?

5. A UK-based company sources locally and sells its entire output to Holland. What kind of operating and financial actions could be taken to reduce the company's cash flow exposures?

NOTES

1. For a more complete framework for the analysis of cash-flow exposure patterns, see Walker (1978).
2. If the exchange rate change is expected, this means that the exchange rate is not deviating from its long-run equilibrium path. Hence the cash flow effects of the currency movement are neutralized by movements in relative inflation and interest rates.
3. Whilst we are considering here only exchange risk, the same kind of analysis can also be applied to interest rates, (see Dufey and Giddy, 1978).

BIBLIOGRAPHY

Dufey G. and Giddy I.H. (1978), 'International Financial Planning: the use of market based forecasts', *California Management Review*, Fall.
Dufey G. and Min S. (1975), 'A comparison of the variability of spot and forward rates', unpublished working paper, Graduate School of Business Administration, University of Michigan.
Dufey G. and Walker D.P. (1978), 'Alternative strategies for managing foreign exchange risk', in McRae and Walker (1978).
Giddy I.H. (1976), 'Why it doesn't pay to make a habit of forward hedging', *Euromoney*, December.
Howlett K. (1977), 'Forward hedging does pay because the long run is too long', *Euromoney*, April.
Kettell B. (1978), 'The forward rate as an accurate predictor of future spot rates', in McRae and Walker (1978).
Korth C.K. (1972), 'The future of a currency', *Business Horizons*, June.
Lietaer B.A. (1971), *Financial Management of Foreign Exchange*. Cambridge, Mass., MIT Press.
McRae T.W. and Walker D.P. (1978), *Readings in Foreign Exchange Risk Management*. Bradford, MCB Publications.
Shapiro A.C. and Rutenberg D.P. (1976), 'Managing exchange risks in a floating world', *Financial Management*, vol. 5, no. 2, Summer.
Shulman R.B. (1970), 'Are foreign exchange risks measurable?', *Columbia Journal of World Business*, June.
Wheelwright S.C. (1975), 'Applying decision theory to improve corporate management of currency exchange risks', *California Management Review*, Summer.

CHAPTER 7

Exposure Management: Internal Techniques

A CLASSIFICATION OF EXPOSURE MANAGEMENT TECHNIQUES

There is a large and perhaps confusing variety of techniques which can be used in corporate exchange risk management. To understand the rationale underlying their use it is helpful to classify them according to their basic origin. Following Prindl (1976), the distinction will be made here between those techniques which are *internal* to the company, which are mainly used as part of a company's regulatory financial management aimed at minimizing its continuing exposure (however defined) to exchange risk; and those which are *external* to the company, consisting basically of contractual measures to insure against an exchange loss (realized or unrealized) which may arise from an existing transaction or exposed position. The major internal and external techniques are listed in Table 7.1.

To simplify the distinction, the first group of policies is generally aimed at reducing or preventing an exposed position from arising; the second group is used to insure against the possibility that exchange losses will result from the exposed position which the internal measures have not been able to eliminate. The distinction is not quite as clear-cut as this, as will become evident in the following analysis, but it is nevertheless a useful way of summarizing the overall range of choices available.

Table 7.1. Internal and External Exposure Management Techniques

INTERNAL	— Netting
	— Matching
	— Leading and lagging
	— Pricing policies
	— Asset and liability management
EXTERNAL	— Forward contracts
	— Short-term borrowing
	— Discounting
	— Factoring
	— Government exchange risk guarantees

This distinction is also useful because it pinpoints a common weakness of corporate exposure management — an overemphasis on external (market-related) techniques. In all too many companies the exposure manager simply receives exposure reports from operating units and then, based on a currency forecast, decides whether or not to cover on the money markets. With this kind of approach little or no consideration is given to internal (business-related) tactics, such as matching the currency denomination of cash inflows and outflows by changing sourcing and currency of invoicing patterns. We believe, however, that emphasis should be placed on business-related exposure management tactics. The role of market-related techniques, which can be very costly and may even disappear when exposures are of greatest concern, should not be the sole focus.

It should also be emphasized that the various exposure management techniques described here are not available in all circumstances. This is mainly because of limitations imposed by the market-place (no forward market exists in many of the 'exotic' currencies of the less-developed nations) and by regulatory authorities (the hedging of translation exposures on the forward markets is not allowed in many countries).

The availability of internal techniques is largely a function of the international involvement of each company. The international business literature abounds with definitions of what a 'multinational' company really is, but for our present purpose a twofold classification of international penetration will suffice. *International* companies, which are simply defined here as importers or exporters, have a fairly limited range of internal exposure management options available. By contrast, *multinational* companies, defined as those which have overseas operating subsidiaries, will probably have a much more complicated network of foreign operations and hence currency exposures. Consequently, the multinational company will have access to a much broader range of exposure management techniques, both internal as well as external. We will now discuss these techniques in detail in this and the following chapter.

NETTING

Netting simply means that affiliated companies which trade with each other receive or pay, at regular intervals, only the *net* amount of the intergroup debt. Gross intergroup trade receivables and payables are netted out. In the simplest kind of scheme, known as *bilateral netting,* each pair of subsidiaries nets out their own positions with each other. Flows are reduced by the lower of each company's purchases from or sales to its netting partner. There is no attempt to introduce the net positions of other group companies.

Bilateral netting, illustrated in Figure 7.1, is easily demonstrated by the use of a simple example. If Worldwide Corporation (Germany) owes Worldwide Corporation (UK) the sterling-equivalent of $1 million, and if WWC (UK) owes WWC (Germany) the Deutsche Mark equivalent of $3 million, then the actual cash remittance is netted out so that WWC (UK) pays WWC (Germany) the Deutsche Mark (or some other currency) equivalent of only $2 million. The two companies have saved between them the exchange and transfer costs associated with $1 million of eliminated flows. Hence netting is not so much an exposure management technique but more a way of reducing the amount of intercompany receipts and payments which go through the foreign exchanges. In their more developed forms, however, netting schemes do have important organizational implications for exposure management.

Bilateral schemes are fairly straightforward to operate. The two main practical problems are that participants must decide on the currency denomination of the net remittance and on a reconciliation

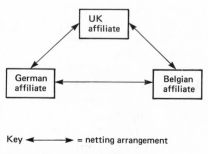

Key ◄───────► = netting arrangement

Figure 7.1 Bilateral Netting

and settlement schedule. A centralized control system is not necessary.

Whereas bilateral netting is possible only when there are reciprocal flows between two companies, *multilateral netting* can take place whenever affiliates both import from and export to companies within the same corporate group. Flows are reduced by the lower of each company's *total* purchases from/sales to affiliates. We can illustrate multilateral netting (Figure 7.2) by the following example. Worldwide Corporation's intergroup trading in Europe is as follows: WWC (UK)'s monthly purchases from WWC (Germany) are $3 million and monthly sales to WWC (Belgium) are $1 million; WWC (Germany)'s monthly purchases from WWC (Belgium) are $1 million. The netting potential in this trading pattern is demonstrated in Figure 7.3. The netting

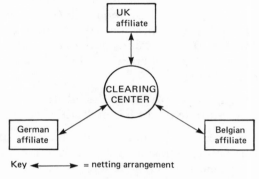

Key ◄————► = netting arrangement

Figure 7.2 Multilateral Netting

Paying unit / Receiving unit	Germany	UK	Belgium	Total receipts	Net receipts	Eliminated receipts
Germany		3	0	3	2	1
UK	0		1	1	—	1
Belgium	1	0		1	—	1
Total payments	1	3	1	5		
Net payments	—	2	—		2	
Eliminated payments	1	1	1			3

Netting potential   Gross flows   = $5 million
                      Net flows   = $2 million
                      Eliminated flows = $3 million

Figure 7.3 Netting Matrix ($ million)

matrix shows that multilateral netting would eliminate $1 million in transfers from each affiliate's monthly payments, even though in this example there is no scope for bilateral netting. After multilateral netting, intercompany payments consist solely of $2 million monthly from the UK to Germany.

The focal point in a multilateral netting scheme is the central information point. Participating units must report all intercompany positions at the end of a given period, and the center then advises the units of the net amount which they are to pay or receive at a certain date. Multilateral netting therefore requires a centralized communications system and a lot of discipline on the part of participating units. The major external requirements are those imposed by local exchange controls. The three most common constraints are (a) prior approval for netting may be required; (b) trading (rather than financial) transactions only may be netted; and (c) intercompany (rather than third party) transactions only may be netted.

The mechanics of netting schemes are always some variation of the following basic timetable:

The basic step is to set up a fixed schedule for periodic settlements — the settlement date might be the 25th of each month

At S minus 5 days (in our example, the 20th of each month) participating units telex details of intercompany positions, stated in a common currency at agreed exchange rates

At S minus 4 subsidiaries agree to reconciled intercompany positions

At S minus 3 the clearing center decides on the extent netting is to be used — the full netting potential may not be realized because of broader treasury management considerations. Payment instructions are then issued to subsidiaries

At S minus 2 the paying units instruct their banks to deliver the appropriate funds with value compensation on day S

At S same-day value transfers are made between paying and receiving units

The major benefits of netting are reduced banking costs and increased control of intercompany settlements. The reduced number and total amount of payments produces savings in the form of lower float and lower exchange costs (i.e. the buy/sell spread in the spot and forward markets plus the elimination of bank charges, if any). No simple savings percentage can be universally applied to the amount netted since savings will be determined by prevailing buy/sell spreads and the structure of the payment flows eliminated. For instance, since foreign transfers typically involve a fixed cost and a decreasing marginal cost, then the elimination of small payments produces higher percentage savings than the elimination of large payments. As a broad guideline, however, such savings can be estimated at around one-sixth of one per cent of the flows eliminated.

Additionally, the introduction of a netting system does create opportunities for exposure and liquidity management and tax planning. The two relevant variables here are the credit period and the currency of invoicing, both of which may be subject to exchange controls. The utilization of leading and lagging and currency-of-invoicing policy as tools for exposure management are discussed below. It is merely necessary to note here that, at the S minus 3 date, the treasury manager at the clearing center can analyze the tax and interest rate differentials and the transactional exposure and translation exposure impacts of manipulating these two variables. A quick and easy decision format can then be applied to produce an inter-company settlement pattern which will help to achieve the company's liquidity and exposure management objectives.

MATCHING

The terms 'netting' and 'matching' are often used interchangeably but the following distinction will be made here. The former, as we have seen, refers to the netting out of group receipts and payments. It is typically used only for intercompany flows and as such is applicable only to the operations of a multinational company rather than the exporter or importer.

In contrast, matching can be applied to both third party as well as intercompany cash flows, and it can be used by the exporter/importer as well as the multinational company. It is a process whereby a company matches its currency inflows with its currency outflows with respect to amount and (to an approximate degree) timing. Receipts in a particular currency may then be used to make payments in that currency, so that the need to go through the exchanges (spot and forward) is limited to the unmatched portion of foreign currency cash flows. It should be added, of course, that matching may not be done automatically. As discussed in Chapter 6, this depends on each company's exposure management strategy. The aggressive company may decide to take forward cover on its currency payables and leave the currency receivables exposed to exchange risk, if it takes the view that the forward rate looks cheaper than the expected spot rate.

The basic requirement for a matching operation, then, is a two-way cash flow in the *same* foreign currency. This kind of operation is sometimes called 'natural' matching. There is a further possibility, however, which we will call 'parallel' matching. Here the match involves *two* currencies whose movements are expected to run closely parallel — the Deutsche Mark and the Swiss franc, perhaps, or two of the narrow-band European Monetary System (EMS) currencies. In a parallel matching situation, gains in one foreign currency (e.g. appreciation of Deutsche Mark receivables) are expected to be offset by losses in another (e.g. appreciation of Swiss franc payables). Needless to say, with parallel matching there is always the risk that the exchange rates will move contrary to expectations, so that both sides of the parallel match lead to exchange losses (or gains).

To revert to 'natural' matching, given the existence of two-way foreign currency cash flows in the same currency, matching can be carried out by companies with relatively simple foreign exchange exposures, such as the importer/exporter. However, the international operations of the multinational corporation — with its greater trading flows and also dividend and quasi-dividend payments — offers the highest matching potential. Clearly, the more widespread are the currency flows encompassed by a matching operation then the greater is the scope for matching. Hence in any corporate group the existence of an effective matching operation is almost synonymous with some degree of centralization.

The major practical problems in implementing matching concern the timing of third party receipts and payments. Unexpected delays can cause the mistiming of a match and may consequently leave both receivable and payable exposed to exchange risk. For instance, if the currency payable is settled on the expected date but the receivable is delayed, then the company may have to purchase the currency requirement at the payment date spot rate, and then sell the offsetting currency receipts at a later date and probably at a different spot rate. In effect, the company would have a receivable exposure for the period between payment date and receipt date. The success of a matching operation is therefore very much dependent on the quality of the information available, as embodied in the exposure projections. Success requires accurate prediction of the amount of settlement and, more particularly, the timing of settlement dates. Where exchange controls allow, the timing problem can be overcome by the utilization of foreign currency accounts, which allow the retiming of currency conversions to facilitate matching. The cost of neutralizing exposures in this way is represented by the effective interest rate differential (including the deposit/borrowing rate spread) between the foreign and domestic currency.

LEADING AND LAGGING

This simply refers to the adjustment of intercompany credit terms, 'leading' meaning a prepayment of a trade obligation and 'lagging' a delayed payment. This is primarily an intercompany technique because in third party trade there is a clear conflict of interest between buyer and seller. Whilst netting and matching are purely defensive measures, intercompany leading and lagging can be used as part of either a risk-minimizing strategy (to facilitate matching) or an aggressive strategy (to maximize expected exchange gains). In either case a central information and decision point is usually required, to ensure that the timing of intercompany settlements is effective from a group point of view rather than a purely local one.

As with other schemes involving central (corporate or regional treasury) decision making, leading and lagging requires a lot of discipline on the part of participating subsidiaries. Apart from the exposure impacts, such operations can seriously affect the liquidity — and hence profitability — of each subsidiary. To overcome the consequent evaluation problem, multinational companies which make extensive use of leading and lagging may either evaluate subsidiary performance on a pre-interest basis or impute interest charges and credits where appropriate.

Perhaps of more importance is the net cost of the leading and lagging operation to the corporate group. There are three elements in this calculation: (a) a cash cost/benefit represented by the interest rate differential between the lead and lag countries; (b) an expected cash gain/loss to be realized on the altered transactional exposures arising in the lead/lag countries; and (c) an expected translation gain/loss arising on the altered translation exposures in the lead/lag countries. Two relevant factors which must not be ignored in this translation computation are the effective tax rates in the countries concerned and the currency of intercompany invoicing.

A simple decision format can be used to calculate the cash (interest and realized foreign exchange) effects and the translation impact. It is then up to each company to decide on the appropriate trade-off between these two kinds of effect. With clear guidelines from senior management, the lead/lag decision is a relatively straightforward one for the treasury department.

One very important complicating factor, however, is the existence of local minority interests. If there are powerful local shareholders in the 'losing' subsidiary there will be strong objections because of the added interest costs/lower profitability resulting from the consequent local borrowing. In such cases of leading and lagging the interests of the minority shareholders are subordinated to those of the majority shareholder (the parent company). Host governments, via credit and exchange controls, may well restrict such operations.

It should be obvious from this discussion of liquidity effects that the applications of leading and lagging extend beyond pure exposure management — it is, for instance, a very useful tool for shifting intercompany funds for the purpose of liquidity management. As a financing technique, leading and lagging is often more appropriate than straightforward intercompany loans. In the USA, for example, the Internal Revenue Service now generally allows intercompany accounts to be extended to at least six months without imputing interest, while interest must be charged at reasonable rates on intercompany loans. However, if payments are lagged beyond six months then the IRS may impute interest income, thereby increasing the company's taxable revenues. Hence US companies tend to limit their lags to six months or convert the positions into intercompany loans thereafter.

The main external constraints on leading and lagging are tax and exchange controls. Given the much-publicized effects of leading and lagging on exchange rates and balance of payments figures, many governments have restricted the scope for such operations by imposing maximum credit terms on international trading. These controls are reviewed in Chapter 12.

PRICING POLICY

Clearly, marketing (and sourcing) factors will be the major influence on any company's pricing policies, but for the purpose of our analysis we will try to isolate the exposure management role of pricing policy. In other words, the inherent assumption in the following analysis is that marketing and sourcing considerations do not place insuperable barriers on exposure management-oriented pricing decisions. In practice, of course, this assumption will not always hold since exchange risk is but one input into a company's overall pricing strategy, but the assumption is necessary for our analysis.

For exposure management purposes there are two kinds of pricing tactics: price variation and currency-of-invoicing policy. (In effect, the latter tactic is a subtle variant of the former.) For each of these it is necessary to distinguish between external and intercompany trading, since each kind of trading gives rise to a different set of problems and opportunities.

Price Variation

Price Variation: External Trade

One obvious way for a company to protect itself against exchange risk is to raise selling prices to offset the adverse effects of exchange rate fluctuations. Indeed, in some environments this may be the only exposure management technique available. In Latin America, for instance, other internal tactics are severely restricted by exchange controls, and external techniques (forward cover, local borrowing) may either be non-existent or prohibitively costly.

The question which always arises with the pricing option, of course, is that if the company is able to raise prices then why has it not done so already, irrespective of exposure considerations? If we assume prices are *not* lower than necessary before the currency movement, then the only two rejoinders here are that, firstly, pricing policy involves a number of non-financial considerations — the treasury input may be the additional justification which persuades marketing management that a price change is now appropriate; and secondly, competitive conditions may have changed as a result of the currency movement, thereby allowing a price increase to be made.

The second point leads to the crucial question of pricing flexibility. A key determinant of the economic exposure of a foreign market (either that of the regular exporter or the foreign sales subsidiary) is the price adjustment lag. Given an adverse exchange rate change (or trend), how quickly can local selling prices be increased to bring the parent currency equivalent of the foreign operation's cash flows back to the pre-depreciation level? The determination of this lag requires an analysis of the following questions:

1. *Competitive situation* — what sector of the market are we in? A firm selling in the import or import-competing sectors is likely to have greater pricing flexibility than one in the purely domestic sector. The question of timing is also important: is there any scope for anticipatory price increases, given an expectation of an adverse currency movement?

2. *Customer credibility* — when did our company last increase its prices and will there be customer resistance to another price rise?

3. *Price controls* — are these in existence or likely to be introduced in the near future? Given the existence of such controls, to what extent do they allow the adverse impact of an exchange rate change to be recouped by subsequent price increases, and how quickly?

4. *Internal delays* — what are the administrative lags involved in raising prices? Foreign currency price lists can be the source of significant delays, depending on how regularly they are reviewed and how lengthy is the review process. For a price list involving thousands of items such delays can be serious.

A related factor here is the choice of exchange rates used to translate parent currency price lists into foreign currencies. The use of spot rates will accentuate price adjustment delays. Instead, the exchange rate used should be a forecasted rate (or alternatively, the forward rate) for the period in which the price list is expected to be in operation. Hence pricing automatically includes a factor to cover any expected depreciation of the currency during the adjustment lag (exposure) period. Alternatively, where the product and sales pattern permits, such exposures can be eliminated by deriving local currency prices from a parent currency price list at the current exchange rate (plus a risk premium for the receivables turnover period). Local currency prices will then automatically adjust for changes in the local currency/parent currency exchange rate, thereby eliminating the price adjustment lag.

5. *Trading/financing pattern* — if a firm does not have pricing flexibility for any of the above reasons, does it have a trading pattern or can one be created in which adverse currency impacts in one area of the business will be offset by positive effects elsewhere? For example, a foreign subsidiary which imports raw materials and sells locally is exposed to a local currency depreciation. To the extent that it can shift its sourcing (to domestic suppliers) or its selling (to foreign customers), this economic exposure may be reduced. This kind of action, which can be applied to both trade and financial flows, is analyzed in the section on Asset and Liability Management on p. 113.

Price Variation: Intercompany Trade
Intercompany (or transfer) price variation refers to the arbitrary pricing of intercompany transfers of goods and services at a higher or lower figure than the 'fair' or 'arm's length' price (the market price if there is an established market or the price which would be charged to a third party customer if there is not). However, multinational companies must always now set intercompany prices on an arm's length basis, as generally required by tax and exchange control authorities. In the USA, for example, the Internal Revenue Service

has power to reallocate income among members of a corporate group where transfer price manipulation is suspected. Similarly, in many countries the customs authorities have the power to mark up the invoice price (and hence the excise duty payable) where transfer price manipulation is suspected.

Currency-of-Invoicing

External Trade

Currency-of-invoicing tactics can be either aggressive or defensive. An aggressive strategy would be to try to invoice exports in relatively strong currencies — relative to the exporter's home currency (HC) — and imports in relatively weak currencies. Here the company is increasing its exposure to exchange risk in the expectation that this exposure will produce exchange gains rather than losses.

Ostensibly, at least, the defensive strategy might appear to be to try to invoice all exports and imports in HC, irrespective of the strength or weakness of the currency involved. In practice, however, a certain amount of currency exposure (typically on the payables' side) is unavoidable for many international companies given the nature of their cross-border operations. In this situation the defensive approach will not necessarily mean HC invoicing whenever possible, since the introduction of foreign-currency invoicing could provide greater scope for matching. For example, if a UK-based company exports to Europe in sterling and imports from the USA in dollars or has dollar loan payables, a matching opportunity could be created by invoicing its European exports in dollars, thereby reducing the net dollar payable exposure. For the multinational company the scope for such cash flow matching is considerably extended, since the export receivables of subsidiary A might be globally matched with the import or local currency payables of subsidiary B.

For the strong currency exporter (Germany, Switzerland) the defensive approach is the only one available for export invoicing since the HC is probably also the strongest currency acceptable to the customer. For the weak currency exporter, however, there may be significant opportunity gains from an aggressive currency-of-invoicing policy. In such circumstances foreign currency invoicing may be attractive to the exporter, in the expectation that the HC-equivalent sales proceeds would be increased by a foreign currency appreciation over the credit period. It should be added, however, that there are risks involved in switching from a weak currency to a supposedly stronger one. The relative strengths of the two currencies could reverse themselves in the future and, once having changed to foreign currency billing, companies will find it difficult to switch back to HC-invoicing if the currency situation alters. In any case, currency-of-invoicing cannot be changed regularly – quite apart from customer objections and the loss of customer credibility, there is the problem of price list adjustment lags.

Currency-of-invoicing changes will also have to be 'sold' to subsidiary management as well as to customers. Indeed, resistance at operating unit level may present major problems to a corporate treasury trying to make the initial switch to foreign currency invoicing. Subsidiaries may be reluctant to give up the perceived marketing advantages of weak currency invoicing, particularly since – if corporate exposure management is to be centralized (often a corollary of the switch to foreign currency invoicing) – the benefits of foreign currency billing may accrue at corporate treasury.

Intercompany Trade

On a pre-tax basis, the distinction between aggressive and defensive approaches to currency-of-invoicing disappears in the context of intercompany trade, since what is one subsidiary's benefit (higher profit or lower risk) is another subsidiary's loss. On an *after*-tax basis, however, there is scope for an aggressive intercompany currency-of-invoicing policy. As an extreme example, if subsidiaries A and B trade with each other and A pays a higher tax rate, then A might be directed to invoice B in a weak currency and B to invoice A in a strong currency. After-tax group income may be increased, although such an approach can also create internal (motivation and evaluation) and external (tax) problems.

In practice, therefore, the major role of intercompany currency-of-invoicing policy is often an organizational one. Intercompany currency-of-billing procedures can be structured in such a way that transactional exposures are centralized within one (or more) specialized unit(s) within the group. For instance, if a US company exports to its worldwide marketing subsidiaries in US dollars, these subsidiaries then have the problem of managing their foreign currency ($) payables' exposures. An alternative approach is for US-based manufacturing units to invoice foreign subsidiaries in their local currencies. This eliminates the intercompany payables' exposures of overseas companies – the exchange risk now arises centrally as a parent country (US) receivables' exposure problem. Further concentration of the exposure management function may then be achieved by the implementation of structural or reporting-based systems for centralization. These organizational approaches are discussed in Chapter 9.

ASSET AND LIABILITY MANAGEMENT

Asset and liability management techniques can be used to manage balance sheet, income statement and/or cash flow exposures. They can also be used aggressively or defensively. The aggressive approach is to increase exposed assets, revenues, and cash inflows denominated in strong currencies and to increase exposed liabilities, expenses, and cash outflows in weak currencies. In contrast, the defensive firm will seek to minimize foreign exchange gains and losses by matching the currency denomination of assets/liabilities, revenues/expenses, and cash inflows/outflows, irrespective of the distinction between strong and weak currencies.

In analyzing how these objectives can be achieved, it is useful to make the distinction between operating variables (trade receivables and payables, inventory, fixed assets) and financial variables (cash, short-term investments and debt).

The currency denomination of *operating variables* is largely determined by intrinsic business conditions, such as production and marketing factors. Nevertheless, some fine tuning of existing exposures is often possible. Consider the case of a foreign subsidiary located in a weak currency country. If the 'all-current' method of translation is used then operating variables will tend to generate positive balance sheet exposures. Hence, the aim of asset/liability management here might be to reduce the subsidiary's local currency (LC) asset exposures and increase LC liabilities. LC receivables could be reduced by shortening the length of credit terms, offering special discounts and discounting or factoring — all of which involve costs (lower sales, higher cash discounts or factoring charges) which may well outweigh the potential benefits. Similarly, local inventories could be run down to lower levels. The reverse process is applied on the liability side. Trade payables can be increased by deferring payment, which may mean missing trade discounts and a loss of goodwill if applied to third party suppliers. Such costs must be compared with the perceived benefits of reducing the net asset exposure in a given currency.

The manipulation of operating variables can also be used in cash-flow-oriented exposure management. Take the case of a German exporter with a continuing and significant flow of Canadian dollar receipts. Given the marketing costs of Deutsche Mark invoicing and the size of the forward discount and interest rate differential between the Canadian dollar and the Deutsche Mark, this company chose to source from Canada as a means of nullifying its receivables' exposure. Clearly such changes will not always be possible. Nevertheless, the choice of exposure management technique should begin with a consideration of the opportunities for this kind of action.

The next step is to consider how *financial variables* can be manipulated for exposure management purposes, and it is here that corporate financial management has most discretion over currency denomination. Let us revert to the case of the positive balance sheet exposure of a foreign subsidiary located in a weak currency country. The treasury management objective here would normally be to reduce net exposed financial assets, which means reducing local currency (LC) cash/near cash balance and increasing LC denominated debt.

The LC cash balance is, in effect, the residual of all other asset/liability management actions. In the weak currency situation, the subsidiary's cash position will be increased by such tactics as increasing LC trade payables and borrowings and reducing LC receivable balances. For such asset/liability management actions to be effective, the resultant weak currency cash must be converted into non-exposed assets. This is typically achieved by transferring this cash back to the parent company or to strong-currency-based subsidiaries, by such tactics as intercompany leading and lagging, the payment of higher dividends and quasi-dividends (royalties, management fees) and the repayment of parent company debt.

The capital structure of the weak-currency-based subsidiary can be organized to facilitate such transfers of funds. For example, retained earnings might not be capitalized so that extra dividends can be paid out of reserves; a high ratio of intercompany debt to parent equity in the subsidiary's capital structure might enable the timely repayment of funds in circumstances where a high dividend payment might be restricted. This assumes, of course, that LC financing is available to replace the intercompany funds which are to be withdrawn and also that host government regulations allow such foreign subsidiary capital structures. (In practice, the host government may impose limits and/or heavy taxes on dividends and other forms of funds repatriation, and it may require that a certain proportion of parent debt and retained earnings be capitalized.) Other advantages of parent company debt are that repayments are not normally taxed (unless these are held to be a 'constructive dividend') and are less frowned upon by exchange control authorities.

This leads us to the second, and major, area of financial asset/liability management: currency-of-financing policy. For the weak-currency-based subsidiary with a net asset exposure, the aim of both the defensive and aggressive risk/return approaches will typically be to increase LC debt. This debt falls into two basic maturity categories: short term and long term. The scarcity of weak currency finance is often a major constraint here but, subject to availability, the parent company would typically borrow the weak currency long term, whilst the subsidiary is usually restricted to local bank (short-term) borrowing. This is because (a) most subsidiaries are not individually listed on a stock exchange, so that the public issue of debt instruments is very difficult (hence the bulk of long-term loans taken out by foreign subsidiaries are private placements); (b) many foreign subsidiaries are relatively small and not well known to the local financial community; and (c) host governments may be reluctant to allow long-term borrowing by expatriate subsidiaries, arguing that — for balance of payments reasons — long-term funds should be supplied by the parent company.

In practice the most important of these two forms of finance is local bank borrowing, mainly because such short-term debt is more likely to be available. Also, for the parent company of a multinational operation, borrowing long term in each of its subsidiaries' currencies would involve incremental administrative and interest costs.

In the context of cash flow exposure management, the distinction between aggressive and defensive currency-of-financing policies is an important one. With an aggressive financial management strategy the aim of currency-of-financing policy is simply to borrow in those currencies which have the cheapest effective interest cost, after tax. 'Cost' here consists of three elements: (a) nominal interest cost; (b) the projected exchange gain/loss on repayment of principal and interest — for example, if a US corporation is faced with the choice of borrowing Deutsche Marks at 4% per annum or US dollars at 8% per annum and it expected the Deutsche Mark to appreciate against the dollar by 5% per annum over the life of the loan, then the company may prefer to borrow dollars because the effective interest cost is cheaper by 1% per annum; and (c) the tax treatment of exchange gains/losses arising on the repayment of foreign currency principal and interest and on any related covering operations. Tax treatment can be a vital consideration since in many countries exchange gains/losses on the repayment of principal are not taxable/tax allowable. Hence the effective after-tax cost of borrowing relatively strong foreign currencies is thereby made considerably more expensive. Similarly, the high pre-tax cost of borrowing weak currencies is reduced if exchange gains on repayment of principal do not fall into the tax net. (These considerations are analyzed in Chapter 11.)

For the defensive firm the aim of international financial management should be to arrange the financing pattern of the company so that the detrimental effects of currency movements are minimized, whatever the exchange rate scenario. This can be done by structuring the group's liabilities in such a way that any change in cash inflows (operating revenues) induced by a currency movement is offset as much as possible by a countervailing change in cash outflows (effective interest costs). The application of this principle to the exporter and multinational cases has been analyzed in Chapter 6. The basic conclusion was that, to neutralize cash flow exposures, a company should finance in those currencies in which its operations generate net cash inflows. In effect, then, the cash flow approach to financing represents a long-term application of the 'matching' technique discussed earlier. The only difference is that here the foreign currency trade receipts are being 'matched' against foreign currency loan (rather than trade) payments.

REVIEW QUESTIONS

1. Express, in the form of a netting matrix, the netting potential of the following annual intercompany trade flows: the US sells to the UK ($30 million), France ($20 million), Germany ($10 million) and Italy ($5 million); the UK sells to Italy ($15 million) and Germany ($5 million); France sells to Italy ($10 million) and Germany ($5 million); and Italy sells to the US ($15 million).

2. Suggest two currency groups which might each be used for 'parallel' matching. Graph past currency movements to support your case.

3. The UK sells to its German affiliate in sterling on three-month credit terms. For the UK and Germany respectively, marginal annual interest rates are 15% and 8% and tax rates are 52% and 56%. The annualized Deutsche Mark premium against sterling is 6%. Assuming linear interest and exchange rate relationships, calculate the incremental percentage cash impacts of leading (Germany pays immediately) and lagging (Germany pays after six months). Also discuss the broader implications for a multinational group using this technique.

4. A Japanese parent company exports in yen to its European sales companies (France, Germany, Italy) which sell on into their domestic markets. The European sales companies have cash flow, income statement, and balance sheet exposures (the parent company uses the 'all-current' translation method). Discuss how operational (pricing, currency-of-invoicing) and financial (currency-of-financing) policies can be used to reduce exposures at the local (European) level.

BIBLIOGRAPHY

See Chapter 9 for a combined bibliography on both internal and external exposure
management techniques.
See *Business International Money Report* and *Euromoney* for regular articles by
practitioners on corporate exposure management techniques.

Aubey R.T. and Cramer R.H. (1977), 'The use of international currency cocktails
    in the reduction of exchange rate risk', *Journal of Economics and Business*,
    29, No. 2, Winter.
Business International (1971), *Hedging Foreign Exchange Risks: Management
    Monograph 49*. New York, Business International Corporation.
Chown J. and Finney M. (1977), *Foreign Currency Debt Management*. London,
    J.F. Chown and Co. Ltd.
Euromoney (1978), *Management of Foreign Exchange Risks*. London, Euromoney
    Publications.
Goeltz R.K. (1971), 'Managing liquid funds on an international scale', Presentation
    to the American Management Association Conference on International Cash
    Management, November.
Hague D.C., Oakeshott W.E.F., and Strain A.A. (1974), *Devaluation and Pricing
    Decisions*. London, Allen and Unwin.
Prindl A.R. (1976), *Foreign Exchange Risk*. London, Wiley.
Robbins S.M. and Stobaugh R.B. (1976), *Money in the Multinational Enterprise:
    A Study in Financial Policy*. London, Longman.

CHAPTER 8

Exposure Management: External Techniques

External techniques are specific contractual arrangements, 'external' to the firm, which are designed to insure against the possibility of a loss arising from an existing exchange risk position. External techniques can be applied to both transaction and translation exposures. However, the exchange control authorities in many countries require that a genuine commercial transaction must underlie a resident company's request for forward currency or other similar exposure management facilities. In most major industrial countries (the chief exceptions are the USA, the UK, West Germany and Switzerland), the external hedging of unrealizable translation exposures is forbidden.

In contrast to internal exposure management methods, the complete range of external techniques can be used by both exporters and importers as well as by multinational companies. Another difference is that, ostensibly at least, the costs of the external exposure management methods are fixed and predetermined. However, there is some disagreement as to precisely how the 'cost' of certain external techniques should be defined. This controversy will be explained below.

The external exposure management techniques to be examined here are:

1. Forward exchange contracts
2. Short-term borrowing
3. Discounting bills receivable
4. Factoring receivables
5. Government exchange risk guarantees

Major emphasis will be placed on the first two techniques, forward exchange contracts and short-term borrowing, because they are the most commonly used and the most generally applicable of the external techniques — they can be used to cover transactions' exposures (both receivables and payables) as well as to hedge translation exposures.

Incidentally, let us clarify the distinction between 'covering' and 'hedging' at the outset. There is some disagreement as to the precise meaning of these two terms, and indeed they are sometimes used interchangeably. The distinction between covering and hedging is, however, a useful one. The basis of this difference is that covering is connected with a self-liquidating arrangement whereas hedging is not. Covering therefore implies protection against a cash flow exposure which could otherwise lead to a realized gain or loss. Thus a forward sale to protect the home currency (HC) value of a foreign currency receivable is a covering operation, since on settlement date the foreign currency receivable will automatically liquidate the forward sale. In contrast, hedging involves the protection of the accounting value of foreign-currency-denominated assets and liabilities against *unrealized* losses (and gains). Hence such forward sales of foreign currency would not be self-liquidating, but rather would have to be met by a subsequent purchase in the spot market. In the following analysis, then, 'covering' will be used in connection with transactions' exposure management whereas 'hedging' implies the protection of an unrealizable translation exposure.

FORWARD EXCHANGE CONTRACTS

The 'classical' exposure management technique is the purchase or sale of a company's future currency commitments in the forward market. The currency commitment to be protected may be either in the form of a transaction or a translation exposure. For tax and exchange control reasons it is necessary to distinguish between forward contracts relating to each kind of exposure.

Before considering covering and hedging in the forward markets, we must first state a brief qualification as to the availability of forward currency. Such markets exist in the currencies of most major industrial countries in the world. Elsewhere, they are far less common, as Appendix 3A to Chapter 3 demonstrates. Also, the period of cover available is a function of the size of a particular deal (very large amounts may be difficult to place) and the volume of a particular forward market. Periods of up to 12 months are readily available in the major forward markets (e.g. dollar/sterling, dollar/Deutsche Mark, dollar/Swiss franc), but elsewhere the market may thin out at shorter maturities. Very large forward contracts with maturities of ten years or more can be put together, typically with a major international bank acting as intermediary between two commercial customers (multinational corporations or government agencies) with offsetting long-term currency needs. Nevertheless, generally the principle applies that the bigger the required deal and the more exotic the currencies involved, the less is the likelihood that a forward contract is obtainable.

Forward Covering (Transactions' Exposure)

The operation of this type of forward deal can be easily demonstrated by the use of a simple but not atypical example. On 31 March 1979, a UK company enters into an export contract with a French customer. The goods are shipped immediately, the credit period is 90 days, and the invoice amount is FFr 1million. Hence on 30 June 1979, our UK treasurer expects to receive FFr 1million. This receivable is then booked at the exchange rate prevailing on the invoice date (8.9700), giving a sterling equivalent receivable of £111,483.

Yet what sterling amount will our company actually receive for its one million francs on 30 June 1979? If the franc/sterling spot rate remains unchanged over the exposure term (the period during which the receivable or payable is exposed, which in this case is the credit period of 90 days[1]) then there will be no discrepancy between the sterling-equivalent receivable booked and the actual sterling receipt. However, in our present currency environment such stability is unlikely, so that as at 31 March the actual sterling receipt is unknown. In other words, the one million franc receivable is 'exposed' to exchange risk over the 90 days, the 'risk' element being that currency movements (in this case a depreciation of the franc vis-à-vis sterling) will adversely affect the final sterling receipt. What can our treasurer do to avoid the possibility of such a loss?

The 'classical' prescription, as illustrated in Table 8.1, would be as follows. Simultaneously with the signing of the export contract the UK company sells the franc receipts in the forward exchange market at a fixed price for delivery at the receivable payment date. This fixed price will be the 90-day forward rate, which in this case is the current spot rate (8.9700) plus the forward franc discount (0.425), i.e. 9.0125.[2] This means that our exporter has contracted to deliver FFr 1million in 90 days time at the forward rate of 9.0125. Whatever happens to the franc/sterling spot and forward rates over the next 90 days, this contracted forward rate remains irrevocably fixed. Hence on 30 June 1979, the UK company should receive its customer's payment of FFr 1million. This is then delivered to the bank handling the forward

Table 8.1 Forward Cover

Exposure

Seller	UK company
Buyer	French company
Contract and invoice date	31 March 1979
Credit terms	90 days
Expected settlement date	30 June 1979
Invoice value	FFr 1 million

Rates

The UK treasurer obtains the following exchange rate quotations as at 31 March 1979 (all quotations are selling rates):

Spot rate	£1 = FFr 8.9700
90-day forward discount on FFr	FFr 0.0425
Thus 90-day forward rate	£1 = FFr 9.0125

Prescription

The UK treasurer decides to cover the exposed receivable in the forward market, as follows:

31 March 1979	sells FFr 1 million forward for 90 days at 9.0125
30 June 1979	receives FFr 1 million from customer. Delivers FFr 1 million at 9.0125 as per forward contract, yielding £110,957

deal and, as agreed in the forward contract, our exporter receives a sterling credit of £110,957.

By covering forward our exporter (or importer) need no longer worry about the exchange risk element in the foreign transaction.[3] What price has been paid for this protection? This is clearly an important question since, in deciding between various covering techniques (including internal techniques, such as 'doing nothing') it is the least-cost alternative which should be chosen. There is, however, some disagreement on how to calculate the cost of forward cover, mainly because there are two kinds of 'cost' involved: an *ex ante* cost and an *ex post* (opportunity) cost.[4]

The *ex ante* cost of a forward contract is simply the difference between the booked receivable or payable (the foreign currency amount converted into the home currency (HC) at the spot rate prevailing on the invoice date) and the amount actually received or paid (the foreign currency amount converted into HC at the forward rate). In the above example this *ex ante* cost is £526 or 1.92% per annum — see Table 8.2(a) — and this amount will be booked as an additional cost of sales.

Table 8.2 The 'Cost' of Forward Cover

(a) Ex ante cost

$$= \pounds\frac{\text{Foreign currency receivable/payable}}{\text{Spot rate at contract date}} - \pounds\frac{\text{Foreign currency receivable/payable}}{\text{Forward contract rate}}$$

$$= \pounds\frac{1,000,000}{8.9700} - \pounds\frac{1,000,000}{9.0125}$$

$$= \pounds111,483 - \pounds110,957$$

$$= \pounds526$$

This can be converted into annual percentage terms as follows:

$$\begin{matrix}\text{Annualized discount}\\\text{(premium) on domestic}\\\text{currency}\end{matrix} = \frac{\text{Forward rate* } - \text{ Spot rate*}}{\text{Spot rate*}} \times \frac{365}{\begin{matrix}\text{Contract term}\\\text{(days)}\end{matrix}} \times 100$$

$$= \frac{0.1110^\dagger - 0.1115^\dagger}{0.1110^\dagger} \times \frac{365}{90} \times 100$$

$$= \frac{0.0005}{0.1110} \times 4.0555 \times 100$$

$$= 1.92\% \text{ p.a. premium}$$

The *ex ante* cost is often interpreted as representing *the* cost of forward cover. This view is incorrect if, as is normal, 'cost' is used as a decision making criterion. The *ex ante* cost is simply the annualized percentage discount (or premium) of the foreign currency *vis-à-vis* the HC. A discount/premium in the forward market does not represent a cost, but rather it reflects (a) the difference between the free (Euro-)market interest rate of the exporter's currency and that of the foreign currency: (Any difference between forwards and Euro-currency interest rates would very quickly disappear since this represents a profitable opportunity for covered interest arbitrage. The only exception to this rule is in those countries where exchange controls restrict the access of residents to the Euro-markets. In such countries — France, Italy — the 'domestic' forward rate is determined by the differential between the *domestic* interest rate available to residents and the Euro-interest rate of the foreign currency. This 'domestic' forward rate will generally be different from the 'Euro' forward rate available to non-residents.) and (b) the combined judgment of all market participants on the future spot rate — otherwise par-

(b) Ex post (Opportunity) cost

$$= £\frac{\text{Foreign currency receivable/payable}}{\text{Spot rate at settlement date}} - £\frac{\text{Foreign currency receivable/payable}}{\text{Forward contract rate}}$$

At settlement date (30 June 1979) spot rate = 8.4550

$$\text{Thus ex post cost} = £\frac{1,000,000}{8.4550} - £\frac{1,000,000}{9.0125}$$

$$= £118,273 - £110,957$$

$$= £7,316$$

815661

* To express the cost in domestic currency percentage terms, spot and forward rates must be expressed as the amount of domestic currency per unit of foreign currency (i.e. direct quotation). Where rates are expressed as the amount of foreign currency per unit of domestic currency (indirect quotation, as used in the UK, e.g. £spot = FFr8.9700), then the reciprocals of the quoted rates should be used to calculate cost in domestic currency terms:

$$\text{Cost of forward cover} = \frac{1/FR - 1/SR}{1/SR} \times \frac{365}{\text{Contract term}} \times 100$$

$$= \frac{SR - FR}{FR} \times \frac{365}{\text{Contract term}} \times 100$$

Applying the standard formula (FR − SR)/SR to direct and indirect quotations will always give different results, unless the forward rate is at par. This is because costs are expressed in domestic currency terms and foreign currency terms respectively. However, unless the premium/discount is large, then (ignoring the signs) the difference in the results will be small.

† To avoid rounding errors, the exact reciprocals are 0.110957004 (FR) and 0.11148272 (SR).

---

ticipants could enter into forward contracts and expect to make a profit on settlement date. Unfortunately, it is usually impossible to distinguish between these two elements because of the feedback effects which changing forward premiums and discounts have on interest rates.

The most useful definition of the cost of forward cover is the *ex post* or opportunity cost approach. This defines the cost of forward cover as the HC amount which would have been received (paid) if the exposed receivable (payable) had been left uncovered, less the HC amount which the forward contract yields. In other words, it represents the difference between the foreign currency amount converted into HC at the settlement date spot rate and the foreign currency converted at the forward rate.

In our example the treasurer will find that the settlement date spot rate has moved to 8.4550. In other words the franc has not depreciated against sterling, as the forward discount predicted, but instead it has appreciated. As Table 8.2(b) shows, if our treasurer had done nothing about his franc exposure — which is, of course, a perfectly reasonable exposure management option — he would have received £118,273 (1,000,000 ÷ 8.4550) rather than the £110,957 which the forward contract yielded. Thus the real or opportunity cost of the forward contract is £7,316, a figure which greatly exceeds the *ex ante* cost.

This 'forward rate versus settlement spot rate' approach is, of course, a rather limited definition of the opportunity cost concept. The difference between the forward rate and the settlement spot rate represents just one possible opportunity forgone, of which there are many incurred daily. Strictly speaking, the 'real' opportunity cost of a forward contract is the difference between the forward rate taken and the most favorable rate available (between the contract date and the maturity date) for that maturity date. In other words, the forward rate taken should be compared not only with the settlement date spot rate but also with all the possible forward rates available over the exposure term.

Clearly, such a definition of opportunity cost is a very strict measure of the efficacy of a firm's forward cover policy — inevitably, almost every forward cover decision would result in such an 'opportunity loss'. Very few companies try to measure the 'true' opportunity cost of their forward cover actions, and even then only one or two forward rates per day are used in the calculations. For practical purposes, then, the 'forward rate versus settlement spot rate' approach provides a reasonable estimate of opportunity cost.

Another point to emphasize about the opportunity cost of forward cover is that, quite clearly, it cannot be known until settlement date. It is only with the aid of hindsight that the treasurer can judge whether the forward deal was in fact the cheapest exchange risk management option. (As one treasurer told us: 'Any schoolboy's hindsight is worth more than the president's foresight!') Hence the opportunity cost approach does not explicitly provide us with a decision-making criterion that will help determine when a company should cover forward. This is the basis of some practitioners' criticisms of the opportunity cost definition. Yet a decision rule can be easily distilled from the *ex post* approach: a company should compare the forward rate with its *forecast* of the future spot rate. If the forward rate underestimates the expected rate of depreciation or overestimates the expected rate of appreciation, the firm might be willing to sell the currency forward and buy at future spot rates. If the forward rate overestimates the expected depreciation or underestimates the expected appreciation, the firm might prefer to sell at future spot rates and buy at present forward rates. (The inherent assumption in these decision rules is, of course, that the firm believes its currency forecasts can outpredict the forward rate).

Some Practical Complications:
Forward Option and Forward Swap Contracts

In our example it has been assumed that the receivable will be paid in a lump sum on the last day of the three-month credit period. In those industries where individual orders are very large (computers, shipbuilding) and where customer payments are prompt (intercompany trade) such a situation may well apply. For the vast majority of companies, however, cash flows are not so discrete or predictable. Individual sales or purchase transactions generally involve much smaller amounts, credit terms are not always adhered to by customers, and shipping and bank transfer delays occasionally occur. In the typical case, then, forward contracts of a reasonable size and for a specific date are difficult to match with foreign currency cash flows.

Analytically, at least, two kinds of practical difficulties can be distinguished. The first problem is that the settlement date cannot be predicted exactly. (This is especially relevant to the case of the exporter, but even for the importer shipping delays can produce uncertainty of settlement dates.) The second difficulty is that cash flows (receipts and payments) occur on a continuing basis and are not normally composed of large and discrete transactions — hence they do not readily lend themselves to large and discrete forward deals. We will now examine these two common problems, and the way in which the forward cover technique can handle them.

Imprecise Settlement Dates

The two basic ways of covering a foreign currency receivable (or payable) with an imprecise settlement date by using the forward market are forward option and forward swap deals. The way in which these operate will again be illustrated by using the example of a UK exporter with a French franc receivable. This time, however, the customer's settlement date is unspecified within the range of the 90th—120th days after the contract/invoice date, rather than being fixed on the 90th day.

The first alternative is that our exporter can purchase an *optional date forward contract* with a 90—120 day option. As with all forward deals the exchange rate is irrevocably fixed when the forward contract is made. Yet with an option contract the exact maturity date is left for the company to decide subsequently — with the proviso, of course, that the maturity date must fall within the 90—120 day option period. Hence, in this case (see Table 8.3) the UK exporter could sell the one million francs forward on a 90—120 day option contract at the rate of 9.0300. Whatever the date between the 90th and 120th days when the option is taken up, the one million francs will be sold at the forward option rate, yielding £110,742.

Table 8.3 Forward Option Contract

Exposure
    Seller   UK company
    Buyer   French company
    Contract and invoice date   31 March 1979
    Expected settlement period   30 June—31 July 1979
    Invoice Value   FFr 1 million

Rates
    The UK treasurer obtains the following exchange rate quotations as at
    31 March 1979 (all quotations are selling rates):

Spot rate	£1 = FFr 8.9700
90-day forward discount on FFr	FFr 0.0425
90-day forward rate	£1 = FFr 9.0125
120-day forward discount on FFr	FFr 0.0600
120-day forward rate	£1 = FFr 9.0300
90—120-day option FFr selling* rate	£1 = FFr 9.0300

Prescription
    The UK treasurer decides to cover the exposed receivable in the forward
    market, as follows:

31 March 1979	sells FFr 1 million forward for 90—120 days at option rate of 9.0300
15 July 1979 (say†)	receives FFr 1 million from customer. Delivers FFr 1 million at 9.0300, as per forward option contract, yielding £110,742.

---

* The French franc buying rate for a 90—120 day option would be 9.0125, i.e. the least favorable for the customer.
† The precise timing of the settlement date within the option period is irrelevant.

Whilst this is the simplest method of dealing with an uncertain payment date, it can also be costly. Since the bank does not know when the option will be taken up it will charge the premium or discount for the most costly of the settlement dates within the customer's option period. In this example, then, the 90—120 day forward option rate to the seller of francs is the full 120-day discount. Similarly, the buyer of francs on a 90—120 day option would be quoted only the 90-day discount, again the most unfavorable rate for the customer.[5]

Incidentally, the knowledge of which forward rate determines the forward option rate — the 'option-determining rate' — should influence a company in its choice of option period. Option-determining rates for premium and discount currencies (*vis-à-vis* sterling) are illustrated

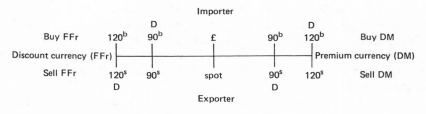

90 = 90-day forward rate
120 = 120-day forward rate
b = foreign currency buying rate
s = foreign currency selling rate
D = option-determining rate

Figure 8.1 Option-determining rates

in Figure 8.1. For the seller of foreign currency (the exporter) if the foreign currency is at a premium (e.g. Deutsche Marks) then the first date of the option is the determining rate and so it should be kept as far out as possible. The maximum option date is irrelevant to a premium currency selling option rate. Where the foreign currency to be sold is at a discount (e.g. francs) then the option-determining rate is the maximum option date, and so this furthest date should be kept as near as possible given the company's credit terms. In such circumstances the first date of the option does not affect the option rate and so it can be kept at a minimum. (In our example, then, the UK exporter may as well take out a 0–120 day option contract, since the option rate will still be the 120-day forward rate.) The reverse logic applies to buyers of foreign currency (importers).

The second technique for handling an unspecified settlement date is by the use of a swap deal, which simply means the simultaneous buying and selling of a currency for different maturities. Swap deals can be of two types: a forward/forward swap and a spot/forward swap. In both cases our exporter begins by covering the foreign currency transaction forward to an arbitrarily selected but fixed date, just as in an ordinary fixed-date forward contract. Then either (a) if the precise settlement date is subsequently agreed before the initial forward contract matures, the initial settlement date can be adjusted to the exact date by a forward/forward swap; or (b) if a precise settlement date is not agreed by the date when the initial forward contract matures, the forward cover is extended by a spot/forward swap. How do these two kinds of swaps work?

A *'forward/forward'* or *forward swap* is simply a pair of forward exchange deals involving a forward purchase and a forward sale of a currency, simultaneously entered into but of different maturities.

The first leg is for the delivery date of the original and arbitrarily dated forward contract, but in the opposite direction so that the original contract can be met. The second leg is for the desired new delivery date (now known exactly), in the same direction as the original contract so that the underlying transactions' exposure remains covered.

This abstract description may sound a little complicated, but the technique is very simple and can be readily illustrated by again referring to our French franc example (see Table 8.4). Our UK exporter begins by selling the one million francs forward for some arbitrary period of, say, 90 days (maturity date 30 June 1979). On 15 May 1979 the French customer finally agrees on a settlement date of 15 July 1979. The UK company can now adjust its forward cover to the precise settlement date by using a forward swap. The first leg of the swap is the purchase of FFr 1 million forward for 45 days, to enable the company to supply the francs necessary to meet its original forward sale. This one million francs is simultaneously sold back to the bank on a 60-day forward contract, so that the franc receivable is covered right up to 15 July. Finally, on 15 July the customer's payment and the second forward sale duly cancel out, yielding a final sterling receipt of £110,957 – £117,647 + £117,371 = £110,681.

A *spot/forward swap* is again a simultaneous pair of foreign exchange deals, except here the first leg consists of a spot purchase (sale) and the second leg is a forward sale (purchase). The technique works in much the same way as the forward/forward swap, except that our exporter would meet the original, fixed-date forward sale of francs by a spot purchase at the contract maturity date (the first leg of the swap). At the same time the exporter would enter into a new forward sale contract, thereby extending the cover. Eventually, when the receivable is settled the franc receipts would liquidate the forward sale. In terms of Table 8.4 then, instead of closing out the original contract by a forward purchase on 15 May 1979 our exporter would buy back the franc requirement by a spot purchase on 30 June 1979. Similarly, the second leg of a spot/forward swap would be a forward sale entered into on 30 June 1979 rather than on 15 May 1979.

The main shortcoming of swap (forward/forward and spot forward) deals is that they do not give complete protection against exchange risk. The residual risk is of two types. The most obvious problem is that there may be an adverse change in the premium/discount between the date of the original contract and the date of adjustment. In terms of Table 8.4, for instance, if the French franc became very weak on 15 May, then the cost of covering the exposure through to the exact settlement date will become much more expensive (although

Table 8.4 Forward/Forward Swap

Exposure details and rates as in Table 8.3.

Prescription

The UK treasurer decides to cover the exposed receivable by a forward/forward swap, as follows:

31 March 1979	sells FFr 1million forward for arbitrary period of, say, 90 days (settlement date 30 June 1979) at rate of 9.0125.
15 May 1979	customer settlement date finally agreed at 15 July 1979. To meet original forward sale, buys FFr 1 million forward for 45 days at 8.5000.
	To cover franc receivable to 15 July 1979, sells FFr 1 million forward for 60 days at 8.5200.
30 June 1979	original sale of FFr 1million at 9.0125 yields £110,957
	This short franc position met by subsequent purchase of FFr 1million at 8.5000, costing (£117,647)
15 July 1979	receives FFr 1million from customer.
	Delivers FFr 1million at 8.52000, as per second forward sale, yielding £117,371
	Net sterling yield* £110,681

* Pre-tax and ignoring interest expense for 15 days on £(117,647 − 110,957).

this increased cost may, of course, be partly offset by a reduction in the cost of buying francs forward for 45 days, the first leg of the swap). The second risk is that a breakdown of the forward market might prevent our company making the adjusting swap. The longer the period and the more exotic the currency, the fewer are the market makers and the fewer the possibilities (higher the cost) of adjusting an unwanted forward position. It should also be added, however, that unless there are heavy speculative pressures or significant interest rate changes between the two currencies involved, swaps are generally cheaper than forward option contracts.

A Continuing Stream of Foreign Currency Exposures

Where a firm's foreign business is composed of a large number of low-value foreign currency transactions it will obviously be expensive, both in terms of administration as well as transaction costs, to cover each exposed transaction individually. One way of handling this continuing exposure problem is to take out a single, large forward contract to cover a number of different receivable (or payable) exposures. Since the receivable exposures to be covered would normally be of different settlement dates, forward option contracts are preferable to fixed-date contracts for this kind of operation. Also, the value of the forward contract would usually be rounded off, to reduce the higher transaction costs associated with 'odd-values'. For this reason, and also because some of the receivables may not be settled in the option period as expected, such 'bulk' forward contracts are often closed-out by a spot purchase or sale.

The way this type of operation works is illustrated in Table 8.5, which represents the kind of forward contract report which our exporter (or importer) ought to maintain. In this example we are looking at the case of a UK exporter who has a continuing stream of Canadian dollar receipts. He decides to cover a bunch of these receivables exposures by selling Can.$ 1,000,000 forward on an option contract for settlement between 10 October 1979 and 9 December 1979 at the option rate of 1.9225. On 17 November he receives his first Canadian dollar settlement from XYZ Corporation for an amount of $243,198.92. The sterling equivalent receipt is £126,501.39 (243,198.92 ÷ 1.9225) and the balance outstanding on the forward contract is now $756,801.08 (1,000,000 − 243,198.92). Subsequent receipts on 21 and 30 November and on 6 December reduce the contract balance to $43,671.80. The UK treasurer does not expect to receive any more Canadian dollars in the near future, and so on 7 December he decides to close out the contract by a spot purchase of the balance of $43,671.80 at the prevailing spot rate of $2.00. The sterling cost of closing out is £[(43,671.80) (2.00 − 1.9225)], since our exporter is simply buying $43,671.80 at 2.00 to resell at 1.9225 (as per the forward contract).

If our exporter expected to receive more of the foreign currency

Table 8.5 Forward Option Contract Report

Forward contract number: 00001 *Amount*: Can $1,000,000 sale *Rate*: 1.9225
Bank: Morgan Guaranty Trust Company of New York
Option: 10 Oct. 79 to 9 Dec. 79

Date of payment	Customer	Foreign currency amount received Can $	Balance of contract Can $	Actual UK £ proceeds
			1,000,000	
17 Nov.	XYZ Corp.	243,198.92	756,801.08	126,501.39
21 Nov.	ABC Corp.	127,422.40	629,378.68	66,279.53
30 Nov.	DPW Corp.	313,282.28	316,096.40	162,955.67
6 Dec.	TWM Corp.	272,424.60	43,671.80	141,703.30
7 Dec.	Contract closed out at 2.00			
	£ cost = 43,671.80 X (2.00 − 1.9225)			(3,384.57)
	Net £ receipt			£494,055.32

in the near future (perhaps the expected receipts did not materialize during the option period) then he could simply roll-over the forward contract by a spot/forward swap, i.e. close out the present forward contract by a spot purchase or sale and then enter into a new forward contract, with new option dates, by a simultaneous forward sale or purchase. As already noted, of course, the danger with all such swaps is that there may have been an adverse change in the premium/discount between the date of the original contract and the date of the adjusting swap.

Forward Hedging (Translation Exposure)

Up to now we have been looking at various ways of covering the exchange risk inherent in a foreign currency transaction. Forward contracts are also used to hedge translation exposures and, for exchange control and tax purposes, it is necessary to distinguish between these two types of operation.

The point about exchange controls is simply that in most countries resident firms are not allowed to enter into forward contracts unless these relate to firm underlying commercial transactions. In other words, forward contracts designed to cover unrealizable translation exposures are forbidden. The basis of the tax distinction is that, whilst translation gains/losses (not realizable) are usually *not* taxable/tax-allowable, gains/losses on forward exchange contracts (which are realizable) are generally subject to tax. The word 'generally' is, however, used advisedly. There are two important tax qualifications which should be emphasized here.

The first point is that, whilst gains and losses on transactions-oriented forward deals (forward covering) are added to or subtracted from taxable profits, the tax treatment of translation-oriented forward contracts (forward hedging) may be asymmetrical. In particular, forward hedging losses may not be tax-allowable. Such losses are generally allowable in the USA but elsewhere the loss might be disallowed. The revenue authorities could argue that, if the forward contract was in connection with a capital asset, then it would be unreasonable to allow the loss against the parent's unrelated income when the corresponding profit on the capital asset was not brought into charge. It should also be added that this argument may not prevent the same revenue authorities from taxing the hedging gain as an unrelated gain, even though the corresponding loss was not allowed. As one international tax consultant has warned (Chown, 1975):

> wherever the law is vague it may be possible for the taxation authorities to argue, after the event, that a profit was a trading profit and therefore taxable. If the transaction goes the other way, the loss may not be allowed as a deduction.

The second tax qualification is that, even where forward hedging gains/losses are taxed/tax-allowable, the group treasurer must obviously ensure that the company which enters into the forward hedge has earned sufficient taxable profits to absorb any loss on the contract. Otherwise, of course, the tax treatment becomes in effect asymmetrical because of poor tax-planning. Not all US parent companies are profitable, and many UK companies now have low effective corporate tax rates because of Stock Appreciation Relief.

After making these two tax qualifications we will now proceed to ignore them! In other words, in the following analysis we will make the *generally* valid assumption that both gains *and* losses from forward hedging enter into corporate tax computations whilst translation gains and losses do not. What is the significance of this for a company which takes out a forward contract to hedge a projected translation loss? The company would be offsetting a taxable projected gain on the forward contract against a non-tax allowable projected loss on translation. Hence the size of forward contracts aimed at hedging translation exposures must be grossed up to take account of the differential tax treatment.

The need for 'grossing-up' can be illustrated by a simple example. A US company (year-end 31 December) owns a subsidiary in the UK. On 31 December 1978 the US treasurer calculates that, according to the 'temporal' convention, the UK subsidiary presents a translation exposure of £1 million. Although 12-month forward sterling is being quoted at par with the current spot rate, the US parent is concerned about the consolidation effects of a possible sterling depreciation *vis-à-vis* the US dollar. It therefore decides to cover the translation exposure by a forward sale of pounds to reduce its long sterling net asset position to zero, but the question then arises of exactly how much should be sold forward.

Ostensibly, at least, it might seem that a forward sale of £1 million should cover a £1 million translation exposure. The fallacy of this pre-tax approach is demonstrated in Table 8.6. On 31 December 1978 the US company sells £1 million forward for one year at the forward rate of $2.0000. Hence on 31 December 1979 the company must deliver £1 million, for which it will receive $2 million. To fulfill the forward contract the company buys £1 million in the spot market at the time of delivery. In our example we assume that sterling depreciates by 10% *vis-à-vis* the dollar during 1979 so that the spot rate at the forward contract maturity date (31 December 1979) is equal to $1.80. On 31 December 1979 our company buys £1 million at the spot rate of $1.80 (cost = $1,800,000) and delivers £1 million at the forward rate of $2 (yielding $2,000,000), producing a pre-tax gain on the spot/forward deals of $200,000. This *pre-tax* gain exactly

Table 8.6 Forward Hedging Before Grossing-up

Exposure

Parent base	USA
Subsidiary base	UK
Present date	31 December 1978
Next year-end	31 December 1979
UK subsidiary's translation exposure	£1 million long

Rates

The US treasurer obtains the following exchange rate quotations as at 31 December 1978 (for simplicity, assume buying rate = selling rate):

Spot rate	£1 = $2.0000
12-month forward premium on dollar	$0.0000
12-month forward rate	£1 = $2.0000

2,840,000

Prescription

Ignoring tax effects, the US treasurer decides to hedge the translation exposure by a forward sale of £1 million for delivery in 12 months, as follows:

31 December 1978	sells £1 million forward for 12 months at $2.
31 December 1979	to meet short sterling position produced by forward sale, buys £1 million at current spot rate of (say) $1.80.
	US dollar cost ($1,800,000)
	Delivers £1 million at $2 per forward contract, yielding $2,000,000

Pre-tax dollar gain on offsetting forward/spot deals	$200,000
With 48% corporate tax rate, *after-tax* gain = $200,000 (1− 0.48)= $104,000	
Translation loss (not tax-allowable)	
= $(1,000,000 × 2) − $(1,000,000 × 1.80)	($200,000)
Net reported exchange loss	($96,000)

offsets the translation loss arising on the consolidation of the 'exposed' UK assets at the new rate of $1.80.

Unfortunately, however, the realized gain on the forward/spot deals is taxable. Assuming a corporate tax rate of 48% the after-tax gain amounts to only $104,000. The translation loss, of course, is not realizable and cannot be offset for tax purposes against the realized gain on the spot/forward deals. Hence the after-tax gain on the forward/spot deals offsets only $(1 − t)$% of the translation loss, where t is the corporate tax rate. Accordingly, our US company reports a net exchange loss of $96,000.[6]

To avoid such a net loss the US treasurer must gross up the amount of sterling sold forward by $[1/(1 − t)]$, as shown in Table 8.7. On 31 December 1978, the US company would thus sell £1,923,076

Table 8.7 Forward Hedging After Grossing-up

Exposure details and rates as in Table 8.6.

Prescription
  The US treasurer grosses-up the amount of the forward sale by $[1/(1-t)]$ where t is the corporate tax rate. Therefore the US treasurer sells forward:

  £1 million X $[1/(1-0.48)]$
  = £1 million X 1.923076
  = £1,923,076

Hence,
  31 December 1978: sells £1,923,076 forward for 12 months at $2.
  31 December 1979: to meet short sterling position produced by forward sale, buys £1,923,076 at current spot rate of (say) $1.80.

US dollar cost	($3,461,537)
Delivers £1,923,076 at $2 as per forward contract, yielding	$3,846,152
Pre-tax gain on offsetting forward/spot deals	$384,615
With 48% corporate tax rate, after-tax gain	
= $384,615 (1 − 0.48)	$200,000
Translation loss (not tax-allowable)	
= $(1,000,000 X 2) − $(1,000,000 X 1.80)	($200,000)
Net reported exchange loss	0

forward for 12 months at the forward rate of $2. The same amount of sterling is then bought back at the settlement date (31 December 1979) spot rate of $1.80, yielding a realized pre-tax gain of $384,615. A corporate tax deduction of 48% then leaves an after-tax gain of $200,000, which will exactly offset the translation loss. Our US company can now report a zero net exchange loss arising from its sterling balance sheet.

Some Practical Complications:
Forward Discounts/Premiums and
Unknown Reporting Date Spot Rates
In the above example it was assumed that the forward rate was at par with the initial balance sheet date spot rate (i.e. there was no discount or premium in the 12-month forward market). Given this condition the parent company can calculate the exact amount of forward cover necessary to offset the translation loss, and this amount will be fixed irrespective of the future balance sheet spot rate. However, when the forward rate for delivery at the future reporting date is *not* equal to the prior reporting date spot rate, then the extent of both realized and unrealized exchange gains and losses will depend on the initial forward discount (or premium) and on the eventual

spot rate at the subsequent reporting date. Clearly, whilst today's forward rate is known with certainty, the future balance sheet date spot rate will not be known until the reporting date. Therefore the actual size of the translation loss (gain), the gain (loss) to be made by the forward hedge, and hence the size of forward contract required to offset the translation loss cannot be known in advance. In most circumstances, then, companies must use exchange rate forecasts to decide the extent of forward sale required to exactly nullify a prospective translation loss. If this forecast is inaccurate then the company will report either a net exchange loss (foreign currency depreciates more than forecast) or a net exchange gain (foreign currency depreciates less than forecast). These uncertainties, and a method of eliminating them, are analyzed in Appendix 8A at the end of this chapter.

SHORT-TERM BORROWING

An alternative to covering or hedging on the forward market is the short-term borrowing technique. Again, the currency commitment to be protected may be either a transaction or a translation exposure and we will distinguish between these two exposure types because of tax and exchange control considerations.

Covering by Short-term Borrowing ('Transactions' Exposure)

This method can be used to cover both foreign currency receivables (exporter borrows the foreign currency and immediately converts into his own currency) and foreign currency payables (importer borrows his own currency and immediately converts into foreign currency). The availability of this technique is subject, of course, to local credit availability and exchange controls. An example will illustrate the operation of this technique by exporters and importers.

For the export case we can use our earlier example (Table 8.1) of a UK company which has an exposure of FFr 1million for three months. Recall that the invoice and contract date is 31 March 1979 and the settlement date is 30 June 1979. Our exporter again decides to cover the transactions' exposure but this time he decides to do so by borrowing in the money market rather than by buying forward currency (see Table 8.8). Simultaneously with the signing of the sales contract our exporter:

Table 8.8 Short-term Borrowing—Receivables' Exposure

Exposure

Seller	UK company
Buyer	French company
Contract and invoice date	31 March 1979
Credit terms	90 days
Expected settlement date	30 June 1979
Invoice value	FFr 1million

Rates

The UK treasurer obtains the following exchange rate and interest rate quotations as at 31 March 1979 (all quotations are single buying/selling or borrowing/lending rates):

Exchange rates:

Spot rate	£1 = FFr 8.9700
90-day forward discount on francs	FFr 0.0425
90-day forward rate	£1 = FFr 9.0125

Interest rates:

Three-month sterling	8% p.a.
Three-month French francs	10% p.a.

Prescription

The UK treasurer decides to cover the exposed receivable in the money markets, as follows:

31 March 1979	Borrows FFr 1 million for three months at 10% p.a. Converts proceeds into sterling at current spot rate of 8.9700, yielding £111,483 Lends £111,483 for three months at 8% p.a. FFr interest payable (1,000,000 × 0.10 × $^{3}/_{12}$) = FFr 25,000, due 30 June 1979. Buys FFr 25,000 forward for three months at 9.0125
30 June 1979	Receives FFr 1million from customer; delivers this to lender as repayment of principal. Receives FFr 25,000 as per forward contract, costing (£2,784) Delivers this to lender as repayment of interest. Receives sterling interest of (111,483 × 0.08 × $^{3}/_{12}$) £2,230 Net sterling yield £110,929

1. borrows FFr 1million for three months (the exposure term) at 10% per annum and converts this into sterling at the current spot rate of 8.97, yielding £111,483. This sterling amount is then placed on deposit at 8% per annum for three months, earning a further £2,230.[7]
2. buys FFr 25,000 (the interest payable on the franc loan) forward for three months at the forward rate of 9.0125.[8]

Our exporter's exposure is now completely covered against exchange risk. On 30 June 1979 the UK company receives FFr 1million from its export customer and this amount is then delivered to the franc lender as repayment of principal. The exporter simultaneously receives FFr 25,000 per the three-month forward contract, and this amount is then delivered to the franc lender as repayment of interest. All these transactions can take place at predetermined rates, which are not affected by currency or interest rate movements over the exposure term.[9] Our exporter's exchange risk is fully covered. What price has been paid for this cover? Just as with forward cover there is both an *ex ante* and an *ex post* (opportunity) cost associated with the borrowing technique.

The *ex ante* cost is simply the foreign currency (borrowing) rate less the home currency (lending) rate; 2% in terms of Table 8.8. The reader should note that in our example the *ex ante* costs of forward cover (1.92% as calculated in Table 8.2) and of short-term borrowing cover (2%, see Table 8.9) are almost identical. This is precisely what we would expect if we were borrowing/lending in the Euro-currency markets, given the free-market validity of the interest rate parity theorem.[10] Indeed, even a covered interest differential of 0.08% per annum in the Euro-currency markets would soon be wiped out by covered interest arbitrage. Domestic markets are, of course, a different matter. These are not usually free from capital restraints, so that domestic interest rates do not usually relate perfectly to each other through the foreign exchange market. Hence the opportunity for profiting by selecting the currently most favorable of either forward cover or currency borrowing.

Table 8.9 Cost of Short-term Borrowing

Ex-ante cost % p.a.   = Borrowing rate — Lending rate
                      = 10% p.a. — 8% p.a.
                      = 2% p.a.

Ex-post (opportunity) cost =

$$\text{£} \frac{\text{Foreign currency receivable/payable}}{\text{Spot rate at settlement date}} - \frac{\text{Net HC proceeds from}}{\text{short-term borrowing}}$$

At settlement date (30 June 1979) spot rate = 8.4550

$$\text{Ex post cost} = \text{£} \frac{1{,}000{,}000}{8.4550} - \text{£}110{,}939$$

$$= \text{£}118{,}273 - \text{£}110{,}939$$

$$= \text{£}7{,}334$$

As with forward cover, we will again use a rather limited definition of the concept of 'opportunity cost'. The *ex post* cost of short-term borrowing cover is thus defined as the HC amount which would have been received if the exposed receivable had been left uncovered (i.e. the foreign amount converted into HC at the settlement date spot rate), less the HC amount which the short-term borrowing technique yields. In our example this *ex post* cost is £7,334 (Table 8.9). Again, the opportunity cost is high because the French franc actually *appreciated* against sterling over the exposure term, rather than *depreciate* as indicated by the higher franc interest rate (or forward discount on the franc).

The short-term borrowing technique can also be used to cover a foreign currency payables' exposure, but this time it is the home currency which is borrowed. When the purchase contract is signed the importer immediately borrows his home currency and converts the proceeds into the foreign currency, which is then placed on deposit for the credit period. The maturing deposit is subsequently used to make the foreign currency payment, so that the importer is fully covered against exchange risk.

Some Practical Considerations:
Imprecise Settlement Dates and a Continuing Stream of Foreign Currency Exposures

As suggested earlier in the context of forward cover, two kinds of practical transactions' exposure management difficulties can be distinguished: settlement dates cannot be predicted exactly and cash flows are not normally composed of large and discrete amounts. Both these problems can be handled quite easily by the short-term borrowing technique — indeed, short-term borrowing has some advantages here over forward cover. Whilst the principle is exactly the same as that shown in Table 8.8 it might be helpful to clarify how these practical problems are overcome by the use of a further example.

Imprecise settlement dates. To illustrate how the problem of an imprecise settlement date can be handled by short-term borrowing we will again use the example (Table 8.3) of a UK exporter with a French franc receivable where the settlement date can only be specified within a range of 90–120 days after contract/invoice date. As an alternative to a forward option contract the exposure could be covered by arranging a franc overdraft with a fixed interest rate[11] for a period of up to 120 days. The operation works as follows (see Table 8.10). When the contract is signed our exporter borrows FFr 1million on an overdraft basis at 10¼% for 120 days (the company's estimate of the maximum exposure term). These francs are

Table 8.10 Short-term Borrowing — Receivables' Exposure with Unspecified Settlement Date

Exposure
Seller	UK company
Buyer	French company
Contract and invoice date	31 March 1979
Expected settlement period	30 June—31 July 1979
Invoice value	FFr 1 million

Rates

The UK treasurer obtains the following exchange rate and interest rate quotations as at 31 March 1979 (all quotations are single buying/selling or borrowing/lending rates):

Exchange rates
Spot rate	£1 = FFr8.9700
90-day forward discount on francs	FFr0.0425
90-day forward rate	£1 = FFr9.0125
120-day forward discount on francs	FFr0.0600
120-day forward rate	£1 = FFr9.0300
90—120-day option FFr selling rate £1 =	FFr9.0300

Interest rates:
£ borrowing	8¼% p.a.
FFr borrowing	10¼% p.a.

Prescription

The UK treasurer decides to cover the exposed receivables in the money markets, as follows:

31 March 1979	Borrows FFr 1 million at 10¼% fixed for 120 days. Converts proceeds into sterling at current spot rate of 8.9700, yielding	£111,483
	Re-lends £111,483 on call in UK at 8¼%[12]	
15 July 1979 (say)	Receives FFr 1 million from customer; delivers this to lender as repayment of principal. Franc interest payable = (1,000,000 × 0.1025 × 105/365) = FFr29,486. This amount bought at current spot rate[13] of (say) 8.4550, costing and delivered to lender as repayment of interest.	(£3,487)
	Receives interest on sterling loan of (£111,483 × 0.0825 × 105/365), yielding	£2,646
	Net sterling proceeds	£110,642

immediately converted into sterling, producing £111,483, and this is re-lent on call at 8¼%.[12] Let us assume that the franc receivable is settled on 15 July 1979. The franc receipt is then delivered to the lender, as repayment of principal. The interest payable on the franc loan, which we now know to be FFr 29,486, may be bought at the prevailing spot rate of 8.4550 producing a sterling-equivalent interest cost of £3,487.[13] This interest expense is partly offset by UK interest of £2,646, yielding net sterling proceeds from the franc receivable of £110,642.

Continuing foreign currency exposures. As an alternative to entering into 'bulk' forward option contracts a company may cover a continuing stream of foreign currency exposures by arranging a borrowing facility, either in the currency of invoicing (in the case of the exporter) or the home currency (for the importer). This technique can be used to simultaneously handle the problems of continuing foreign currency exposures and uncertain settlement dates.

To illustrate, let us take the case of a UK exporter with a continuing stream of US dollar export receipts. These can be covered by arranging a fixed rate dollar borrowing. When each export contract is finalized, the exporter immediately draws down the dollar loan by the amount of the dollar sale and converts the proceeds into sterling. As the receivables are settled the dollars are paid into the exporter's dollar account, so that the borrowing is automatically reduced. As long as the dollar borrowing rate is fixed over the exposure term, the receivable is fully covered against exchange risk.

Hedging by Short-term Borrowing

Let us now turn to the application of short-term borrowing as a means of hedging translation exposures. Government controls and differential tax effects are again relevant to the distinction between hedging and covering, since (a) the borrowing of a foreign currency and its conversion into a stronger currency for the purposes of protecting a translation exposure will often be restricted by government credit and exchange controls; and (b) translation gains and losses are unrealized and hence do not enter into corporate tax computations.

Interest receipts and payments *are* realized and *are* taxed or tax-allowable. Again, then, the amount of the money market hedge needs to be grossed up for tax purposes, using the formula $[1/(1 - t)]$ where t represents the company's effective tax rate.

To illustrate how after-tax money market hedging works we will again use the example (Tables 8.6 and 8.7) of a US corporation with a £1 million translation exposure. As an alternative to selling £1,923,076 [£1,000,000 × 1/(1 − 0.48)] forward for 12 months up to the reporting date, our US treasurer may instead decide to borrow £1,923,076 at 8% per annum for one year and convert the

Table 8.11 Short-term Borrowing as a Hedge, After Grossing-up

Exposure
   Parent base   USA
   Subsidiary base   UK
   Present date   31 December 1978
   Next year-end   31 December 1979
   UK subsidiary's translation exposure   £1 million long

Rates
   The US treasurer obtains the following exchange rate and interest rate quotations as at 31 December 1978 (all quotations are single buying/selling or borrowing/lending rates):

   Exchange rates:
      Spot rate   £1 = $2.0000
      12-month forward premium on dollars $0.0000
      12-month forward rate   £1 = $2.0000

   Interest rates:
      12-month sterling   8% p.a.
      12-month dollar   8% p.a.

Prescription
   The US treasurer decides to hedge the translation exposure by borrowing £1,923,076, i.e. [£1 million X 1/(1 − t)] where t is the US corporate tax rate, 48% as follows:

   31 December 1978   borrows £1,923,076 at 8% for one year.
                      Converts proceeds into dollars at current spot rate of $2.0000, yielding $3,846,152.
                      Lends $3,846,152 at 8% for one year.

   31 December 1979   receives $4,153,844 ($3,846,152 X 1.08) from US borrower. Converts proceeds into sterling at current
                      spot rate of (say) $1.80, yielding   £2,307,691
                      Pays (£1,923,076 X 1.08) to UK lender,
                      costing   (£2,076,922)

Pre-tax gain on money market operation	= £230,769
With 48% corporate tax rate, after-tax gain	= £120,000
US dollar value of after-tax gain (£120,000 X 1.80)	= $216,000
Translation loss (not tax-allowable) = $(1,000,000 X 2) − $(1,000,000 X 1.80)	= ($200,000)
Net reported exchange gain	= $16,000

proceeds into dollars over the life of the loan (see Table 8.11). On 31 December 1978 the £1,923,076 loan is converted into dollars at the current spot rate of $2, yielding $3,846,152. These dollar funds are then re-lent, also at the rate of 8% per annum (12-month sterling is at par with the dollars, and so there is no interest differential between dollars and sterling).

Hence on 31 December 1979 the US corporation receives $4,153,844 ($3,846,152 principal and $307,692 interest) as repayment of the dollar loan. This is converted back into sterling at the current spot rate, which is now $1.80, yielding £2,307,691. After repaying its sterling debt of £2,076,922 (£1,923,076 principal and £153,846 interest) our US company is left with a pre-tax gain of £230,769 on its money market hedge. Assuming a corporate tax rate of 48%, the after-tax gain is £120,000 or $216,000. The translation loss arising on the 10% depreciation of sterling is $200,000, so that the company reports a net exchange gain of $16,000. This net gain is due to two factors: (1) the interest rate differential effect of ($3,846,152 × 0%) — which in this particular case, of course, is zero; and (2) the exchange gain on the payment of sterling interest, amounting to $(5,153,846 × $0.20/£ × 0.52) = $16,000. Such gains (or losses) can be eliminated if the sterling loan is taken on a discounted basis, i.e. loan proceeds amount to only £920,000 although the amount to be repaid is £1 million.

Some Practical Complications:
Interest Rate Differentials and Unknown Reporting Date Spot Rates
In the above example it was assumed that the 12-month sterling interest rate exactly equalled the 12-month dollar interest rate (the two currencies were at par in the forward market). Given this condition the parent company can calculate the amount of borrowing necessary to offset the translation loss (or gain), and this will be unaffected by the subsequent balance sheet spot rate. But when an interest differential exists the size of both the money market gain (or loss) and the translation loss (gain) will depend on the interest rate differential and the closing spot rate. In these circumstances a forecast of the closing rate must be used in order to decide the amount of borrowing required to offset the projected translation loss. These complexities are analyzed in Appendix 8B at the end of this chapter.

DISCOUNTING FOREIGN CURRENCY BILLS RECEIVABLE

Unlike the first two techniques, discounting can be used to cover only export receivables. It cannot be used to cover foreign currency payables or to hedge a translation exposure. Where an export receivable is to be settled by bill of exchange the exporter can discount the bill and thereby receive payment before the receivable settlement date. The bill may be discounted either with a foreign bank in the customer's country, in which case the foreign currency proceeds can be repatriated immediately at the current spot rate; or it can be discounted with a bank in the exporter's country so that the exporter may receive settlement direct in home currency (HC). Either way the exporter is covered against exchange risk, the explicit cost being the discount rate charged by the bank.

The technique can be illustrated by adapting our first example (Table 8.1) of a UK company with a French franc receivable due in three month's time. If, on 31 March 1979 our exporter receives FFr 1million of discountable three-month trade bills drawn on the French customer, then the three-month exposure can be covered by discounting the bills with a French bank (see Table 8.12). At a 10% per annum discount rate this yields an immediate receipt of FFr 975,000. Our exporter then converts this immediately into sterling at the prevailing spot rate of 8.9700, yielding a sterling receipt of £108,696. By placing this amount on deposit in the UK the ensuing

Table 8.12 Discounting Foreign Currency Bills Receivable

Exposure
Seller — UK company
Buyer — French company
Contract and invoice date — 31 March 1979
Credit terms — 90 days
Expected settlement date — 30 June 1979
Invoice value — FFr 1 million

Rates
Spot rate — £1 = FFr 8.9700
Discount rate on franc bills — 10% p.a.

Prescription
The UK treasurer decides to cover the exposed bills receivable by discounting, as follows:

31 March 1979 receives FFr 1 million of three-month bills of exchange. These are discounted at 10% p.a. (net interest cost = FFr 25,000), yielding FFr975,000. Proceeds are converted into sterling at current spot rate of 8.9700, yielding £108,696
Lends £108,696 for three months at 8%, earning (£108,696 X 0.08 X $^3/_{12}$) £2,174
Net sterling receipt £110,870

interest yield (£2,174) reduces the gross discounting cost, producing a net pre-tax sterling receipt of £110,870.

The discounting technique for covering receivables exposures is very similar to the alternative of short-term borrowing except here the *ex ante* cost is the effective discount rate less the HC deposit rate, rather than the foreign currency borrowing rate less the HC deposit rate. With both techniques, of course, the basic aim is to convert the proceeds from the foreign currency receivable into the HC as soon as possible. As with straight borrowing operations, discounting is a non sequitur in many exchange-controlled countries since foreign currency borrowing of any sort is permitted only under certain conditions.

FACTORING FOREIGN CURRENCY RECEIVABLES

Like discounting, factoring can only be used as a means of covering export receivables. When the export receivable is to be settled on open account, rather than by bill of exchange, the receivables can be assigned as collateral for related bank financing. Under normal circumstances such a service will give protection against exchange rate changes, though during unsettled periods in the foreign exchange markets appropriate variations may be made in the factoring agreement. Both commercial banks and specialized factoring institutions offer such factoring services.

For the exporter the technique is very straightforward. He simply sells his export receivables to the factor and receives HC in return. The costs involved include both credit risks (the customer may default) and the cost of financing (if the exporter wants to receive payment before the receivable maturity date), as well as the cost of covering the exchange risk (the forward discount/premium). Factoring therefore tends to be a high-priced means of covering exposure, although there may be offsetting benefits such as obtaining export finance and reducing sales accounting and credit collection costs (the exporter may simply hand over the invoices against payment, the book-keeping and credit collection being done by the factor).

GOVERNMENT EXCHANGE RISK GUARANTEES

To encourage exporting, government agencies in many countries offer their exporters insurance against export credit risks and special export financing schemes. In recent years a few of these agencies have begun to offer exchange risk insurance to their exporters, as well as the usual export credit guarantees. Typically the exporter will pay a small premium on his export sales and, for this premium, the government agency will absorb all exchange losses (and gains) beyond a certain threshold level.

Initially such exchange risk guarantee schemes were introduced to aid capital goods' exporters, where receivable exposure terms can be of a very long-term nature. For example, the export credit agency in Germany, HERMES, provides exchange cover where export credit terms exceed two years. For a premium of 0.4% the exporter invoicing in US dollars, sterling or Swiss francs is covered against currency movements of more than 3% — but HERMES takes the gains as well as the losses. In Holland, the Netherlands Credit Insurance Company Ltd also covers exchange risks on export contracts exceeding two years. The premium here is 0.7% (2¼% for sterling and the lira), all internationally marketable currencies can be covered and again a 3% threshold is applied. The Ministry of International Trade and Industry in Japan provides exchange cover on capital goods exports on credit terms of between two and 15 months. The US dollar, sterling, the Deutsche Mark and Swiss franc can be covered, again against currency movements exceeding 3%, and the maximum refund is 12% of the contract value. The cost is 0.8% (comprehensive cover) or 3% (individual transactions). Similar schemes are available in Belgium, Switzerland and France (COFACE's scheme is the only one to cover both receivables and payables exposures).

More recently, however, some schemes have been extended to cover the exchange risk arising on consumer as well as capital goods' exports. COFACE now offers cover where export terms are less than one year and in currencies where a forward market is available — the scheme is designed for exporters who are not familiar with the forward exchange market. Similarly, Switzerland's Exchange Risk Guarantee Department now offer exchange cover on consumer goods exports where credit terms are three months or more.

Government exchange risk guarantees are also given to cover foreign currency borrowing by public bodies. In the UK, for example, nationalized industries, local authorities and other statutory bodies have borrowed large amounts of foreign currency under the Treasury's exchange cover scheme, in operation from 1969 to 1971 and reintroduced in 1973. With this scheme the borrower surrenders most of the interest rate differential between the foreign currency loan and the appropriate rate on sterling loans from the National Loans Fund (or in the case of local authorities, the Public Works Loan Board), but is allowed to keep an interest 'subsidy' of about 1%.

Hence most major trading nations now provide some form of exchange risk insurance through their export credit or other government agencies. Most of these schemes have been brought into operation since the 1971 devaluation of the US dollar, and with the continuing flexibility of exchange rates it is likely that such schemes will become increasingly available to exporters.

REVIEW QUESTIONS

1. On 1 January 1980 a US company enters into a purchase contract for £100,000 on six months credit terms. Calculate the dollar payment required if this exposure is eliminated by (a) forward cover and (b) short-term borrowing, using the following rate assumptions as at 1 January 1980:

Exchange rates		*Interest rates*	
Spot	= $2.00	Six month sterling	18%p.a.
Six month			
dollar premium	= $0.10	Six month dollar	16%p.a.

What is the opportunity cost of each covering option if the 30 June 1980 spot rate is $2.20?

2. Calculate the amount of forward hedge required for the following example, both (a) on a pre-tax basis and (b) after-tax:

Exposure	
Parent	UK
Unrealizable balance sheet exposure	DKr 10 million, long
Present date	1 January 1980
Future reporting date	31 December 1980

Rates, as at 1 January 1980	
Spot	11.00
12-month DKr discount	0.50
Expected spot rate at 31 December 1980	9.00
Corporate tax rate, UK	52.00%

Assume that the company's DKr/£ forecast is accurate.

3. What is the 60–90 day 'option determining rate' for (a) the seller of dollars and (b) the buyer of dollars given the following rates? What are the implications for a company entering into a forward

contract to cover a transactional exposure with an uncertain settlement date?

Spot rate	£1 = 2.25
60-day forward rate	£1 = 2.10
90-day forward rate	£1 = 2.00

4. Discuss alternative methods of covering a continuing stream of foreign currency receipts where settlement dates cannot be accurately predicted.

NOTES

1. It should be emphasized that, even for a single transaction the exposure term is not necessarily synonomous with the credit period. For example, a sale or purchase contract may be signed before the goods/invoice are despatched, and hence before the beginning of the credit period; and where an exporter offers firm foreign currency quotations we must go back even further to ascertain the beginning of the exposure term. More fundamentally, if a firm has committed substantial resources to servicing its export markets (or alternatively if it has based its production technology on imported inputs) then the concept of a single 'exposure term' must be replaced by one of a more permanent nature. In such circumstances the exposure horizon will depend on the validity of the PPP theorem and on the restructuring period necessary for a company to reduce its dependence on foreign customers or producers.

2. As explained in Chapter 3, exchange rates are quoted in the world's foreign exchange markets either directly (the amount of home currency per one unit of foreign currency) or indirectly (the amount of foreign currency per one unit of home currency). In our example, sterling is quoted indirectly. For direct quotations, which are used in all major foreign exchange markets other than London and New York, the forward discount would be *deducted* from the spot rate to give the forward rate. The principle remains the same, of course: more units of the discount currency will have to be spent in the forward market to buy the premium currency, relative to the spot rate of exchange.

3. Of course there is the additional, albeit miniscule, risk that the bank of negotiation may fail or suspend its dealings in the interim period before maturity (e.g. Herstatt, Franklin National). In such cases the foreign currency will not be taken up (or delivered, in the case of the importer) by the bank at the contracted forward rate. Hence the company will not be covered, and it will subsequently have to sell (or buy) its currency commitment in the spot/forward market.

4. See, for example, the debate between Bradford and Pelli (Bradford, 1974a and b; Pelli 1974).

5. We abstract here from the very rare case where a currency switches from a forward discount to a forward premium (or vice versa) at some future date.

6. This net exchange loss is, of course, composed of two very different elements: a realized cash-flow gain ($104,000) and an unrealized translation loss ($200,000). For a discussion on the relative merits of these two definitions of gains/losses, see Chapter 4.

7. Of course, our exporter may not actually re-lend the sterling proceeds from the French franc loan. He may instead decide to reinvest the proceeds in UK operations. A cash shortage is one good reason why the short-term borrowing technique may be preferred to forward cover, and if this is the case then the value to the company of receiving the funds three months earlier than otherwise may be greater than that indicated by the three-month lending rate. Conversely, for a cash *rich* company the borrowing technique can be costly. The company will have to pay an interest rate based on the offered side plus the profit spread for the lender, whilst surplus domestic funds would simultaneously be invested at the bid rate. In such circumstances forward cover will generally be the cheaper alternative.

8. There are two alternatives to covering the French franc interest payable in the forward markets:

    (a) wait until the settlement date and buy the French franc at the prevailing spot rate; or

    (b) instead of converting all the French franc loan into sterling, thereby leaving an exposed French franc interest payable, our exporter could simply discount the French franc loan at the 10% interest rate ($1,000,000 \times 0.10 \times {}^{3}\!/_{12} = $ FFr 25,000 interest) and convert only the remaining FFr 975,000 into sterling. Hence the exporter would already hold the necessary amount of French francs to pay off the interest at the end of three months, so that a forward purchase of the French franc interest payable would not be required.

9. Borrowing may be negotiated at either fixed or variable (market-related) interest rates. Overdrafts normally carry variable interest rates. Clearly, only the fixed rate loan can be used as an exposure management technique — to the extent that the borrowing rate is variable then the cost of covering or hedging is open-ended.

10. The interest rate parity theorem states that, in free markets, covered interest arbitrage will eliminate any covered interest rate differentials between equivalent interest-bearing securities denominated in different currencies, (see Chapter 10).

11. The flexible nature of short-term borrowing rates causes practical problems with this technique. In Europe, for example, overdraft rates change over time according to predetermined formulae. However, it is possible to borrow part of the currency requirement at a fixed rate for a fixed term, to be rolled over on maturity for a further term, with the fluctuating incremental requirement being borrowed on overdraft.

12. Of course, the sterling proceeds of the French franc loan may well be retained for further investment in the business, rather than being lent out for the duration of the credit period. The call rate is used here as the minimum value to be gained by the early receipt of funds.

13. There are, of course, other alternatives. For instance, our exporter could make an estimate of the French franc interest expense (the precise amount obviously will not be known until settlement date) and buy the estimated French franc requirement on a forward option basis. In our example this would have been the better alternative (the French franc interest amount would have been bought at 9.0300 rather than 8.4550), but the difference is not material.

BIBLIOGRAPHY

Bradford S.R. (1974a), 'Measuring the cost of forward exchange contracts', *Euromoney*, August, pp. 71–75.

Bradford S.R. (1974b), 'Thoughts on the cost of forward cover in a floating system — a reply', *Euromoney*, November, pp. 32–33.

Chown J. et al. (1975), 'Hedging balance sheet exposure after tax — a reply', *Euromoney*, June, pp. 89–93.

Pelli G. (1974), 'Thoughts on the cost of forward cover in a floating system', *Euromoney*, October, pp. 34–35.

APPENDIX 8A

Forward Hedging Complexities—Forward Premiums/Discounts and Unknown Reporting Date Spot Rates

It has been stated above that, when the forward rate for the translation exposure period is not at par, the amount of forward hedge required to eliminate translation gains/losses is dependent on the size of the forward premium/discount and on the eventual reporting date spot rate. Since future spot rates are unknown, a company must use a currency forecast to calculate the amount of forward sales required to exactly nullify a prospective translation loss. If this forecast is inaccurate the company will incur a net (unrealized translation plus realized forward contract) foreign exchange gain or loss at the future balance sheet date.

All this may seem a little complicated but it can be easily clarified by the use of a few examples (for simplicity tax effects will be ignored). In Table 8A.1 we start off with the simple, albeit rare case where our US treasurer's forecast of a sterling depreciation to $1.70 at the next balance sheet date is accurate. Based on this assumption the US company projects a translation loss of $300,000, (1,000,000 × $(2.00 − 1.70)). Using the $1.70 forecast, the amount of forward sale of sterling required to produce an offsetting gain can be calculated by the following formula:

$$\frac{\text{Amount of forward sale required}}{} = \frac{\text{Required hedging gain}}{\text{Forward rate} - \text{expected reporting date spot rate}}$$

Accordingly, on 31 December 1978 the US company sells £3 million forward for one year at the forward rate of $1.80. On 31 December 1979 the company must deliver £3 million, for which it will receive $5.4 million. To fulfill this forward contract the company then buys £3 million in the the spot market at the time of delivery. Assuming our treasurer's forecast is accurate, on 31 December 1979 the company buys £3 million at the spot rate of $1.70 (cost = $5.1 million) and delivers £3 million at the forward rate of $1.80 (yielding $5.4 million), producing a pre-tax gain on the spot/forward deals of $300,000. Given our pre-tax assumption, this exactly offsets the translation loss arising on the consolidation of the 'exposed' UK assets at the new rate of $1.70. As long as the balance sheet date spot forecast is

Table 8A.1 Forward Hedging, with Accurate Forecast of Spot Rate at Balance Sheet Date

Exposure

Parent base	USA
Subsidiary base	UK
Present date	31 December 1978
Next year-end	31 December 1979
UK subsidiary's translation exposure	£1 million

Rates

The US treasurer obtains the following exchange rate quotations as at 31 December 1978 (for simplicity, assume buying rate = selling rate):

Spot rate	£1 = $2.0000
12-month forward premium on dollars	$0.2000
12-month forward rate	£1 = $1.8000

Projected Translation Loss

The US treasurer expects the spot rate at 31 December 1979 to be $1.70.

Projected translation loss = $(1,000,000 × 2) − $(1,000,000 × 1.70) = $300,000.

Gain on forward hedge required (ignoring tax*) = $300,000.

Amount of forward sale of sterling required

$$= \frac{\text{Required hedging gain}}{\text{Forward rate} - \text{expected reporting date spot rate}}$$

$$= \frac{300,000}{1.80 - 1.70}$$

$$= \frac{300,000}{0.10}$$

$$= £3 \text{ million}$$

Prescription

The US treasurer decides to hedge the translation exposure by a forward sale of £3 million. Assuming the $1.70 forecast is accurate, the results will be as follows:

31 December 1978	sells £3 million forward for 12 months at $1.80	
31 December 1979	to meet short sterling position produced by forward sale, buys £3 million at current spot rate of $1.70.	
	US dollar cost	($5,100,000)
	Delivers £3 million at $1.80, as per forward contract, yielding	$5,400,000
Pre-tax gain* on offsetting forward/spot deals		$300,000
Actual translation loss = $(1,000,000 × 2) − $(1,000,000 × 1.70)=($300,000)		
Net reported exchange loss		0

* For an after-tax gain of $300,000, the amount of forward sale must be grossed up by [1/(1 − t)], i.e., £3 million × [1/(1 − 0.48)] = £5,769,231.

accurate, the company can calculate precisely how much of the foreign currency must be sold forward to offset the translation loss.

Yet what if this forecast is *inaccurate*? There are two broad possibilities here: either the foreign currency (sterling) may depreciate more or appreciate less than expected, or it may depreciate less or appreciate more than expected. These two possibilities are depicted in Tables 8A.2 and 8A.3 respectively.

Table 8A.2 Forward Hedging: Foreign Currency depreciates by more than expected

Exposure details, rates and projected translation loss as in Table 8A.1.

Prescription
The US treasurer again decides to hedge the translation exposure by a forward sale of £3 million. The actual spot rate at 31 December 1979 is now $1.60, instead of the forecasted rate of $1.70.

31 December 1978	sells £3 million forward for 12 months at $1.80.	
31 December 1979	to meet short sterling position produced by forward sale, buys £3 million at current spot rate of $1.60.	
	US dollar cost	($4,800,000)
	Delivers £3 million at $1.80 as per forward contract, yielding	$5,400,000
Pre-tax gain on offsetting forward/spot deals		$600,000
Actual translation loss = $(1,000,000 X 2) − $(1,000,000 X 1.60)=($400,000)		
Net reported exchange gain		$200,000

Table 8A.3 Forward Hedging; Foreign Currency depreciates by less than expected

Exposure details, rates and projected translation loss as in Table 8A.1.

Prescription
The US treasurer again decides to hedge the translation exposure by a forward sale of £3 million. The actual spot rate at 31 December 1979 is now $1.75, instead of the forecasted rate of $1.70.

31 December 1978	sells £3 million forward for 12 months at $1.80.	
31 December 1979	to meet short sterling position produced by forward sale, buys £3 million at current spot rate of $1.75.	
	US dollar cost	($5,250,000)
	Delivers £3 million at $1.80 as per forward contract, yielding	$5,400,000
Pre-tax gain on offsetting forward/spot deals		$150,000
Actual translation loss = $(1,000,000 X 2) − $(1,000,000 X 1.75) =($250,000)		
Net reported exchange loss		($100,000)

In Table 8A.2 we assume that sterling depreciates by more than expected, so that the balance sheet date spot rate is (say) $1.60. Based on the $1.70 forecast, on 31 December 1978 our US company again sells £3 million forward for 12 months at $1.80. One year later the company must then buy £3 million at the actual spot rate of $1.60 (cost = $4.8 million) so that it can deliver £3 million at $1.80 as per the forward contract (yield = $5.4 million). The resultant pre-tax gain on the forward hedge ($600,000) more than offsets the translation loss (now increased to $400,000), producing a net reported gain of $200,000.

The reverse logic applies in Table 8A.3 where we assume that sterling depreciates less than expected to (say) $1.75. Again, based on the $1.70 forecast, the US company sells £3 million forward for 12 months as from 31 December 1978. Then on 31 December 1979, our company buys £3 million at the spot rate of $1.75 (cost = $5.25 million) and sells £3 million at the forward rate of $1.80 (yield = $5.4 million). This time the resultant pre-tax gain ($150,000) only partially offsets the translation loss ($250,000), so that a net exchange loss of $100,000 is reported.

There are, of course, many other scenarios. If sterling were to depreciate less than that predicted by the forward rate (in our hedging examples, if the 31 December 1979 spot rate lies within the range $1.80 − $2) a forward hedge would result in both an unrealized translation loss *and* a realized loss on the forward/spot deals. Alternatively, if sterling *appreciates* during 1979 (i.e. the 31 December 1979 spot rate is greater than $2) there will be an even heavier loss on the forward hedge which will more than outweigh the resulting translation gain.

In view of these uncertainties an alternative, low-risk approach to forward hedging is often adopted by US companies. Up to now we have assumed that companies enter into a forward hedge with the intention of exactly nullifying translation effects, by the use of the formula:

$$\frac{\text{Amount of forward sale required}} {} = \frac{\text{Required hedging gain}}{\text{Forward rate} - \text{expected reporting date spot rate}}$$

Other things being equal, the higher the discount on the foreign currency then the higher the amount of forward sale required to exactly nullify a translation loss − and hence the higher the net exchange loss if the treasurer's forecast is wrong.

A 'low-risk' alternative is to sell exactly the amount of the exposed net assets forward, thereby locking in a net exchange loss (gain) equal to the forward discount (premium) on the foreign currency. This is illustrated in Table 8A.4 which shows that, irrespective of the future reporting date spot rate, the net exchange loss on translation is locked in to the forward discount ($0.20/2.00 = 10%) as a function of the dollar-equivalent translation exposure (1,000,000 X $2), i.e. $200,000. Similarly, if the foreign currency was at a premium then such a forward hedge would lock in a net translation *gain* amounting to the percentage premium. Future exchange rates affect only the composition of the net figure, split between a forward hedging gain (loss) and a translation loss (gain), but the net reported effect will remain fixed.

Table 8A.4 Forward Hedging; Net Exchange Loss locked in to Forward Discount on Foreign Currency

Exposure details and rates as in Table 8A.1.

Prescription
The US treasurer decides to hedge the translation exposure by a forward sale of £1 million, as follows:

(a) Let the 31 December 1979 spot rate be $1.50

31 December 1978	sells £1 million forward for 12 months at $1.80	
31 December 1979	to meet short sterling position produced by forward sale, buys £1 million at current spot rate of $1.50.	
	US dollar cost	($1,500,000)
	Delivers £1 million at $1.80 as per forward contract, yielding	$1,800,000
Pre-tax gain on offsetting forward/spot deals		$300,000
Translation loss = $(1,000,000 X 2) − $(1,000,000 X 1.5)		($500,000)
Net exchange loss		($200,000)

(b) Let the 31 December 1979 spot rate be $2.50

31 December 1978	sells £1 million forward for 12 months at $1.80.	
31 December 1979	to meet short sterling position produced by forward sale, buys £1 million at current spot rate of $2.50.	
	US dollar cost	($2,500,000)
	Delivers £1 million at $1.80 as per forward contract, yielding	$1,800,000
Pre-tax loss on offsetting forward/spot deals		($700,000)
Translation gain = $(1,000,000 X 2) − $(1,000,000 X 2.50)		$500,000
Net exchange loss		($200,000)

APPENDIX 8B

Money Market Hedging — Interest Rate Differentials and Unknown Reporting Date Spot Rates

It has been stated above that, when an interest rate differential exists between the parent currency and the exposed currency, the amount of borrowing required to eliminate translation gains/losses depends on the size of the interest rate differential and on the eventual reporting date spot rate. Hence, a forecast of the future spot rate is required to calculate the amount of borrowing needed to eliminate the translation gain/loss.

The way this can be done is shown in Table 8B.1. Exposure details are as in Table 8.11, but this time the interest rate on 12-month sterling is 10% higher than that on 12-month dollars (the dollar is at a 10% premium in the forward markets). We also assume here that the US treasurer's forecast of a sterling depreciation of 15% by the next balance sheet date is accurate. Based on this forecast, the US company projects a translation loss of $300,000. The amount of borrowing required to offset this loss can then be calculated by the following formula:

$$\text{Amount of borrowing required} = \frac{\text{Required hedging gain}}{(1 + \text{HCI}) - (1 + \text{LCI})(1 + \text{ELCC})},$$

where HCI = home currency ($) interest rate (0.04)
       LCI = local currency (£) interest rate (0.14)
       ELCC = expected local currency change, % (−0.15)

Accordingly, on 31 December 1978 the US company borrows £2,112,676 at 14% for one year and converts this into dollars at the current spot rate of $2. The proceeds, $4,225,352, are then invested at 4% for one year. Hence, the company has incurred a weak currency (sterling) liability and switched into a strong currency (dollars) asset, at a nominal cost of 10% per annum (the interest rate differential).

At the end of the year the US company receives $4,394,366 from the US borrower which, when converted into sterling at the closing rate of $1.70, produces £2,584,921. After repaying its sterling debt of £2,408,451 our US company is left with a pre-tax gain on the money-market hedging operation of £176,470, or $300,000. This

Table 8B.1 Money Market Hedging, with Accurate Forecast of Spot Rate at Balance Sheet Date

Exposure details as in Table 8.11 (page 141).

Rates
The US treasurer obtains the following exchange rate and interest rate quotations as at 31 December 1978 (all quotations are single buying/selling or borrowing/lending rates):

Exchange rates:

Spot rates	£1 = $2.0000
12-month forward premium on dollars	= $0.2000
12-month forward rate	£1 = $1.8000

Interest rates:

12-month sterling	14% p.a.
12-month dollars	4% p.a.

Projected translation loss
The US treasurer expects the closing spot rate to be $1.70.
Projected translation loss = $(1,000,000 × 2) − $(1,000,000 × 1.7) = $300,000
Gain on money market hedge required (ignoring tax*) = $300,000
Amount of borrowing required

$$\$ \frac{\text{Required hedging gain}}{(1 + HCl) - (1 + LCl)(1 + ELCC)} = \frac{300,000}{(1 + 0.04) - (1 + 0.14)(1 + (-0.15))}$$

$$= \$ \frac{300,000}{0.071} = \$4,225,352 \text{ or } £2,112,676.$$

Prescription
The US treasurer decides to hedge the translation exposure by borrowing £2,112,676. Assuming the $1.70 forecast is accurate, the results will be as follows:

31 December 1978:	borrows £2,112,676 at 14% for one year. Converts proceeds into sterling at current spot rate of $2, yielding $4,225,352. Lends $4,225,352 at 4% for one year. .		
31 December 1979:	receives $4,394,366 ($4,225,352 × 1.04) from US borrower. Converts proceeds into sterling at current spot rate of $1.70, yielding	£	2,584,921
	Pays £2,408,451 (£2,112,676 × 1.14), costing	(£	2,408,451)

Pre-tax gain on money market operation	=	£	176,470
Dollar value of pre-tax* gain (£176,470 × 1.70)	=	$	300,000
Translation loss = $(1,000,000 × 2) − $(1,000,000 × 1.70) =		$	300,000
Net reported exchange effect	=		0

* For an after-tax gain of $300,000, the amount of borrowing must be grossed up by [1/(1 − t)], i.e., £2,112,676 × [1/(1 − 0.48)] = £4,062,838

exactly offsets the translation loss, so that the net reported exchange effect is zero.

But what if the company's forecast is *inaccurate*? There are two possibilities here: either the foreign currency (sterling) depreciates more or appreciates less than expected, or it depreciates less or appreciates more than expected. The first of these possibilities is depicted in Table 8B.2. Exposure details, rates and projected translation loss are as in Table 8B.1 but this time sterling depreciates to $1.60 rather than to $1.70 as forecast. Based on the $1.70 forecast, the company again borrows £2,112,676 and converts into dollars. But because sterling depreciated by more than expected, the gain on the hedging operation now amounts to $540,845. This more than offsets the increased translation loss (since the amount borrowed was greater than the translation exposure) thereby producing a net exchange gain of $140,845. The reverse would apply if the company's forecast overstated the actual sterling depreciation (i.e. a net exchange loss would be incurred). Hence the effectiveness of hedging by short-term borrowing — just as with hedging in the forward markets — depends very much on the accuracy of the balance sheet date spot forecast.

Table 8B.2. Money Market Hedging: Foreign Currency Depreciates by More Than Expected.

Exposure details, *rates* and *projected translation loss* as in Table 8B.1.

Prescription
The US treasurer again decides to hedge the translation exposure by borrowing £2,112,676. The actual spot rate at 31 December 1979 is now $1.60, instead of the forecasted rate of $1.70.

31 December 1978	borrows £2,112,676 at 14% for one year. Converts proceeds into sterling at current spot rate of $2, yielding $4,225,352. Lends $4,225,352 at 4% for one year.
31 December 1979	receives $4,394,366 ($4,225,352 X 1.04) from US borrower. Converts proceeds into sterling at current spot rate of $1.60, yielding

	£	2,746,479
Repays sterling loan (£2,112,676 X 1.14), costing	(£	2,408,451)
Pre-tax gain on money market operation	£	338,028
Dollar value of pre-tax gain (£338,028 X 1.60)	$	540,845
Translation loss = $(1,000,000 X 2) − $(1,000,000 X 1.60)	($	400,000)
Net reported exchange gain	$	140,845

CHAPTER 9

Organization of the Exposure Management Function

THE TREASURY FUNCTION

Before analyzing the specific organizational requirements of exposure management it might be useful to step back and briefly consider the many other functions which can be carried out within a corporate treasury. Treasury functions are various, and the following list is probably not exhaustive:

> capital structure considerations: the development and implementation of long-term financing strategy;

> liquidity management: ensuring adequate short-term funds throughout the group at minimum cost;

> banking relations: monitoring the effectiveness of the company's banks on a group-wide basis, in terms of the cost and availability of credit and the quality of non-credit services;

> cash management procedures: rationalization of collection and disbursement procedures at operating unit level, to reduce the overall working capital funding requirement and associated interest charges;

exposure management: protecting the company's net assets, income streams and/or cash flows from the adverse impact of currency movements;

controllership: the treasury should also be involved in financial accounting and the budgeting process;

taxation: ensuring treasury decisions are effective on an after-tax basis;

insurance coverage;

pension fund management;

shareholder relations' considerations.

In what follows the reader should remember that, when the organization of the exposure management function is examined, we are looking at only one of a number of functions carried out by treasury staff. Thankfully, the organizational requirements of exposure and liquidity management, which are the two basic problem areas of international treasury management, are very similar. Nevertheless, the analysis which follows is a partial one.

TWO ORGANIZATIONAL OBJECTIVES

No single exposure management system is right in all situations. Each corporation has its own peculiarities in terms of operating characteristics, business environment, management philosophy, legal structure, personnel strengths, and so on. Companies differ, and their exposure management systems should reflect these differences. A treasury structure which is right for IBM is unlikely to be appropriate for Unilever. Nevertheless, there are two organizational objectives which we believe all international companies should try to attain in the treasury area. Firstly, treasury (exposure) management must be *integrated* with the operating side of the business. This means that treasury must get involved with production, purchasing, and marketing decisions. Treasury influence should not be limited to traditional, purely financial functions. Secondly, treasury (exposure) management, must be *coordinated* if it is to be fully effective. Coordination requires a centralized (corporate and/or regional) information system — in both exposure and liquidity management a group-wide focus is essential. However, coordination does not require that all decisions or actions be taken centrally. The operating and other characteristics of each company will often provide constraints here and so the costs of centralization (such as demotivation at the local level) should be weighed against the costs of decentralization (reduced control, unnecessary transactions' costs).

The method of attaining these two objectives and the extent to which they can be achieved will clearly vary from company to company. However, in our opinion these objectives are almost inviolate, so let us examine the advantages of integration and coordination.

INTEGRATED EXPOSURE MANAGEMENT

A common failing of exposure management systems is that the management process begins after the exposure has been generated. This is too late. Exposure management decision making must begin *before* exposures are generated, otherwise (a) fundamental operating decisions are being taken on the basis of unnecessarily incomplete information, which may mean that incorrect decisions are made; and (b) from the very beginning, exposure management choice is limited to a narrow range of tactics. To avoid these weaknesses senior management must recognize that exposure management should be a fundamental business consideration. Everything that a company does internationally has some impact on its foreign exchange exposure. Each major function contributes to the generation of exposures or has the opportunity to reduce or increase them:

capital budgeting: the choice of product and the location of manufacturing operations;

purchasing: the selection of country of sourcing or the choice between bids denominated in different currencies;

selling: the selection of country and currency denomination of sales;

marketing: the trade-off between advertising effort, easier credit terms, and lower sales prices;

controllership: the manipulation of working capital by enforcing changes in credit terms;

budgeting: the behavioral impact of performance evaluation systems;

finance: the currency of financing decision.

Since exposures arise primarily from operating decisions, exposure management cannot and must not be separated from the operating activities of the company. This objective can only be met if the treasury function is fully integrated into the firm. Operating personnel (purchasing, manufacturing, sales and marketing) and financial management (taxation, treasury and controller) should meet routinely to review the fundamental strategic and tactical decisions which create currency exposures. A two-way flow of information and advice is necessary. The exposure manager must educate operating personnel on the foreign exchange implications of fundamental operating decisions, and operating personnel must ensure that the exposure manager understands how the business operates and how it generates exposures.

A fundamental characteristic of an integrated exposure management system is that it enables the utilization of a wide range of exposure management techniques. Initial emphasis is on internal (business related) responses such as utilizing better local cash management techniques, changing sourcing patterns, raising prices or changing the currency of intercompany sales. It is only after the application of internal techniques that treasury need go to the markets, to apply such external techniques as forward exchange contracts or Euro-currency borrowing.

In contrast, if the treasury function is isolated from operating decisions then exposure management becomes a much narrower and more straightforward process. In this kind of set-up the foreign exchange manager receives exposure numbers from operating units and, based on a currency forecast, decides whether or not to cover on the forward markets. Too much emphasis is placed on external tactics; internal responses are almost entirely pre-empted. In a centralized system there may be some netting or matching, but it is too late to consider changing the price levels or the currency of invoicing, far less to consider whether the manufacturing unit might have been better located elsewhere.

In this kind of system the focus of exposure management is on curing the symptoms rather than the causes of the problem. The exposure manager is more concerned with where the foreign exchange markets seem to be going rather than with where the company's business is taking group exposure. This preoccupation with the foreign exchange markets means that the company (and the exposure manager) will often get hurt when currencies move abruptly.

COORDINATED EXPOSURE MANAGEMENT

Treasury (exposure and liquidity) management must be coordinated if it is to be fully effective. For a company with real concerns about exposure (and liquidity) management, the organizational question is not so much whether the treasury function should be coordinated or not. Rather, the relevant question is what degree of coordination is possible given the firm's specific characteristics. For efficiency reasons, a centralized treasury bias will exist in all companies, regardless of the degree of (de)centralization in other functional areas. A coordinated viewpoint is essential if exposure identification and exposure management decisions are to be effective on a group basis.

No matter which exposure definition is chosen as the primary focus, the identification of a company's exposures will only be completely meaningful on a consolidated, group-wide basis. Similarly, rational exposure management decision making is possible only if a coordinated group viewpoint is taken. Otherwise two separate operating units could each have offsetting positions and each could independently be taking offsetting actions. Moreover, the exposure definitions applied by these units could be contrary to the concerns of senior corporate management. Other typical weaknesses of a decentralized exposure management system include unnecessary foreign exchange costs, overemphasis on external tactics and inadequate control over foreign exchange trading.

The concept of treasury coordination is easy to justify; its implementation can be much more difficult. In practice, the efficiency bias towards coordination is constrained by decentralizing biases in other parts of a company. Examples of such constraints are:

operating characteristics: a divisional organization based on heterogeneous product groups

corporate development: growth by acquisition (and rationalization by divestiture); foreign subsidiaries which are mature, financially strong and powerful; a historically small and uninfluential corporate treasury

profitability: the more profitable the company, the less pressing will be the need for strict financial controls; this is often related to the product life cycle, since the need for coordinated treasury management strengthens as the company and its product mature

legal structure: the existence of minority interests places severe limits on the ability of a company to defer local interests to the good of the group as a whole;

personnel and personality strengths: these can also create very real barriers to coordination.

Nevertheless, the potential exposure (and liquidity) management benefits of a treasury system will often outweigh its costs. Let us now examine how this centralization can be achieved.

METHODS OF CENTRALIZATION

Conceptually, there are two methods of centralizing exposure management: (a) reporting-based approaches which shift some decision making authority from the operating units where exposures arise to a central exposure management body; and (b) structural approaches which shift the actual incidence of exposures from operating units to a central location. These two methods are not mutually exclusive. Indeed, they are often complementary since some kind of reporting/communication system is always necessary if internal business-related exposure management tactics are to be identified. Nevertheless, for the purpose of understanding how centralization can be achieved the distinction is a useful one.

Reporting-based Centralization

The essence of this approach is that central treasury (corporate or regional) receives exposure information from operating units, makes certain exposure management decisions and then communicates these decisions back down to operating units. Exposure information systems have been discussed in Chapter 5, so our focus here is on exposure decision making and action.

Three levels of centralization of exposure management are identified in Table 9.1. Central treasury may issue only *general guidelines* to operating units; it may also regularly issue *specific directives* on how certain exposures are to be managed; and finally, central treasury

Table 9.1. Levels of Reporting-based Centralization

Exposure management role	Level of centralization		
	General guidelines	Specific directives	Centralized action
Sets overall exposure management guidelines	C	L	L
Makes specific decisions on each operating unit's exposures	C	C	L
Takes exposure management action	C	C	C

C = Central treasury (corporate or regional)
L = Local unit (division, subsidiary)

may actually take the exposure management *action* on behalf of operating units. These three levels of centralization are analyzed below.

General Guidelines. At the very lowest level of centralization, corporate treasury sets overall guidelines on how exposures are to be managed. These guidelines can take various forms depending on the nature of the company's exposures. However, they are often too rigid and simplistic or else so vague as to be meaningless, as the following examples indicate:

> cover all net transactional exposures,
> cover all weak currency receivables and strong currency payables (currencies specified),
> do not use forward cover,
> minimize foreign exchange losses,
> minimize foreign exchange losses/maximize foreign exchange gains.

With this approach, exposure management action (e.g. forward cover) is taken at operating unit level. So also are specific exposure decisions (e.g. should next month's Deutsche Mark payables be covered forward), although local responsibilities can be heavily constrained if corporate guidelines are inflexible. The information requirements of such a system can be minimal. Indeed, corporate treasury may not even monitor exposures except for a review of the foreign exchange gain/loss calculation in the periodic reporting package. An example of this kind of approach is described in Case A on p. 173.

Specific Directives. At the next level of centralization, treasury makes specific currency exposure decisions which operating units are then directed or recommended to act upon. This can take two basic forms. In the first case the central foreign exchange manager or committee makes regular (weekly, monthly) forecasts on each currency in which the company operates. These forecasts are then transmitted to operating units together with the related currency-specific advice (cover US dollar receivables, French franc payables). As with general directives, the exposure information requirements of this approach are minimal. Alternatively, the foreign exchange manager or committee discusses future currency movements in the context of the company's existing and anticipated exposures. Hence operating units must now submit exposure information to the center. This approach allows a much wider range of exposure management techniques to be applied, such as matching, leading and lagging, and pricing policies. With either of these approaches, operating units get regular and specific exposure management advice from treasury.

Centralized Action. At the highest level of centralization the treasury not only makes specific exposure management decisions but it also takes the appropriate action on behalf of operating units, where this is cost-effective. Benefits arise from the greater treasury expertise which can be brought to bear on exposure management and the more favorable terms which can often be obtained on the broader range of available techniques.

Whilst the second and third levels of centralization produce a more coordinated approach they can also create important evaluation and motivational problems. In terms of evaluation the basic concept to be applied is that management should be responsible only for the decisions which it controls. Clearly, irrespective of who takes the exposure management action, it is the unit/individual who made the underlying decision who should be evaluated on the effectiveness of that decision. (The same principle can be applied to the liquidity implications of exposure management. For instance, if treasury directs subsidiaries to lead or lag intercompany payments then subsidiary profitability should be evaluated on a pre-interest basis.) This means that if treasury only *advises* operating units, then responsibility lies at operating level; if treasury *directs,* then responsibility rests with treasury.

Even with such an evaluation system, however, the centralized approach is not necessarily free of motivational and management problems. With a compulsory system, for example, operating units may not fully accept that they are not held responsible for exposure management actions taken under the direction of treasury. After all, it is their cash balances which are affected by such decisions. Alternatively, with an advisory system the problem is that, if operating units reject treasury advice, should subsidiaries be allowed to take actions which treasury believe will harm the group?

One simple way to avoid such problems is the implementation of an *internal forward cover (hedging) system.* This can be either optional or compulsory. The basic idea of the optional approach is that operating units make their own forward cover decision but, if they decide to cover, it must be done with central treasury. Treasury then issues an internal ('paper') forward contract, and this 'paper' rate (based on the current forward rate) is used for subsidiary evaluation purposes. Treasury is left with the decision of whether the company as a whole should actually take the forward rate or stay uncovered — and the foreign exchange manager is evaluated on this decision. Table

Table 9.2. Internal Forward Cover Scheme — Responsibility Allocation

Cover/no cover decision			
Operating unit	Treasury	External action	Internal responsibility allocation
Cover	Cover	Treasury takes cover	Costs/benefits for account of operating unit
		Or operating unit takes over	Automatic
	No cover	None	Internal forward contract between treasury and operating unit. Costs/benefits for account of operating unit
No cover	Cover	Treasury takes cover	Costs/benefits for account of treasury
		Treasury directs operating unit to take cover	Memorandum adjustment to operating unit accounts. Costs/benefits for account of treasury
	No cover	None	None

9.2 illustrates the allocation of responsibilities within an optional system for each combination of treasury/operating unit forward cover decisions. In practice, however, most internal hedging systems are compulsory: operating units *must* take the internal forward rate and treasury is left with the company's 'spot versus forward' decision.

Structural Centralization

This approach seeks to redirect exposures to a central location within the company, where both exposure management decisions and action can be carried out. The two basic ways of achieving this are (a) the manipulation of intercompany currency-of-invoicing policy, and (b) utilization of an exposure management-oriented intermediary company, typically either a factoring or a re-invoicing vehicle. Whilst the following analysis focuses on the exposure management role of such policies or vehicles, it should be emphasized that these also have very important liquidity management and tax-planning functions.

Vehicle companies have also been set up for non-financial reasons, to control the purchasing, marketing or accounting functions of a corporation. Clearly, these other functions are integral elements in the choice of an exposure management system.

(a) Intercompany Currency-of-Invoicing Policy

For companies with extensive intercompany trade, transactional exposures can be easily redirected to one or more locations by the restructuring of intercompany currency-of-invoicing policy. The simplest case is where foreign operations consist merely of sales companies which sell locally and are sourced from parent country manufacturing affiliates. If intercompany exports are invoiced in exporters' currencies, as is often the case, then transactional exposures are dispersed throughout the group. This makes it more difficult to manage group exposures on a coordinated basis. Also, overseas sales companies are typically thinly staffed and hence unlikely to have the expertise to manage these exposures effectively. A policy of invoicing such exports in the buyers' currencies will automatically redirect the transactional exposures back to parent country operating units, where corporate treasury influence is likely to be much stronger. Centralization can then be completed by a reporting-based system or an intermediary vehicle involving parent-country manufacturing units only.

The same principle can be applied to more extensive intercompany trading patterns. For the company which sources its sales companies from manufacturing affiliates located in a number of countries, transactional exposures can be concentrated at the major manufacturing locations (parent country and overseas) by invoicing sales' affiliates in their local currencies. This again facilitates a group exposure management viewpoint, since an exposure reporting system or vehicle company need only involve the principal manufacturing subsidiaries. An example of how intercomapny currency-of-invoicing policy can be used to centralize exchange risk is given in Case D on p. 179.

(b) Intermediary Companies

The basic intermediary concept is that payment for goods provided by one entity to another is channeled through an agent or 'intermediary'. The intermediary acts as a conduit for the transfer of funds between the parent company, its subsidiaries (as exporters/importers), and/or third parties. Hence the intermediary is ideally placed to manage exposures (and liquidity) on a global or regional basis.

The intermediary's function is often limited to a designated geographic area of the firm's foreign operations. The location of the intermediary within that area is dependent on such factors as exchange controls, customs regulations, fiscal treatment, the sophistication of the capital and labor markets, and the presence of existing group entities. Specific regional examples of countries with the appropriate environmental background are the UK, Netherlands and Switzerland in Europe, Panama and Puerto Rico in the Americas, and Hong Kong and Singapore in Asia.

The two most common types of intermediary company are the export (import) finance vehicle and the re-invoicing vehicle. These carry out essentially the same exposure management function, the main practical difference being the broader scope of the intermediary function of the re-invoicing vehicle.

Export Finance Vehicle. This operates as an export factor, buying the export receivables of affiliate companies for settlement in the affiliate's local currency. If intercompany exports are then invoiced on to the foreign affiliate in the importer's currency, transactional exposures are shifted from operating units to the vehicle company. This creates opportunities for internal exposure management (matching, leading and lagging) and low-cost export financing (taking advantage of interest differentials between domestic and Eurocurrency rates).

The export factoring function can be applied automatically to all export sales or on a 'best efforts' basis. With a best efforts scheme the finance vehicle offers external sources of financing to the exporter, who then compares this with the domestic interest rate. Subsidiary treasurers thereby remain autonomous.

A simple (pre-tax) example of how a single export financing deal works is depicted in Figure 9.1. The Belgian company exports to its Italian affiliate on one-year terms. Due to limited local credit availability and high cost (Belgium 12%, Italy 18%) the two subsidiaries were unwilling or unable to finance the transaction domestically. Nor did either party want to carry a foreign currency exposure for one year. Instead, the export finance company borrows Euro-French francs for one year at 10% and immediately converts to Belgian francs to settle the Belgian receivable, thereby eliminating the Belgian company's receivables exposure. Export Finance Ltd's receivable from the Italian affiliate is denominated in lira, which again removes exchange risk from the operating unit. Export Finance Ltd now has an unmatched book (lira receivables, French franc payables, both for settlement in one year) which is neutralized by a forward contract at a cost of 6%. (Alternatively, the finance vehicle might have matched these positions with opposite flows from other parts of the group, or left them uncovered.) The pre-tax cost of funding is 16% and all exposures are fully covered.

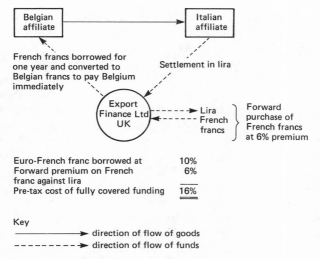

Euro-French franc borrowed at   10%
Forward premium on French   6%
franc against lira
Pre-tax cost of fully covered funding   16%

Key

⟶ direction of flow of goods

--------➤ direction of flow of funds

Figure 9.1 Export Financing Deal

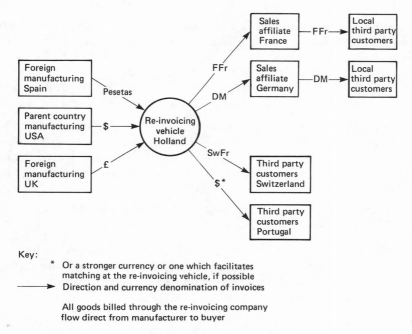

Key:

* Or a stronger currency or one which facilitates matching at the re-invoicing vehicle, if possible

⟶ Direction and currency denomination of invoices

All goods billed through the re-invoicing company flow direct from manufacturer to buyer

Figure 9.2 Exposure Centralization with a Re-invoicing Vehicle

This example has described the export financing of intercompany trade. The same approach can be applied to third-party exporting and importing, as demonstrated in Case B on p. 174.

Re-invoicing Vehicle. The mechanics of re-invoicing are illustrated in Figure 9.2. Goods exported from an affiliate company are shipped direct to either third party or affiliate customer, but the invoice (and hence payment) is channeled through the re-invoicing vehicle. Transactional exposures can be centralized at the vehicle company by invoicing affiliates (exporters and importers) in their local currencies. This centralization facilitates internal exposure management by the application of such techniques as leading and lagging, multilateral netting, and matching. The centralization of the exposure management system around a re-invoicing vehicle is described in Case F on p. 181.

For the purpose of analyzing the costs and benefits of an intermediary company, export finance and re-invoicing vehicles can be analyzed jointly since they function in much the same way. Benefits go beyond purely exposure management considerations — the rationale for an intermediary could equally be based on liquidity or operating (purchasing, marketing) considerations. Major benefits are:

> Exposure management: centralizes exposures at one location where information and expertise is developed.

> Exposure (and liquidity) management: the doubling of trade flows maximizes the flexibility to lead and lag. The central decision point also allows leading/lagging decisions to be made on a group basis, involving the after-tax trade-off between expected translation gains/losses, transactional gains/losses, forward cover gains/losses and interest income/expense.

> Liquidity management: creates a central liquidity pool, to be funded or invested in supranational markets. In particular, profitable opportunities arising from after-tax interest rate differentials between domestic and Euro-money markets can be utilized.

> Liquidity management: creates a channel for reallocating funds between previously unconnected units by leading and lagging.

> Banking costs: reduces foreign exchange transactions, producing savings of around one-sixth of one per cent of the amount netted. Also, finer rates, commissions and value compensation charges may become available to the central unit.

> Operating management: improves bargaining power with external markets (purchasing and sales) without placing negotiating burden on operating units.

This list of benefits seems very impressive, so why are intermediary vehicles still relatively uncommon? One reason is simply management inertia and opposition from the operating unit level of decentralized companies. Another is start-up and running costs. The former can be significant if a sophisticated communications system is used. Once established, running costs are surprisingly low since only a small management team (plus clerical back-up) is normally required to run the system. A third reason is that for many companies the same benefits can be achieved by a reporting-based system if authority is sufficiently centralized.

STAGES IN INTERNATIONAL CORPORATE DEVELOPMENT

The scope for exposure management centralization will depend on the type of international activities performed by each company. Three prototype stages of international corporate development are shown in Table 9.3. Specific examples of exposure management systems drawn from each stage are examined in the next section. Before analyzing these cases, let us briefly outline in general terms the scope for exposure management centralization for each of the three prototypes.

Exporter/Importer. All subsidiaries are located in a single country and international business consists solely of sales to or purchases from third parties overseas. Operations generate transactions' exposures only; this type of company has no foreign subsidiaries. The only kinds of exposure management centralization available here are the application of reporting-based or structural centralization to export/import exposures.

Parent-Country-Oriented Multinational Operations. Principal manufacturing operations still remain in the parent country. Instead of exporting direct to third parties, this type of company exports to foreign sales subsidiaries, which then sell in their local markets. Exposures are still heavily transactions-oriented.

With the predominance of intercompany cross-border trade, intercompany currency-of-invoicing policy becomes a very useful means of bringing foreign subsidiaries' potential transactional exposures back to the parent country. To the extent that the overseas sales companies' cross-border trade consists of imports from parent country manufacturing operations, transactional exposures can be switched to the parent country simply by invoicing this trade in subsidiaries' local currencies. As in the case of the exporter/importer, group transactional exposure management can then be centralized by the introduction of an appropriate reporting system or vehicle company.

Table 9.3. International Life Cycle — Treasury Organization and Exposure Characteristics

Stage of international life cycle	Treasury organizational trend: Decentralized Centralized	Exposure characteristics Transactional	Translation
Exporter/ importer	A ————————→ B	Third party export/import trade from/to parent country	Foreign currency loans No foreign assets
Multinational: foreign sales companies only	C ◄———————— ►D	Intercompany export trade from parent country	Foreign currency loans
		Limited intercompany financial (dividend) flows back to parent country	Limited foreign assets
Multinational: foreign manufacturing and sales operations	E ————————→ F	Intercompany export trade from worldwide manufacturing centers	Extensive foreign currency loans
		Third-party import trade into worldwide manufacturing centers	Extensive foreign assets
		Intercompany financial (dividend and loan) flows	

'Pure' Multinational Operations. Manufacturing operations are now located overseas as well as at home. Intercompany cross-border trade is extensive, existing between foreign subsidiaries as well as emanating from the parent country. Third-party transactional exposures also arise in a number of countries. Cross-border financial flows (dividends, intercompany loans, and third party financings) become extensive. Translation exposures increase significantly. In short, group exposures tend to be very large, various and dispersed. The organizational opportunities for centralizing the management of such a complex pattern of exposures are extensive. These include both reporting-based systems and structural manipulation of the exposures themselves, and can be applied on a regional or group-wide basis.

CENTRALIZATION VERSUS DECENTRALIZATION: SOME CASE STUDIES

Six case studies are presented here: a decentralized and a centralized example for each of the three stages of international corporate development. The objective is to show that, wherever firm-specific characteristics permit, coordination of exposure management from corporate or regional treasury should be adopted.

Case A: Decentralized Exporter

Background. Company A is a UK consumer products company. Annual sales exceed $300 million. Reflecting a multi-product base, operations are organized along independent subsidiary lines. Parent company influence over the operations of these subsidiaries is minimal. Basically, if profitability is adequate then subsidiaries are left alone.

Exposure Characteristics. Exposures are purely transactional, arising from third party import and export trade. The company has no foreign subsidiaries and no foreign currency loans. On a group basis the gross transactional exposures consist (in dollar-equivalent terms) of approximately $40 million of currency payables and $100 million of currency receivables. A simplified picture of these exposures is depicted in Figure 9.3.

Exposure Management System. This is highly decentralized, reflecting the company's operating characteristics and the way it has developed. There is no corporate treasurer. This function, insofar as it exists, is one of a number of tasks carried out at head office by the group chief accountant. Subsidiaries do not report their exposures to head office.

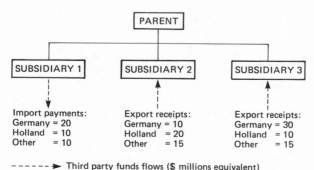

Figure 9.3 Company A — Exposure Characteristics

In effect, the corporate exposure management role consists of a general directive from the board of directors that all foreign exchange exposures should be covered immediately. Subsidiaries do not always adhere to this policy, however, and the group chief accountant cannot detect this from the existing uni-currency information system. Head office does review an exchange gain/loss item in subsidiaries' monthly accounts. However, this number simply represents the difference between monthly booking rates and the aggregate of all exchange rates actually taken by each subsidiary – its exposure management implications are unclear. The approach taken by the group chief accountant is that, as long as this number is not significantly negative, then exposure management is satisfactory. In effect, then, subsidiaries manage their exposures independently of each other and of the parent company.

Strengths and Weaknesses. The principal advantage of this system is that, from a head office viewpoint at least, the administrative costs are low. Also the system is easily accommodated within the existing organizational structure of Company A. However, the opportunity costs of this exposure management system are significant.

1. The subsidiary focus restricts an overall identification of exposures and exposure management opportunities, and this has led to a number of inefficiencies. Most obvious is the fact that existing matching opportunities (two-way Deutsche Mark and guilder flows) are not being realized. More generally, there is inadequate awareness of exposure management techniques and an overemphasis on external tactics.

2. Subsidiary responsibilities are unclear: if they adhere to the 'always cover' directive this can affect their profitability (including foreign exchange gains/losses) upon which they are evaluated.

3. Control over subsidiaries' exposure management action is weak.

Case B. Centralized Exporter

Background. Company B is a UK textile manufacturer. Annual sales exceed $500 million. The company is highly divisionalized, primarily the result of a long history of growth by acquisition and merger. Operating decision making is highly decentralized but in recent years the company has made an effort to centralize the finance function.

Exposure Characteristics. Exposures are purely transactional. Annual exports and imports, all third party, equal $70 million and $50 million respectively. Exposures are spread across the company's six operating divisions. The international textile markets are very competitive and so pricing flexibility is limited.

Exposure Management System. Exposures are handled by a vehicle company which performs import paying agent and export factoring functions.

The export factoring function works as follows. When a division receives an export order a confirmation note is sent to the vehicle, Company B Export Ltd. Internally, the division receives the current forward rate for the appropriate maturity (i.e. the order date to settlement date period). Externally, the foreign exchange manager must then decide, within guidelines set by senior management, whether to sell the currency receivable forward immediately or carry the receivables exposure on his books. This decision will depend on the exchange rate outlook and the existing portfolio of currency positions.

Irrespective of this decision, Export Ltd will settle its debt (at the in-house forward rate) with the division on the 20th day of the following month. In this particular case no factoring charge is made. Export Ltd is a cost center and divisions pay only an annual management fee.

Import exposures are picked up at the purchase order stage. Unlike the export factoring business, where Export Ltd actually takes title of the goods, on the import side the vehicle acts only as paying

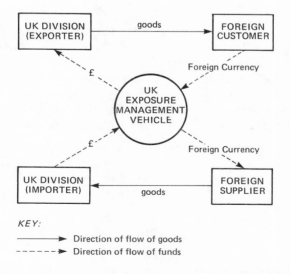

Figure 9.4. Company B – Export Factoring/Import Payment Vehicle

agent. However, the exposure management function is exactly the same: divisions automatically receive an internal forward rate and exposure management responsibilities rest firmly with the foreign exchange manager of Export Ltd. The operation of the vehicle is depicted in Figure 9.4.

Costs and Benefits For Company B. Set-up costs primarily involve the treasury management time and effort required to 'sell' the idea to divisional management — often a very difficult hurdle to be overcome. Running costs are surprisingly small, consisting of the following three elements: (a) labor — a single professional and a clerical assistant; (b) Reuters foreign exchange rate service, plus equipment rental and the cost of a telephone line to the nearest computer installation; and (c) the subscription fee for a currency forecasting service.

Benefits go beyond purely exposure management considerations and are predominantly intangible, which makes the justification for such vehicles difficult to quantify. The major quantifiable benefit is that foreign exchange commissions and costs are reduced because of the matching of currency receivables and payables of different operating units. The intangible benefits of the export vehicle are potentially far more significant:

1. It enables a coordinated group currency-of-invoicing policy. This can be used to facilitate matching and netting and to implement a policy of foreign currency invoicing — none of which would typically occur if currency-of-invoicing is left entirely to divisional management.

2. It aids export marketing in two ways. First, Export Ltd will hold open a forward quotation for one week, which is a great help to a division in the final and critical stages of contract negotiations. Second, Export Ltd also provides expert advice on exchange rates to be used in foreign currency price lists, which are reviewed every six months. This 'long-term rate' is also used for small (less than $20,000) internal forward contracts.

3. A central dealing situation offers economies of scale: concentration of management expertise, sophisticated equipment and information system, better quality banking advice and better rates.

4. Financing benefits primarily include the possibility of cheaper interest charges by selective use of Euro-currency financing.

5. There are cash management improvements: reduced administrative burden and better forecasting at operating unit level; cen-

tralized credit control and collection allows better identification of credit risk.

6. In Company B's case, the distribution function is also handled by Export Ltd (involving significant non-treasury manpower), producing higher transport capacity utilization and better rates.

7. Reponsibility allocation is clearly defined: divisions manage the operating side of the business and the foreign exchange management at Export Ltd are evaluated on their forward cover policy by comparing the actual (spot or forward) rate obtained with the internal forward rate. So long as the internal forward rate is an objective and consistently calculated market rate, this comparison effectively evaluates the selective forward cover policy against the 'all cover' alternative.

It should be emphasized that many of these benefits could be realized without a vehicle company. This approach has, however, been successful at Company B.

Case C. Decentralized Parent-Country-Oriented Multinational

Background. Company C is a US manufacturer of equipment and components for the engineering, electrical, and automotive industries. Total third party sales are $1,500 million, split between US domestic ($1,100 million), US export ($100 million) and overseas companies' sales ($300 million). The company is organized along divisional lines and a decentralized management philosophy prevails. Divisions operate as autonomous profit centers and corporate treasury does not have the staff or, in practice, the authority to intervene except in a very general way.

Exposure Characteristics. These are mainly transactional. US based companies have both third party export ($100 million) and import ($300 million) exposures and also export in US dollars to assembly and sales affiliates overseas ($100 million). Overseas subsidiaries also have limited third party imports but sell almost entirely in local markets (more than 30 countries). Overseas companies rely largely on local financing; net translation exposures are not significant.

Exposure Management System. The corporate role is minimal and the exposure management function is devolved to the divisions. For US-based subsidiaries this function is highly centralized at divisional head office. Subsidiaries report export and import exposures as they arise. The divisional treasury manager then decides if forward cover should be taken and, if so, takes out the contract on behalf of operating units. Exposure management at overseas' subsidiaries is subject to much less divisional control, due to the wide spread of locations and the existence of minority interests in some of the manufacturing operations. Overseas companies tend to be left alone, unless divisional management has a very strong currency recommendation or the company books significant foreign exchange losses.

Strengths and Weaknesses. The strength of this system is that it fits into the existing management philosophy, organization and legal structure of Company C. Also, the administrative costs of running the system are relatively cheap — or rather, are hidden (dispersed) in the company. So long as this general policy of decentralization produces adequate profits it is unlikely to be changed. However, this approach does involve substantial opportunity costs:

1. The divisional focus means that interdivisional opportunities for matching or netting are not recognized. This generates unnecessary foreign exchange costs, since two divisions with offsetting currency flows will be entering into spot and/or forward exchanges in different directions. (The divisional focus will also very probably mean wasted opportunities for inter-divisional liquidity reallocation.)

2. Similar wasted opportunities arise at overseas subsidiary level, again because of the lack of a global exposure information system and decision point.

3. Lack of corporate guidelines on and control over exposure management.

4. Dispersion of decision making to divisional and, more particularly, to overseas subsidiary level means opportunities for economies of scale (expertise, dealing) are unrealized. Overseas exposures could be largely centralized by a policy of invoicing US inter-company exports in buyers' currencies.

5. Overemphasis on market-related techniques, to the exclusion of internal tactics (matching, leading and lagging, pricing flexibility). A global viewpoint might also lead to a better understanding of the interaction of operating and exposure decisions and a more integrated treasury.

6. Unclear responsibility allocation: US subsidiaries are evaluated on operating performance, which automatically includes the

effects of the forward-cover decision made by divisions. Hence subsidiaries are held responsible for a decision over which they have no control.

Case D. Centralized Parent-Country-Oriented Multinational

Background. Company D is a US manufacturer of consumer and industrial products. Annual sales exceed $2 billion, around two-thirds of which is on the domestic market. Organizationally the company is dispersed: it has over 10 operating divisions with subsidiaries (sales and manufacturing) in over 30 countries.

Exposure Characteristics. Exchange risk arises from translation as well as transactional exposures. US-based companies have both third party export and import exposures. Overseas manufacturing and sales companies are sourced domestically and from US affiliates, and sell only in local markets. Most of the overseas operations are located in Europe.

Exposure Management System. This has been centralized at corporate treasury by the manipulation of intercompany currency-of-invoicing policy and a comprehensive exposure reporting system for US companies. A dual intercompany currency-of-invoicing policy is adopted. All European companies are invoiced in their local currencies from the US, thereby eliminating their payables' exposures. Non-European affiliates are invoiced in US dollars, and so have dollar payables exposures. The rationale here is that the amounts are not significant, many of the local currencies do not have forward markets, and the management time and administrative costs of doing otherwise would be excessive. The intercompany currency-of-invoicing policy is thus a mixture of two themes: centralize exchange risk but do not create an excessive managerial and administrative burden.

This policy has achieved the objective of redirecting the vast bulk of transactional exposures back to the USA. The exposure reporting and management system can then focus on US operations. Each month all US divisions submit to corporate treasury an exposure forecast, by month for six months out, consisting of both invoiced and forecast transactions. The report gives a currency breakdown of intercompany and third party receipts and third party payments. Within policy guidelines set by senior management, the assistant treasurer-international then takes the exposure management decisions and action (e.g. leading and lagging, matching, forward cover) on behalf of the subsidiaries. Irrespective of this action, for evaluation purposes subsidiaries receive the in-house forward rate. Hence responsibility allocation is clear.

Strengths and Weaknesses. The major weakness of this approach is that, with over 10 divisions, the aim of an integrated treasury function is unavoidably difficult. This constrains treasury liaison on sourcing, marketing, and other operating decisions. Given these organizational complexities, however, Company D's system represents a sensible trade-off between the advantages of centralization and the administrative and organizational costs of taking the centralization concept to an unnecessary extreme. The key benefits are:

1. The vast majority of exposures are identified and managed on a group basis. This enables natural matched positions to be identified and also 'artificial' ones to be 'manufactured' (by changing billing currencies). Centralized management also enables a wider range of techniques to be used and produces more favorable rate quotations on the larger deals.

2. The in-house forward rate system is a clear and fair means of allocating responsibilities between treasury and operating units. Performance evaluation and motivation are not adversely affected.

3. Management effectiveness is increased. The central exposure management operation is run by a single, expert professional (plus back-up staff). This leaves operating management free to concentrate on its major tasks.

Case E. Decentralized 'Pure' Multinational

Background. Company E is a German engineering company and this stage of its development occurred around 1970. Annual third party sales exceeded $2 billion. Operations were centered on manufacturing units in four countries: Germany, UK, Holland, and Italy. Each of these companies produced the same products and operated independently, selling to third parties and sales affiliates (at arm's length) both domestically and internationally. Head office's role consisted basically of acting as banker to the group and monitoring the profit performance of subsidiaries.

Exposure Characteristics. Both transactional and translation exposures were significant. The latter were not a major concern because of flexible accounting regulations (German companies are not required to consolidate foreign subsidiaries in their published financial statements).

Exposure Management System. This was highly decentralized: subsidiary companies managed their own transactional exposures and accordingly were evaluated on their overall profit performance. Given the existence at that time of a relatively fixed exchange rate system, foreign exchange risk was not seen as a major concern. The only element of cooperation between subsidiaries was the operation of bilateral netting arrangements between the four manufacturing companies. Its scope was limited, however, because of the limited nature of trade flows between these entities.

Strengths and Weaknesses. Judged in its historical context this organization was reasonable and typical of many European multinational companies. In the context of the floating exchange rate era, however, its weaknesses are fundamental:

1. Exposures are not clearly defined or identified on a group basis. Hence global exposure management is impossible and control over local exposure management actions is inadequate.

2. The organization does not facilitate the application of treasury expertise to operating decisions.

3. Evaluation of exposure management performance is inadequate.

As the next example shows, the advent of floating exchange rates and changes in the company's operating pattern have led to a rethink of how its exposure management function should be organized.

Case F. Centralized 'Pure' Multinational

Background. Company F is Company E ten years on. Annual third party sales have doubled to around $4 billion. Operations are still centered on the four manufacturing units in Germany, UK, Holland, and Italy. However, significant integration of the manufacturing process has taken place, mainly for production reasons. Rather than manufacture complete items, each unit now specializes in the production of certain components which are then traded with the other manufacturing units for final assembly. This massive increase in intercompany trade, together with fluctuating exchange rates, has created a bias towards greater treasury centralization in Company F.

Exposure Characteristics. The same basic exposure pattern exists as before, but it is now significantly larger and more complex because of extensive intercompany trading.

Exposure Management System. Company F decided to centralize exposure management by the establishment of a re-invoicing vehicle, International SA (Switzerland). The rationale for a re-invoicing vehicle was also based on other financial considerations: to minimize the banking costs relating to foreign exchange transactions and intercompany flows and to assist operating companies with cash forecasting and short-term financing. But from an exposure management viewpoint the basic aim is clear: arrange the currency-of-invoicing policy so that transactional exposures arise at International SA and not at subsidiary level. This is achieved by invoicing all exports to the vehicle company in the exporter's currency. The vehicle company then re-invoices affiliate customers in their local currencies and third party customers in either local or a more appropriate currency. The only transactional exposures remaining at subsidiary level are third party payables, which are generally not significant. These, together with translation exposures, are currently monitored by detailed currency reporting to International SA.

Strengths and Weaknesses. The costs of this system are essentially the development and running costs. The vehicle company is run by three professionals plus clerical staff. For this outlay Company F obtains the following benefits:

1. Exposures are identified and managed on a group basis, with all the attendant economies of scale: realization of potential matching opportunities, concentration of management expertise, access to a wider range of exposure management options, greater focus on internal tactics, better currency advice and finer rates from banks.

2. The re-invoicing vehicle facilitates leading and lagging and automatically acts as a clearing center for multilateral netting.

3. Treasury and operating responsibilities are clearly and rationally allocated.

4. Cash and liquidity management improvements are facilitated: better cash forecasting at subsidiary level, liquidity reallocation is easily effected through adjustment of intercompany credit terms, cheaper financing costs at the center.

CONCLUSIONS

Two overall concepts for exposure management organization have been emphasized: integration and coordination. Our basic recommendation is that the treasury function should be *integrated* and *coordinated* as much as the characteristics of each company will allow. More specifically, the organizational objectives of an exposure management system can be summarized as follows:

1. It should enable group-wide exposure identification, decision making and control.

2. It should facilitate the integration of treasury within the company, preferably involving direct liaison between central treasury and operating units.

3. It should not cause motivational problems. In particular, it should be clear that individuals/units are held responsible only for those decisions which they control.

4. It should not involve unnecessary management effort and administrative costs.

5. It should facilitate the achievement of other business objectives, both non-financial (helping the marketing effort) as well as financial (improving cash and liquidity management, reducing financing costs).

REVIEW QUESTIONS

1. Select three dissimilar companies, such as a manufacturing (e.g. consumer products) company, a service (e.g. airline) company and a trading (e.g. oil) company. Discuss how the operating and organizational characteristics of each has affected the exposure management function.

2. Devise a practical internal hedging system (optional or compulsory) for a US company whose operating divisions make hundreds of foreign currency export sales each year. Your proposal should include the following details: (a) how should the 'paper' rate be set?; (b) if the market forward rate is used, for what maturity?; (c) when should treasury settle with the operating unit and what happens if the

customer pays late?; (d) who is responsible for credit collection?; and (e) exactly how should treasury performance be evaluated? Note that, given the number of export sales, it is impractical to monitor foreign currency receipts on a transaction-by-transaction basis.

3. Discuss alternative methods of centralizing group transactional exposures for (a) a US company exporting to domestically oriented sales companies, and (b) a Japanese company with manufacturing operations in the UK and Germany, and with domestically oriented sales companies in the rest of Europe (sourced intercompany from Japan, the UK and Germany) and the Far East (sourced intercompany from Japan).

4. Discuss how an export finance company can be used in group exposure/liquidity management. To illustrate, construct an export financing deal using current interest rates (domestic and Euro-) and exchange rates.

5. Suggest how the exposure management systems of companies A and C might be improved.

BIBLIOGRAPHY

BIMR (1977), 'The committee approach to oversee and coordinate exchange management', *Business International Money Report*. 29 April, pp. 129–30.

Brooke M.Z. and Remmers H.L. (1970), *The Strategy of Multinational Enterprise: Organization and Finance*. London, Longman.

Brooke M.Z. and Remmers H.L. (1977), *The International Firm*. London, Pitman.

Conference Board (1969), *Organizing and Managing the Corporate Financial Function: Studies in Business Policy No. 129*. New York, National Industrial Conference Board.

Lessard D.R. and Lorange P. (1976), *Currency Changes and Management Control. Resolving the Centralization/Decentralization Dilemma through the use of Internal Forward Exchange Rates*. MIT, Sloan School, Working Paper 849–76, April.

PART III

Parameters and Constraints on Exposure Management

T. W. McRAE

CHAPTER 10

Theory and Practice of Forecasting Exchange Rates

We noted in Chapter 6 that the belief as to whether or not we can predict the future value of the exchange rate is a crucial determinant of foreign exchange management strategy. If a foreign exchange manager believes that he *can* predict future rates he will cover on the forward market when that tactic is profitable and not cover when it is not profitable. If it is thought that forecasting is not possible the manager will devise an initial hedging tactic which is used continuously and not move into and out of the forward market.

In this chapter we will examine some methods which have been used to forecast future currency exchange rates and the evidence as to the success or failure of these methods. We know that the foreign exchange managers of many multinational companies believe that they can forecast future rates and that this forecasting procedure is thought to be a profitable activity.[1] We will also discover that at least one leading academic authority on the subject doubts whether future rates of developed countries' currencies can be forecast with profit under a floating regime (see Dufey and Giddy, 1975). Future spot rate prediction is profitable if it can beat the forward rate prediction of the future spot rate.

The predictive power of forecasters appears to be much stronger under fixed parity regimes than floating parity, and in shallow rather than deep markets. Under a fixed exchange rate system, exchange rates do not adjust gradually to changing circumstances. Pressure for an adjustment between two currencies builds up over time and the adjustment is usually sharp and unexpected. The exchange rate moves in sudden jumps interspersed by long periods of relative calm. This makes forecasting of this variable particularly difficult. It may be obvious that a currency is overvalued, like sterling from 1964 to 1967, but the adjustment may be delayed for years by political factors that seem, and often are, irrational. The benign neglect of the value of the US dollar from 1977 to 1979 was dictated as much by international politics as by international trade. We will see that a successful exchange rate forecaster must be as knowledgeable about politics as he is about economics or finance.

The immediate cause of a sudden adjustment of exchange rates is the uncontrollable flow of international funds out of or into the given currency, but the real cause lies much deeper. The value of a country's currency is usually taken as an index of that country's relative economic performance. A falling off in efficiency is reflected in a falling exchange rate. It is this clear correlation between exchange rate and economic performance which injects such a strong political element into exchange rate forecasting. Governments are not sympathetic to impartial indices of their failure and will go to great lengths to conceal the evidence by manipulating the exchange rate. An eventual adjustment is inevitable but the timing of the adjustment may be determined by political not economic events. For most of this century the government of France has been noted for aggressive devaluations not dictated by the economic conditions prevailing at the time of the devaluation.

The basic methodology of exchange rate forecasting is first to determine the underlying economic value of the currency, second to compare this value to the current spot rate, and then to relate any difference to the prevailing political conditions to judge whether the currency will be allowed to adjust or, alternatively, whether the foreign exchange reserves are sufficient to maintain its value at an artificial level.

WHAT ARE WE FORECASTING?

The simplest type of forecast is one which predicts the *direction* of change of the adjustment in the value of the currency: 'The Swiss franc will rise in value relative to the US dollar over the next three months.' A second, more difficult level of forecast attempts to evaluate the *amount* as well as the direction of the adjustment: 'The Swiss franc will rise by 3% to 4% against the US dollar over the next three months.' The third, and by far the most difficult level of forecast, is the attempt to predict the timing of the adjustment: 'The Swiss franc will rise by between 3% and 4% against the US dollar in early April 198X.' A few forecasters attempt the third level of prediction but most only attempt the second level.

FORECASTING METHODOLOGY

Some forecasting is entirely quantitative in approach, some entirely qualitative, but the best forecasting is a mixture of the two methods. The difference between forecasters lies in the degree of emphasis placed by them on the quantitative and qualitative components of the forecasting model; see Wheelwright and Makridakis (1977) for a fuller discussion.

Quantitative forecasting models use a wide range of techniques from regression (Box—Jenkins) type models to full blown econometric models using dozens of 'constraint' equations to limit the possible solution 'forecast'. The Box—Jenkins approach is relatively simple, using an autoregressive moving average to estimate the future value of the exchange rate from past data. Discriminant analysis has also been used to select out the best predictive variables (Folks and Stansell, 1975).

Full blown econometric forecasting models have been developed by several of the world's leading banks and business schools. The World Service of the Wharton Econometric Forecasters Associates and the Chase Manhattan Bank are perhaps the best known, on the western side of the Atlantic. The London Business School forecasting service and FOREX Research Ltd both base their exchange forecasting initially on large-scale econometric models, although the model outputs are modified by qualitative judgements before final publication.

Pure qualitative forecasts not based on some form of quantitative analysis are practised by some banking organizations.[2] In this case great weight is given to inside knowledge of trends in the international financial markets and the current political situation in the various countries. Quantitative models usually attempt second-level forecasts with a political analysis determining third-level forecasts.

Nonlinear exchange forecasting models appear to be less common although attempts are being made to apply systems dynamics to foreign exchange forecasting. Spectral analysis has been applied to the movements in foreign exchange rates to see if they form a 'random walk' (Upson, 1972).

LONG-TERM FOREIGN EXCHANGE FORECASTING

Let us first define long-, medium- and short-term forecasting. Long-term forecasting examines the terrain beyond a five-year horizon. This type of forecasting is usually qualitative using the scenario type approach. By medium-term forecasting we mean a period of about two to five years ahead. Thus, by elimination, short-term forecasting covers the period up to two years, but concentrating particularly on the period up to one year ahead.

The value of a developed country's currency depends, under normal conditions, on the industrial efficiency of that country. If we can predict the relative industrial efficiency of two nations, we should be able to predict with reasonable accuracy the movement in the rate of exchange between their respective currencies in the long term. The exceptions to this rule consist of countries like Saudi Arabia and the United Kingdom with a considerable volume of natural resources for export and countries, like Switzerland, which attract refugee money in times of financial crisis.

So far as foreign exchange management is concerned the corporate treasurer tends to concentrate on short-term exchange rates. We shall see that in the long term, certain foreign assets tend to adjust in value to changes in exchange rates (Aliber and Stickney, 1975) and that many long-term contracts have some kind of exchange adjustment clause built into them. The one possible exception to this rule are those corporations operating in weak currency countries who, unwisely, borrow significant amounts from hard currency countries, see Chown (1977), and corporations operating long-term royalty agreements.

In short, long-term foreign exchange forecasting seems of limited use for 'pure' treasury management.

MEDIUM-TERM FORECASTING

Economic forces express themselves in the long run but in the short run they can be suppressed by a determined government. Economics defeats politics in the long run, but political considerations can delay the emergence of economic reality in the short run. The economic future is easier to predict than the political future. The best known and best tested economic theory for predicting foreign exchange values in the medium term is the purchasing power parity (PPP) theory.

The PPP Theory

The key to medium-term exchange rate forecasting lies in the celebrated purchasing power parity theory of Gustav Cassal. Cassal postulated that the exchange rate between two currencies *in the medium term* simply reflects the ratio of the prices of a representative basket of goods, both domestic and foreign, in the two countries (Cassal, 1921). In other words, a new exchange rate will reflect a relative change in the internal price levels of the two countries, see Balassa (1964) and Officer (1976) for a fuller discussion.

For example if the price level in Country D doubles and the price level in country T trebles and initially the ratio of exchange was 100:100, then the new exchange ratio will be 100 x 200/300 = 66. Thus 100 units of T's currency will only buy 66 units of D's currency. The exchange ratio has moved from 100:100 to 66:100. This is the absolute version of the theory. In the relative version 'changes in the exchange rate are proportional to changes in the ratio of foreign to domestic prices' (Aliber and Stickney, 1975, p. 52). For example:

	Period 1	*Period 2*
Domestic prices in A	100	150
Foreign prices from B	100	200

If the initial rate of exchange was 100:100 the new equilibrium rate of exchange is predicted to be:

$$\frac{200/100}{150/100} \times 100 = \frac{2}{1.5} \times 100 = 133$$

or 100:133

Several studies have examined the relationship between internal price level changes and external change in the value of the currency. These, in most cases, appear to support the hypothesis. Treuherz (1969) averaged out the increase in the cost of living in five South American countries. He then related this fall in the value of internal purchasing power to the fall in the exchange rate of these currencies against the dollar over 4, 7 and 14 years (1954–1965). The results set out in Table 10.1 show a remarkably consistent relationship between changes in the internal and external value of the currency in the long term.

Table 10.1. Percentage Annual Increases in Dollar Rate and Cost of Living (COL) in Five Latin American Countries.

	For a percentage annual increase in the COL of	There was a percentage annual increase in the dollar rate of
Argentina		
4-year average (1964-67)	28%	28%
7-year average (1961-67)	25%	25%
14-year average (1954-67)	31%	29%
Brazil		
4-year average (1964-67)	60%	58%
7-year average (1961-67)	54%	55%
14-year average (1954-67)	39%	39%
Chile		
4-year average (1964-67)	28%	28%
7-year average (1961-67)	28%	26%
14-year average (1954-67)	29%	35%
Colombia		
4-year average (1964-67)	15%	12%
7-year average (1961-67)	14%	13%
14-year average (1954-67)	14%	11%
Peru		
4-year average (1964-67)	12%	12%
7-year average (1961-67)	7%	11%
14-year average (1954-67)	6%	8%

Source: Treuherz (1969) p. 59

Aliber and Stickney (1975) traced the relationship between consumer price levels and exchange values for 48 countries for the 12-year period 1960 to 1971. The results are set out in Table 10.2. The major findings of this important study are as follows.

1. The PPP theory came out well when deviations were averaged over the long term (column (b)).
2. Large deviations from PPP predictions occurred in the short term of under a year (column (c)).
3. Deviations were much greater in the case of developing countries than in the case of developed countries.

Kern (1977) related internal inflation of 13 developed countries to trade weighted exchange rates and the US dollar for the period 1954—1978. The results are set out in Figures 10.1(a) and 10.1(b).

Table 10.2 A Test of the PPP Theory: Percentage Deviations of the Change in Relative Prices from the Change in Exchange Rates for the Period 1960 to 1971

(a) Country	(b) Average Annual Percentage Deviation	(c) Maximum Annual Percentage Deviation
Argentina	1.68	23.97
Australia	.50	8.57
Austria	1.69	9.52
Belgium	1.25	11.01
Bolivia	2.44	8.69
Brazil	1.96	21.08
Canada	− .19	3.80
Chile	−3.68	28.36
Colombia	−1.20	32.08
Costa Rica	−1.82	13.60
Denmark	2.71	7.57
Dominican Republic	− .68	8.00
Ecuador	−2.36	28.48
El Salvador	−2.30	5.32
Finland	− .02	21.11
France	.75	10.40
Germany	2.37	12.57
Greece	− .71	3.61
Guatemala	−2.12	4.59
Haiti	.55	7.89
Honduras	− .66	3.47
Iceland	1.41	29.75
India	− .25	31.97
Iran	− .90	4.04
Ireland	1.46	13.50
Israel	−3.64	35.07
Italy	1.53	5.94
Japan	4.19	15.66
Korea	−3.96	35.68
Malaysia	−1.14	4.96
Malta	−1.32	16.11
Mexico	− .19	2.15
Netherlands	2.98	13.87
New Zealand	.24	16.35
Norway	2.34	8.45
Panama	−1.44	12.56
Paraguay	.63	17.20
Peru	3.36	25.98
Philippines	−5.21	46.12
Portugal	2.63	11.92
South Africa	− .49	5.12
Spain	2.56	11.38
Sweden	2.01	9.45
Switzerland	1.66	12.59
Turkey	1.12	38.79
United Kingdom	.89	14.02
Uruguay	5.60	72.90
Venezuela	−4.18	29.25

Source: Aliber and Stickney (1975), p. 48

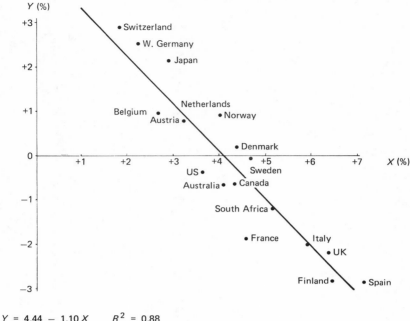

$$Y = 4.44 - 1.10\,X \qquad R^2 = 0.88$$

where:
Y = average yearly % change in trade-weighted exchange rate index
X = average yearly % change in wholesale prices

NatWest exchange rate index (1953 = 100) 18 countries 1977 trade-weights, geometric calculation

Figure 10.1 (a) The Relation between Inflation and Trade-weighted exchange rates 1954—1978: 18 countries

There is a tendency to cluster around the regression line but substantial deviations are noticeable. Galliot (1971) and Rogalski and Vinso (1977) have also tested the PPP theory with similar results.

One final medium-term study should be noted. Folks and Stansell (1975) used the statistical technique of multiple discriminant analysis to select countries which were likely to devalue by 5% or more against the US dollar over the period 1971—1972. The predictive power of their model proved remarkably successful. Out of 51 countries tested, 86% were correctly allocated into the devalue or non-devalue group.

The conclusion of all these studies is that the PPP theory appears to work successfully in the medium term of over two years but that in the short term large deviations occur. Discriminant analysis has also been shown to be a useful tool for predicting devaluations in the medium term. The multinational treasurer will usually be concerned

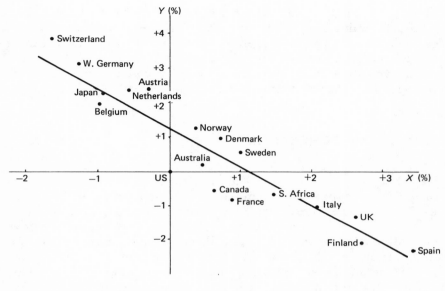

$Y = 1.27 - 1.19 X$ $R^2 = 0.88$

where:
Y = average yearly % change in spot rate of each currency against US dollar
X = average yearly % change in wholesale prices in each country, less average yearly
       % change in wholesale prices in the US

Source: Presented by Mr David Kern, Manager of Economic Analysis Section,
National Westminister Bank Ltd at the 1979 Corporate Finance Conference,
Intercontinental Hotel, London, 10–12 October 1979

Figure 10.1 (b) The Relation between Inflation Rate Differences and Spot
Exchange Rates against the US Dollar 1954–1978: 18 countries

with the short term, and he may be prepared to allow the deviations
to cancel each other out over the long term.

If we are to use the PPP theory as a forecasting technique we must
find out the existing rate of inflation in the two countries and use
these figures to predict the fundamental exchange rate. The actual
spot rate, or the forward rate may differ from the fundamental rate
because of government intervention in the market. If we can predict
the future inflation rate this gives us a longer lead time in predicting
the future exchange rate, but this is a difficult topic which we will
not pursue except to note that monetary economists would use changes
in the money supply and real GNP to predict the future inflation
rate which would in turn predict the future exchange rate.

The key problem in using the PPP theory as a predictor of future
spot rate is the difficulty inherent in measuring the *rate of transmission*

of internal inflation into external devaluation of the currency. The eventual devaluation may be inevitable but the transmission process can take several years to operate. Since this delaying mechanism is not well understood by economists, the value of the PPP theory as a predictive tool is of limited value to the corporate treasurer if precise timing is an important factor in the decision.

SHORT-TERM FORECASTING

We concluded in the previous section that the relative rate of inflation in two countries provides a useful medium-term forecast of the change in the exchange rate of their respective currencies. This approach might be said to provide a *fundamental value* for the currency. However, although economic forces are likely to move a currency towards its fundamental value in the long term, various short-term expedients such as running down the international monetary reserves are available to delay the movement of a currency towards its true value. A large number of small pressures gradually build up until some sudden event, often non-economic, such as a change of government, forces a sudden convulsive movement up or down towards the fundamental value. The analysis of these external pressures, many of which are not economic, is the subject matter of short-term qualitative forecasting.

Short-term forecasting is much more difficult but it is also of much greater significance to the corporate treasurer. Most business contracts operate in the short term of under a year. When the treasurer of a multinational company talks about exchange rate forecasting he almost invariably means forecasting in the short term.

The PPP theory may provide a useful conceptual framework for forecasting the value of exchange rates in the medium term but Table 10.2 demonstrates that it is of limited value as a predictive tool in the short term. In the short term of under a year technical forecasting using momentum models and even the much maligned chartists would appear to be more successful than the economic modellers. For example Goodman (1979) tested a set of foreign exchange forecasts over the two years 1976 to 1978 in six leading currencies. The forecasts were for the currencies three and six months forward.

The technical forecasters, using momentum models[3] and chart analysis, were found to provide rather better forecasts than the economic forecasters. This confirms our earlier statement that economic factors win out, but only in the long run. The technical forecasters have their ear close to the ground, they can gauge well the psychology of the market in the short term up to six months ahead when the market is often ruled by emotion rather than economic logic. Under these conditions the technical forecasters score well. As an antidote to this view readers are referred to Levich (1979), Chapter 7.

Some foreign exchange forecasting models do operate in the short term, such as the asset equilibrium model and the interest rate parity theory.

The Asset Equilibrium Theory

This theory states that the value of a currency in the international market, like the value of any other economic good, is determined by the supply and demand for the currency.

The treasurers of organizations that trade internationally need to hold a certain percentage of their assets denominated in foreign currencies. If an adjustment in the value of a foreign currency is expected the treasurer may attempt to increase or decrease his holding of this currency, and so the total pressures of demand and supply built up from many individual decisions will move the exchange rate to a new equilibrium where the increase or decrease in value exactly offsets the risk of expected future gain or loss on holding the currency.

Note that the PPP theory looks at the price of *goods* in the two countries while the asset equilibrium theory concentrates attention on the demand and supply for liquid assets. The two theories are not necessarily in conflict. The PPP theory can be determining the value of a currency in the medium term while the asset equilibrium theory is determining the short-term value. This will induce the value of the currency to oscillate around the medium-term trend line.

The asset equilibrium theory focuses attention on the *return* on international liquid assets. This return is made up of two parts, the rise or fall in currency value plus the rate of interest. Many years ago Irving Fisher noted this trade off in international loans between the interest rate of return and the expected adjustment in currency value. He called this trade off the interest rate parity theory (Fisher, 1930).

The Interest Rate Parity Theory

A large proportion of the assets traded by the international financial markets are held in highly liquid form. This money can be moved quickly from one currency to another as one currency strengthens and another weakens. The treasurers who control these international assets choose the particular currency in which to invest their funds by trading off the rate of interest received from the bond against the likelihood of devaluation or revaluation of the currency in which the bond is denominated.

It has been known for many years that, under normal conditions, this interest rate differential provides a useful method of predicting the forward rate of a currency. We simply take the current spot rate between two currencies, adjust for the difference between the going free market interest rate in similar types of bonds in the two countries over the period concerned, and this will give us the forward rate at the end of the period. If it does not give us the forward rate then the process of 'arbitrage' will soon remove the difference. The forward exchange rate is at 'interest rate parity' when the interest rate differential is equal to forward rate discount or premium. The process is studied by Giddy and Dufey (1975) who present evidence to suggest that the foreign exchange markets between the US dollar and the Canadian dollar, Euro-sterling and Euro-French franc operate this process efficiently.

It would appear that, barring exchange controls, interest rate differentials determine the forward rate under normal conditions but that under abnormal conditions (i.e. oil price increase) it may be that the reverse process applies and the rapidly changing forward rate feeds back to alter the respective interest rates.

Alternatively one can argue that, like the position of three marbles in a bowl, their value is determined mutually and simultaneously. The adjustment of forward rate discount or premium to interest rate differential is sometimes called the Fisher effect. It is illustrated in Figure

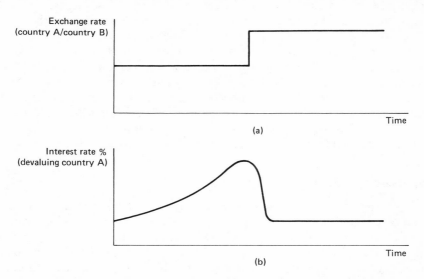

Figure 10.2 The Fisher Effect. The interest rate of devaluing country A rises to offset expected future devaluation. After devaluation, the interest rate returns to its original level.

10.2. Figure 10.2(a) shows the change in exchange rate at time t, Figure 10.2(b) shows the temporary leap in the rate of interest of the devaluing country before the subsequent devaluation removes the interest differential. The interest rate of devaluing country A rises to offset expected future devaluation. After devaluation, the interest rate returns to its original level.

Aliber and Stickney (1975) have tested the interest rate parity theory over 11 years for seven developed countries and six years for six developing countries. The results of this test are somewhat similar to the results of their testing of the PPP theory. They are set out in Table 10.3. The authors concluded that 'the average annual deviations seem to suggest a zero net differential as a central tendency' (p. 51), and again the deviations were greater for developing countries and there were significant short-term deviations from the trend.

One interesting finding was that the interest parity deviations were much less than the PPP deviations for developed countries but much greater for developing countries.

Table 10.3. A Test of the Interest Parity Theory (the Fisher Effect): Percentage Deviations of Relative Differences in Interest Rates from Changes in Exchange Rates for Selected Countries for the Period 1960—1971 (Developed Countries) and 1966—1971 (Developing Countries).*

	Interest Parity	
Country 1960—71	Average Annual % Deviation	Max. Annual % Deviation
Belgium	0.99	11.09
Canada	0.17	5.71
France	0.46	9.34
Germany	1.75	11.27
Netherlands	0.83	16.02
Switzerland	1.04	8.29
UK	0.49	13.27
(1966—71)		
Argentina	10.42	32.00
Brazil	6.35	23.10
Chile	17.18	26.00
Colombia	1.00	10.70
Mexico	5.58	6.50
Venezuela	2.72	6.30

*Note that the deviations on the interest parity theory are greater for currencies of developing countries.

Source: Aliber and Stickney (1975), p. 51

Implications for FEM Policy

The findings of this section have important implications for foreign exchange management policy. If the PPP theory is correct, non-monetary assets held abroad for more than two or three years will tend to rise in value, through inflation, to compensate for the fall in the value of the currency in which they are denominated. Thus non-monetary assets held for two to three years or more are not subject to exchange rate risk and need not be hedged forward.

If the interest parity theory is correct monetary assets held for the medium or long term are also not subject to exchange rate risk since the higher rate of interest on these assets compensates for the risk of devaluation of the currency (or vice versa in the case of revaluation).

Thus if the findings of this section are accepted, assets held abroad for more than two or three years *are not exposed to exchange risk*! The treasurer can ignore these long-term assets and concentrate his attention on protecting those assets due for liquidation and transmission in the shorter term of under two years.

The Forward Rate as a Predictor of Future Spot

One method of handling short-term foreign currency contracts is to make an estimate of the future exchange rate at the payment date, compare this with the forward rate for that date and cover via a forward exchange contract if the forward rate is more favorable than the estimate. The forward rate can be taken as the market's estimate of the future spot rate, although no conscious effort appears to be made by foreign exchange dealers to predict the future spot rate. Thus, the first question we need to ask in short-term forecasting is 'How good is the forward rate as a predictor of the future spot rate?'

Econometric studies of this question have initially concentrated on asking the question 'Is the forward rate an unbiased predictor of the future spot rate?' For example, take the following hypothetical comparison of the three-month forward rate over a four month period between sterling and the US dollar.

	Forward rate (3 month)	Actual spot at this date
	2.10	2.05
	2.05	2.10
	2.02	2.06
	2.07	2.03
Average	2.06	2.06

In no single month did the forward rate predict the actual spot rate of exchange but the *average* of the forecasts were identical, i.e. the forward rate was an unbiased predictor of the future spot rate. If the corporate treasurer did *not* cover forward he would make neither a profit nor a loss in the long term by omitting to cover. Thus, if the forward rate is an unbiased predictor of the future spot rate and if covering has a cost, it may not be worthwhile covering forward (but see Note 4). Giddy (1976) demonstrates that the spread on forward rates is wider than the spread on the spot rate as demonstrated in Table 10.4. Is the forward rate an unbiased predictor of the future spot (see Figure 10.3)? The results of research on this question are somewhat ambiguous. Kettell (1979) examined the predictive bias of the forward rate on the US dollar against the Deutsche Mark and Swiss franc for the period 1967—1976. He concludes that the 30-day forward rate is an unbiased predictor of the future spot rate but that the 90-day forward rate is not. Kohlhagen (1975) examines the 90-day forward rate against the future spot rate in six currencies and concludes that the forward rate *is* an unbiased predictor but, when

Table 10.4. Size and Variability of Spread in the Spot and Forward Markets (from Giddy, 1976).

US Dollar/Swiss franc exchange rates, all Trading Days in 1975

	Spot	One month forward
Average spread*	0.07%	0.10%
Standard deviation of spread	0.75%	0.05%

*Calculated as follows: [(Ask—Bid)/Ask] x 100

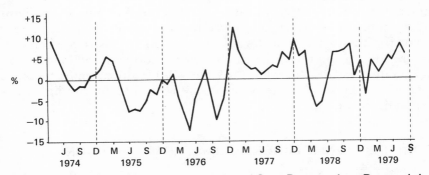

Figure 10.3 The Differences between Actual Spot Rate on given Date and the Three-month Forward Rate for that Date, sterling to dollars 1974—1979

compared to four other exchange rate forecasting methods, it was found to be the least accurate with a large variance. Aliber and Stickney (1975) examined eight currencies at one, three, six and 12 months forward and found the degree of accuracy of forecast to diminish with time. This is supported by Kettell's finding (1978). Aliber and Stickney (1975) found the forward rate to be a less accurate predictor when the given currency was floating as against operating within fixed limits (within a currency 'snake').

Wong (1979) also investigated the predictive power of the forward rate and concluded that it was an unbiased predictor in the very long run over several years but was subject to large medium-term deviations. The predictive power of the absolute value of the deviation was good for one month ahead, fairly good for three months but poor for one year, although the deviations cancelled out in the long run.

Kaiserman (1973) has pointed out that under a free floating regime the forward rate undervalues the future spot when the spot rate is rising and vice versa. This finding is supported by Wong (1979).

It has been pointed out by Bowe (1977) and others that even if the averaged forward rate is an unbiased predictor of the future spot rate in the long run the differences on *individual* transactions in the short run may be so great as to be unacceptable. The deviations of spot above or below the forward rate prediction may be so large as to upset a company's cash flow. We must also remember that only a limited number of currencies enjoy a forward market and that the forward market is usually shallower than the spot market.

Even if the forward market is an unbiased predictor and the deviations are acceptable, there may be other reasons for using the forward market. It allows future liabilities to be exchanged on a favorable day, that is, it gives more leeway than the spot market. Also it gives 'peace of mind' to the treasurer, that is, it provides insurance against uncertain currency fluctuations ahead.

We conclude that the forward rate appears to be a good predictor of the future spot at one and three months ahead but rather a poor predictor thereafter. The forward rate is an unbiased predictor of future spot in the very long run but this is normally too long for the corporate treasurer to 'sit it out'. He will usually attempt to hedge where he believes that the forward rate is out of line with his expectation of future spot.

FORECASTING METHODS — NUMBERS V. INTUITION

There are two approaches to foreign exchange forecasting although as we stated above it is rare today to find a forecaster who depends exclusively on only one of these approaches. The first approach can be described as *qualitative* or 'kitchen sink'. The forecaster gathers together all the information available to him on the political, economic and psychological factors affecting the future exchange rate. He weighs these factors in his mind, discusses them with colleagues and comes up with an intuitive forecast about the future exchange rate. The forecast depends more on 'gut feeling' than calculation.

The most complete examples of the alternative, *quantitative,* approach are to be found in the foreign exchange forecasts devised from computer based international trade models such as the Wharton or London Business School model. These models use complex computer programs to process a wide range of economic statistics to arrive at a forecast of future exchange rates. The computer programs which process these models may take many man-years to write and test.

Today most foreign exchange forecasters employ a mixture of the two approaches. Some are more qualitative, others more quantitative, but almost all forecasters use some sort of formal model for forecasts and modify the output from this model according to the current political climate.

Who Forecasts?

In Appendix 10A to this chapter (page 216) we provide a list of some organizations who provide foreign exchange forecasts. Note that the range of currencies covered, the services provided and the cost of the service varies a great deal between forecasters. Some forecasters provide advice on foreign exchange management techniques in addition to currency forecasts.

SOME FORECASTING MODELS

An example of qualitative foreign exchange forecasting is provided by Korth (1972). He allocates his forecasting data into four categories, financial, relational, political and expectational. The items making up these categories are listed in Table 10.5.

Korth applies a four-step analytical procedure to this data to arrive at his currency forecasts. The procedure is as follows.

1. Does the economic input data suggest that a change in currency value should occur?
2. Does the government have the will, the financial resources, or borrowing power to prevent the change in currency value taking place?

Table 10.5: Elements in Forecasting Currency Value Changes

A. Financial factors
   1. Balance of payments imbalance.
   2. Monetary reserves of the government.
   3. Extent of foreign indebtedness and willingness of foreigners to retain it.
   4. Temporary fluctuations (normal).
   5. Extraordinary factors.
   6. Domestic inflation.
   7. Present and anticipated economic strength of trading partners.
   8. Monetary and fiscal alternatives available to the government.
   9. Trade, exchange and capital controls/incentives.

B. Relational factors
   10. Importance of the currency in world trade.
   11. Importance of the country in total world trade or in certain items of trade.
   12. Elasticities of supply/demand for trade, tourism and capital.

C. Political factors
   13. History of past changes.
   14. Personal philosophies of government officials.
   15. Party (political) philosophies.
   16. Proximity of elections.

D. Expectational factors
   17. Opinions of bankers and other businessmen.
   18. Forward exchange contracts/blackmarket.
   19. Interest-rate levels.
   20. Local investment and spending level.
   21. Real estate values.

Source: **Korth (1972) with permission. Copyright © 1972, by the Foundation for the School of Business at Indiana University. Reprinted by Permission.**

3. How much of a change in the currency value is needed to stabilize the external economic position?

4. When will the change in value occur?

This method delineates the anatomy of the revaluation process but does not formally describe the physiology. It is a kind of *aide memoire* to the forecaster who must reach his own intuitive conclusions from the data.

Lesseps and Morrell (1977) describe the conceptual framework behind the Henley exchange forecasting model. The steps are as follows.

1. Plot the relative movement in the wholesale and retail price index for recent years against the exchange rate.

2. Try to establish the exchange rate trend against inflation rate differential.

3. Tabulate the basic components of the current account (export and import prices, etc.).
4. Tabulate the basic components of the capital account (direct and portfolio investment, government capital flows, interest rate differential, etc.).
5. Use (3) and (4) to predict overall payment flows.

(1) to (5) can now be used to trace the effect of payment flows on official reserves, and via current government policy on the exchange rate. A prediction as to the future exchange rate can now be derived. The final set of currency forecasts should be cross-checked against one another for consistency of forecast.

Simple Formal Forecasting Models

Murenbeeld (1975) uses a statistical technique called multiple discriminant analysis (MDA) to select those variables which can discriminate successfully between devaluing and non-devaluing currencies. He attempts to estimate the direction and timing of change in a currency's value but not the amount of the change. We noted above that Folks and Stansell (1975) also successfully predicted currencies which are due for devaluation by 5% or more over the following two-year period. Murenbeeld uses MDA to select out six variables which appear to predict currency value changes with a fair degree of reliability. These six variables are:

1. Change in wholesale price index.
2. Percentage unemployment change.
3. Foreign exchange reserves divided by imports.
4. Change in foreign exchange reserves expressed as a percentage.
5. Change in money supply as a percentage of total money supply.
6. Change in government budget surplus or deficit as a percentage of GNP.

MDA provides a set of weights which are applied to each of the six variables. The weighted score for each currency is then compared to a set of mean scores representing (a) devalue (−2.375), (b) no change (+0.179), and (c) revalue (+2.796). By comparing any individual currency's score to these mean values the forecaster predicts the likely movement of a currency's value during the next quarter. The Deutsche Mark, for example, had a mean score of 4.36 and therefore was likely to revalue upwards.

The previous analysis was applied to a *fixed rate period*. When floating rates became popular after 1971 the model could only predict successfully one month ahead. Murenbeeld suggests that once

Table 10.6 Method of Estimating Likelihood of Currency Adjustment.

Once the adjustment factor for the currency has been calculated, this factor selects out the row relevant to this currency. For example, a factor of 1.50 suggests a 75% chance of upward revaluation and zero chance of devaluation.

(a) Adjustment Score	(b) Number of Currencies	Probability of Currency-Adjustment		
		(c) Devaluation	(d) No Change	(e) Revaluation
Less than −2.50	4	1.00	—	—
−2.50 to −2.00	0	.75	.25	—
−2.00 to −1.50	1	.50	.50	—
−1.50 to −.50	5	.25	.75	—
−.50 to .50	10	—	1.00	—
.50 to .80	1	—	.75	.25
.80 to 1.00	2	—	.50	.50
1.00 to 1.50	7	—	.25	.75
Greater than 1.50	4	—	—	1.00

the MDA score has been calculated a subjective probability distribution can be applied to the score to indicate the likely future trend of the currency. A suggested scheme is set out in Table 10.6.

Murenbeeld suggests that his model provides 'a workable program of appraising currency strength and weakness from which a simple probability distribution of currency adjustment can be derived.'

Armington (1976) describes a model he has built based on the asset equilibrium theory noted above. The model is based on the expected behavior of international money managers. As expectations about the future value of currencies change so the money managers alter the composition of their portfolios causing money to flow across international frontiers. The exchange rate will move to seek balance of payments equilibrium. By modeling this process Armington claims to be able to provide useful projections of exchange rates in the future. A modification of this model has been used by Forex Research.

The model has two interesting features. First it emphasizes *international,* rather than simply national, equilibrium for a currency's value. Second, Armington doubts that national affiliation plays much part in the international financial policy of multinationals. Exchange-control-free balances or international financial market institutions may provide enough scope for treasuries to avoid local financial restrictions if they should so wish.

Many formal mathematical models are now available which attempt to predict the future value of foreign exchange rates. These models tend to incorporate the same set of variables but they allocate different weights to their relative importance. But how accurate are these forecasts? Do the benefits derived from foreign exchange forecasting justify the cost involved?

HOW ACCURATE ARE FOREIGN EXCHANGE FORECASTS?

In Appendix 10A (pages 216—19) we list 23 organizations who provide foreign exchange forecasts. How accurate are these? This is not an easy question to answer since the forecast can itself influence the future value of the currency. A forecast can become a self-fulfilling prophecy. If all the forecasters agree that sterling will fall relative to the Deutsche Mark over the next three months this may induce company treasurers to take action which will depreciate the pound relative to the Deutsche Mark. However our study of the distribution of forecasts, such as that illustrated in Figure 10.4, appears to indicate that forecasters do not agree on the future value of currencies and that the forecasts tend to scatter around the forward rate, although the scatter is not normally distributed.

Under the fixed exchange rate system, when it is known that the government will intervene to limit the fall or rise in a currency's value, exchange rate forecasters have a relatively easy time. So long as the *direction* of the movement is forecast correctly the maximum value of the rise or fall is known. The introduction of floating rates in the early 1970s made forecasting more significant, since the possible size of losses or gains became very large and also more difficult to predict since government intervention strategy had to be guessed at. For example, in 1976 in the UK and 1978 in the USA forecasters did not know how far the respective governments were prepared to let the international value of their currencies fall in value. For this reason any study of the accuracy of foreign exchange forecasting models must distinguish between fixed and floating rate periods.

It might be expected that foreign exchange forecasters would provide a track record of past achievements to their prospective clients. For example Gray (1974) considers that 'anyone offering a (foreign exchange forecasting) model ought to be able to quote *statistical* measures of the accuracy of his model. Two primary measures are the coefficient of correlation and the standard error of the estimate' (p. 38). In fact it appears that few forecasters are prepared to provide

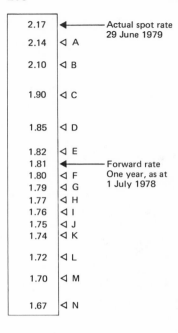

2.17	◄———— Actual spot rate
	29 June 1979
2.14	◁ A
2.10	◁ B
1.90	◁ C
1.85	◁ D
1.82	◁ E
1.81	◄———— Forward rate
1.80	◁ F One year, as at
1.79	◁ G 1 July 1978
1.77	◁ H
1.76	◁ I
1.75	◁ J
1.74	◁ K
1.72	◁ L
1.70	◁ M
1.67	◁ N

Figure 10.4 Forecasts of the Spot Rate for Sterling against the US dollar as at 30 June 1979. The forecasts are taken from 14 leading forecasters as at or near 1 July 1978. Note how the forecasts clustered around the forward rate. The fact that the actual rate on 29 June fell outside the range of forecasts demonstrates the extreme difficulty of forecasting major economic and political events, such as the 1979 oil crisis, which so strongly affected this exchange rate.

statistically validated measures of the accuracy of their prior forecasts. Some will provide raw data but not a measure of accuracy calculated using accepted statistical tests.[5]

Forex Research have provided the data set out in Figure 10.5. Forex attempted to predict the direction of movement of seven major currencies. They were trying to beat the forward market prediction of the future spot rate by predicting which side of the forward rate the future spot would fall. They also provided an ordinal ranking of the currencies as to how undervalued they were relative to the forward rate prediction.

Figure 10.5 shows the distribution of the rank correlation coefficients over the 28-month period. If the ordinal rankings had no predictive value we would expect a rank correlation coefficient of zero. The distribution provided in Figure 10.5 is clearly not zero and is significantly different from zero. An article by B. Hesketh in McRae and Walker (1979) provides more detailed evidence.

Grubel (1965) presents evidence to suggest that if certain 'relatively simple rules of behavior' had been followed in the foreign exchange market during the fixed exchange rate period, 1955—1961, a speculator could have made a reasonable profit. The speculator 'used only the information embodied in past exchange and interest-rate data'. With perfect foresight the speculator could have made 19% rate of

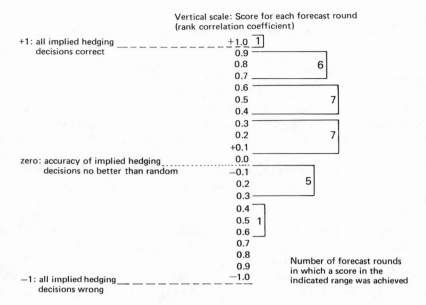

Figure 10.5 Gauging the Accuracy of Forex Forecasts in Comparison with 3-month Forward Rates, October 1975–February 1978

return on money invested. Using Grubel's rules he would have earned 17%. He puts this high rate of return down to 'large and one-sided interest rate differentials that consistently kept the forward rate well below the spot rate' (p. 110).

Poole (1967) studied movements in the exchange rate of the Canadian dollar from 1950–1962. He concluded that past price trends could be used to predict future trends and that annual returns from 10% to 50% could have been made by speculators. He explained this phenomenon as the result of foreign exchange transaction costs.

Upson (1972) tested the predictive power of past exchange rate trends using spectral analysis on the US dollar 90-day forward rate 1961–1967, (weekly). He found several cycles in the data of a length of 32 weeks, 3.8 weeks and 2.5 weeks. He therefore suggests that it should be possible for speculators to make profits if they can uncover these cycles. (The writer did not explain why, if this is so, he did not himself retire as a millionaire before publishing the article!)

The previous studies have suggested that during fixed rate periods future spot rates can be predicted with sufficient accuracy for the forecaster to make a profit out of the activity. Giddy and Dufey (1975) in an important paper claim to prove that under a *floating exchange rate regime* past price trends in exchange rate movements do not provide the exchange rate forecaster with any useful information about future values of the currency. This follows the same reasoning as that used to advance the *efficient markets hypothesis* in share evaluation theory. This hypothesis states that share prices follow a so-called *random walk*, see Fama (1970). Giddy and Dufey claim to prove that exchange rates under a floating regime also follow a random walk. They selected exchange rate data from various floating periods, 1919–1926 and 1971–1974, for the US dollar, the French franc, Canadian dollar, and the UK pound. They found that 'The forecasting accuracy of each method decreases rapidly as an attempt is made to predict exchange rates further into the future' (from 1–90 days) (p. 23). They conclude that 'successive exchange rates do have some memory — but a memory that is short-lived and weak'. Their final conclusion is as follows: 'Except possibly for very short-term (foreign exchange) forecasts the results provide support for the notion that trading rules are of no use in forecasting exchange rates' (p. 29). They claim that predictive models such as that of Grubel and Upson are useless if constructed *after the event* since the parameters of exchange rate forecasting models are continuously changing. They are correct *ex post* but not *ex ante*. In the concluding section of their paper Giddy and Dufey widen the scope of their attack on the feasibility of foreign exchange forecasting by stating that in their opinion successful forecasting of foreign exchange rates is only possible under the following strict set of conditions:

1. that the forecaster has better information or a better forecasting model and has *exclusive use* of this model;
2. that the 'other player in the foreign exchange game is the central bank or trader (a) who is dominant, (b) whose behavior is not governed by the profit maximization objective, and (c) whose behavior is predictable'. These conditions specify a fixed exchange rate regime.

Levich (1979) carried out a further study of forecasting methodology in the foreign exchange market. He concluded that the market efficiently reflects current information about future exchange rates. According to this study it is difficult to make consistent speculative profit out of foreign exchange rate forecasting. However, consistent forward cover reduces the volatility of earnings and this may increase the average share price of the firm.

In contrast to these studies Dooley and Shafer (1976) present evidence to suggest that exchange rates under a floating system *do not* form a random walk. The spot rates for nine currencies were studied from March 1973 to September 1975. It was found that filter rules yielded significant profit for some currencies. The verdict on exchange rate forecasting under a floating regime would seem to be 'unproven'.

CONCLUSIONS

The accuracy of exchange rate forecasting is influenced by three factors: (1) whether a fixed or floating exchange rate regime is in operation, (2) whether we are dealing with a currency of a developed nation with efficient capital markets or not, and (3) the length of the period of the forecast.

In the long term, beyond two or three years, the PPP theory has been shown to work. Therefore, the real value of foreign assets will rise to compensate for devaluation and capital losses on monetary assets will be compensated by higher rates of interest in the foreign financial market. Foreign assets are not exposed in the long term and need not be hedged or covered. Therefore, long-term exchange rate forecasting, even if feasible, has limited value for hedging purposes.

The very short-term forward exchange rate has been shown to be an unbiased predictor of the future spot rate, but although it has been shown to be an unbiased predictor, it has also been shown to be a not very *accurate* predictor compared to other forecasting methods. The forward market (if one exists) has invariably a wider spread and is therefore more expensive than the spot market. If a company is continuously operating in the foreign exchange market and if the forward market is an unbiased predictor of the future spot and more expensive than the spot market, then logically the treasurer should not cover forward but buy or sell currency in the spot market when the time for payment is due. However, since the cost differential between the spot and forward market is not large, the treasurer may be prepared to pay the difference for peace of mind and to obtain flexibility of payment date. We should also recall that some studies have found the medium-term forward rate to be a biased predictor of the spot rate.

Finally, we turn to the difficult question of whether foreign exchange forecasting is a profitable activity. Are the benefits of forecasting sufficient to justify the costs involved? There can be little doubt that under a fixed rate exchange regime when the currency value is controlled within an upper and lower bound, then foreign exchange forecasting can be profitable. Both research studies during fixed exchange regimes and the opinions of foreign exchange managers confirm this view.

Under a floating regime foreign exchange forecasting becomes both more difficult and more important. We have presented evidence to suggest that the forward rate can be beaten. We suggest that the user of foreign exchange forecasts must be highly selective in his choice of forecaster, but those forecasters who are prepared to reveal their track record appear to be able to provide profitable advice to the international currency manager.

REVIEW QUESTIONS

1. Why is a treasurer's foreign exchange management strategy so strongly affected by whether or not he believes that future exchange rates can be predicted with a fair degree of accuracy?

2. What is the immediate cause of change in the exchange rate of a currency?

3. We discuss three levels of forecasts by foreign exchange forecasters. What are these three levels?

4. How does a qualitative foreign exchange forecast differ from a quantitative one?

5. What determines the relative value of the exchange rate between two currencies of developed countries in the long run?

6. Why did sterling rise so sharply in value against the currencies of other developed nations in 1979 while the relative industrial efficiency of the UK was declining?

7. With regard to the external value of a currency 'economics defeats politics in the long run'. Why is this so?

8. What is the purchasing power parity theory?

9. The initial exchange rate between country X and country Y is 3:1. The price level in country X doubles, the price level of country Y increases by 50% during one year. What would the (simple) PPP theory predict the new rate of exchange to be?

10. Why do you think that deviations from PPP-based predictions of currency exchange rates are much greater for developing countries?

11. Why is PPP a poor predictor of exchange rates in the short term of under two years?

12. Explain the interest rate parity theory.

13. The US dollar at 2.04 stands at a three months forward premium of two cents against sterling. Calculate the interest rate differential between Euro-sterling and Euro-dollars over this period.

14. 'The interest rate parity deviations were much less than the PPP deviations for developed countries but much greater for developing countries.' Why do you think this is so?

15. What are the key implications of the PPP and interest rate parity theory for foreign exchange management policy?

16. What is meant when it is said that the forward rate is an unbiased predictor of the future spot rate?

17. What implications *might* this have for foreign exchange policy?

18. Even if 'the forward rate is an unbiased predictor of future spot in the very long run' the knowledge of this fact is of very little use to the corporation treasurer. Do you agree?

19. Describe Korth's four-step analytical procedure for forecasting exchange rates.

20. 'A simple probability distribution is far superior to a point estimate when forecasting exchange rates.' Why is this so?

21. Exchange rate forecasting is much easier under a fixed exchange rate system. Why is this so?

22. What arguments do Giddy and Dufey put forward in claiming that exchange rate forecasting is not a profitable activity under a floating exchange rate regime?

NOTES

1. Foreign exchange seminar chaired by Professor T.W. McRae, London, 15 February 1978.

2. See *Euromoney*, August 1978, p. 25. 'A guide to the banks and firms in the foreign exchange advisory business'.

3. Momentum models study the direction and impetus behind exchange rate movements to predict future movements. This is a short-term prediction technique.

4. A strategy of zero hedging nay be appropriate if the corporation is subject to a steady and continuing flow of exposures. But if exposures are sporadic or if an individual exposure is large enough to cause serious cash flow problems if the exchanges move the 'wrong' way, then this strategy of not covering forward would not be appropriate, see Bowe (1977).

5. The authors, through a research student, asked a large number of forecasters if they would provide their forecasts over a five-year period for testing. Only one forecaster agreed to do this. Two others said they would do so if all the others did too!

BIBLIOGRAPHY

Aliber R.Z. and Stickney C.P. (1975), 'Accounting measures of foreign exchange exposure', *Accounting Review*, Vol. 50, pp. 44-57.

Armington P.J. (1977), 'Floating exchange rates. The balance of payments and the global equilibrium of asset markets', Forex Research Paper No. 3, July, pp. 3-12.

Balassa B. (1964), 'The purchasing power parity doctrine', *Journal of Political Economy*, Vol. 72, December, pp. 584-96.

Bowe K.D. (1977), 'Break-even in the long run? You may be ruined meanwhile!', *Euromoney*, January, pp. 97-100.

Cassal G. (1921), *The World's Monetary Problems*. London, Constable.

Chown J. (1977), 'Taxation aspects of currency management.' Talk to FEM conference, London.

Dufey G. and Giddy I.H. (1975), 'Forecasting exchange rates in a floating world', *Euromoney*, November, pp. 28-33.

Fama E.F. (1970), 'Efficient capital markets', *Journal of Finance*, Vol. 25, No. 2, May, pp. 383-417.

Fisher I. (1930), *The Theory of Interest*. London, Macmillan.

Folks W.R. and Stansell S.R. (1975), 'The use of discriminant analysis in forecasting exchange rate movements', *Journal of International Business*, Spring, pp. 35-50.

Galliot H.S. (1971), 'PPP as an explanation of long term changes in exchange rates', *Journal of Money, Credit and Banking*, Vol. 2, August, pp. 348-57.

Giddy I.H. (1976), 'Why it doesn't pay to make a habit of forward hedging.' *Euromoney*, December, pp. 96-100.

Giddy I.H. and Dufey G. (1975), 'The random behavior of flexible exchange rates', *Journal of International Business Studies*, Vol. 6, No. 1, Spring, pp. 1-32.

Goodman J.H. (1979), 'Foreign exchange rate forecasting techniques', *Journal of Finance*, Vol. 34, No. 2, May, pp. 415–27.

Gray A.K. (1974), 'Foreign exchange forecasting — how far can the computer help?' *Euromoney*, July, pp. 36-43.

Grubel H.C. (1965), 'Profits from forward exchange speculation.' *Quarterly Journal of Economics*, Vol. 79, No. 2, May, pp. 248-62.

Kaiserman D.L. (1973), 'The forward exchange rate as a predictor of the future spot rate', Proceedings of the ASA, pp. 417–22.

Kern D. (1977), 'Inflation implications in foreign exchange rate forecasting.' *Euromoney*, April, pp. 62–69.

Kettell B. (1979), 'Is the forward rate an accurate predictor of future spot rates?' In McRae and Walker (1979).

Kohlhagen S.W. (1975), 'The performance of the foreign exchange markets 1971-1974.' *Journal of International Business Studies*, Fall, pp. 33–38.

Korth C.M. (1972), 'Future of a currency.' *Business Horizons*, Vol. 15, June, pp. 67-76.

Lesseps M. and Morrell J. (1977), *Forecasting Exchange Rates. Theory and Practice*. Henley Centre for Forecasting, March.

Levich R.M. (1979), *The International Money Market, an Assessment of Forecasting Techniques and Market Efficiency*. Connecticut, JAI Press, Inc.

McRae T.W. and Walker D. (1979), *Readings in Foreign Exchange Management*. Bradford, MCB Publications.

Murenbeeld M. (1975), 'Economic factors for forecasting foreign exchange rate changes.' *Columbia Journal of World Business*, Vol. 10, Summer, pp. 81-95.

Officer L.H. (1976), 'The PPP theory of exchange rates', IMF Staff Papers, pp. 1-60.

Poole W. (1967), 'Speculative prices as a random walk — flexible exchange rates.' *Southern Journal of Economics*, Vol. 33, No. 4, p. 468.

Rogalski R.J. and Vinso J.D. (1977), 'Price level variations as predictors of flexible exchange rates.' *Journal of International Business Studies*, Spring, pp. 71-81.

Treuherz R.M. (1969), 'Forecasting foreign exchange rates in inflationary economies.' *Financial Executive*, February, pp. 57-60.

Upson R.B. (1972), 'Random walk and foreign exchange rates — a spectral analysis.' *Journal of Financial and Quantitative Analysis*, Vol. 7, Part 4, pp. 1897-1906.

Wheelwright S.C. and Makridakis S. (1977), *Forecasting Models for Management*. New York, Wiley.

Wong S.K.O. (1978), 'The forward rate as predictor of future spot rate', MBA dissertation, University of Bradford, pp. 59–74.

APPENDIX 10A

Details of Some Foreign Exchange Forecasters Who They Are and What They Offer

Service	Fees		Method and length of forecast	Number of currencies	Number of customers
	Annual	Other			
Amex Bank	Negotiated individually		Kitchen sink* Up to five years informally	All major currencies, others on request	100+
Bank of America	No fee to bank's clients, except £750 for FX and exposure workshop, and negotiable fee for consulting service		Kitchen sink One week, one, three and 12 months	15, others on request	Any bank clients
SI/Metrics	$12,000		Econometric Up to 18 months, Planning three and five year	12	n.a.
Brown Brothers Harriman	$18,000 to $45,000		Kitchen sink Up to 12 months	50, half in limited scope	55

*Kitchen sink may include the use of econometric models, but is mainly judgemental, taking econometric, political and psychological factors into account.

Source: Euromoney, August 1978

Service	Price	Special/notes	Type & horizon	Frequency	Number of currencies
Chase Econometrics	$12,000	$15,000 including time — share access to models	Econometric Up to eight quarters	6 monthly 11 quarterly	n.a.
Chase Manhattan Bank	No fee for forecasts produced internally and available on request to bank's clients. Foreign exchange exposure management is separate service.		Kitchen sink Up to 18 months, or two to seven years, for general planning	12, others occasionally	Any bank clients on request and staff
Chemical Bank	$2,000 to $30,000		Kitchen sink 12 months and four years	26	111
Citibank	$25,000	Special project for negotiated fee	Kitchen sink Up to 12 months	All of interest to clients	60+
ContiCurrency	$25,000	$15,000 to $20,000 for special projects or fewer demands	Kitchen sink 12 months and five to 10 years	33, others on request	52
Eurofinance	FFr 1600 for 11 currencies, one year FFr 5500 for six currencies, five years FFr 50,000 for full corporate finance service		Econometric One year and five years	11	100, all services

Service	Fees		Method and length of forecast	Number of currencies	Number of customers
	Annual	Other			
European American Bank	$10,000 basic	$18,000 maximum. Projects at $550 a day	Momentum for short term, kitchen sink for up to five years	All, emphasis on Europe	80
Forex Research	$10,000 for eight currencies		Kitchen sink Up to 18 months	10	80+
Harris Bank	$21,000 with renewal discounts		Kitchen sink Up to 12 months informal longer	32	25
Gesellschaft fur Trendanalysen		Monthly fee: and 30% of net gains	n.a.	n.a.	31
Henley Centre** for forecasting	£235 for 17 currencies		Momentum Up to 12 months	17	400+
IFC	$8,000 for 10 currencies against the dollar $15,000 for above, plus eight currencies against Can $ and DM		Momentum	10 against $: 8 against Can $ and DM: Yen against SwFr, and £: £ against SKr	20+
Marine Midland	$25,000	Marinfo $2,500 Projections and short term consulting $6-10,000 Major project $75,000	Kitchen sink One, three, six and 15 months	22, also special studies for longer	40+

218

** Added to list.

Company	Fee	Method	Forecast period	Currencies	Clients
Peine Webber Mitchell Hutchins	$1,000 monthly publications $3500 for above plus 4/5 meetings a year	Kitchen sink	Three, six, 12 and 18 months	13	Five, and clients of parent brokerage firm
Morgan Guaranty: Foreign Exchange Services Group	No fee to bank's corporate clients	Kitchen sink		All leading currencies	Any of bank's corporate clients
Patterson, Little and Desmartin	$1,5000 (one currency) $1,100 (2nd to 4th currency) $7,500 (all currencies)	Econometric	One, two, three and six months	16	32
Predex	$5,000 (Predex forecast) $4,800 (Short term forecast) $9,000 (Predex forecast, plus simulations) $15,000 (Predex forecast, plus on-line services)	Econometric		Predex forecast, 17 up to 18 months, Predex short term forecast, 13 up to six months	56
N M Rothschild	$40,000 minimum	Kitchen sink	Up to five years	55	18, plus 'undisclosed number of Central Banks'
Waldner & Co.	$30,000 $6,000 (trial)	Momentum		7	23+

CHAPTER 11

Tax Treatment of Foreign Exchange Gains and Losses

Foreign exchange transactions can result in a profit or loss if the relative value of the two currencies changes between contract date and the date of payment of the contract. There can be a gain or loss in one currency expressed in terms of the other. A similar situation can arise when accounts expressed in one currency are translated into another currency. In either case the profit or loss on foreign exchange may affect the taxation charge imposed on the company at home or abroad. This chapter will discuss the impact of foreign exchange gains or losses on company taxation.

The subject is more complicated than one might expect. Tax rates differ between countries so that an exchange gain may suffer a different tax charge depending on where the revenue authorities deem it to be sourced. Some countries differentiate between foreign exchange deals covering revenue and those covering capital transactions. Foreign exchange gains on capital transactions often suffer a lower rate of tax or may avoid tax altogether. Conversely, foreign exchange losses on appreciation of a foreign loan may not be accepted by the revenue authorities as an allowable charge against tax.

Some tax authorities ignore foreign exchange gains or losses unless they are actually realized, while others consider unrealized gains and losses to be fully taxable. Profits stored in a foreign bank account which is blocked by exchange control regulations are not usually taxed until released, and so on. The tax effects of foreign exchange are complex and so provide considerable scope for the company treasurer to use his ingenuity to minimize the tax bill of his company. The overall policy of the tax adviser is to arrange matters in such a way that gains on exchange rate adjustments are made to arise in a form which are not taxable and losses in a form which are allowable against other income.

BASIC PHILOSOPHIES

Two basic approaches are discernible in the tax treatment of foreign exchange gains and losses. The first approach is to treat the foreign exchange bought or sold as an asset which is quite distinct from the transaction it finances. This is sometimes called the 'separate transactions' approach. The gain or loss on foreign exchange is thus separated from any gain or loss on the underlying transaction. The tax effect will arise when the transaction is closed by payment, not when the contract is signed.

   In contrast to the above approach, the 'integrated' approach ties the foreign exchange gain or loss into the contract it finances. In effect this approach implies that the foreign currency is simply a medium of exchange and not an independent asset. Any profit or loss on foreign exchange would be added to or subtracted from the profit on the underlying transaction, and the tax treatment of this profit or loss might be affected by the nature of the underlying transaction, i.e. whether it is of a capital or revenue nature.

TERMINOLOGY

For tax purposes we define *ordinary income* as income earned in the normal course of trade and differentiate this type of income from a *capital gain* arising from the sale of a fixed asset, etc. Many countries apply different tax rates to these two types of income.

   The tax law on foreign exchange gains and losses often needs to distinguish between an *open* and *closed* transaction. A transaction remains open until the final payment is acknowledged by the seller, when it is closed.

The profit on a foreign exchange transaction is *realized* when the deal is closed by final payment. Many countries do not tax a foreign exchange gain until it is realized.

The sourcing of income can have important tax implications. If the foreign exchange gain is treated as being sourced abroad, i.e. arising in a foreign tax regime, the tax charge may be eliminated or reduced by an imputed foreign tax credit.

We will now examine the tax treatment of four types of foreign exchange transactions:

1. Import—export transactions
2. Foreign currency loans
3. Forward exchange transactions
4. Balance sheet translations

IMPORT—EXPORT TRANSACTIONS

In most countries foreign exchange gains/losses arising from a contract denominated in a foreign currency are treated as if they were ordinary income. The gain is taxable and the loss is allowable against other trading income. In a few countries, such as Switzerland, the gain is taxable as ordinary income but the loss may not be allowable.

In the United Kingdom short-term gains and losses on normal trading transactions are treated as ordinary income for tax purposes. However, debts between companies in the same group may be treated as loans if the debt is held outstanding for more than six months. The UK tax authorities may ignore unrealized gains or losses on foreign exchange if the company have always ignored them in the past or if generally accepted accounting principles in the UK would exclude them from the account until realized. The subject is a matter for negotiation with the UK revenue authorities.

Exchange rate gains or losses on transactions which are not of a normal trading nature are treated as being capital gains or losses. The gain or loss has a tax effect only when the gain or loss is realized. If fixed assets held abroad and denominated in a foreign currency are sold, the foreign exchange gain or loss is amalgamated with the gain or loss on the underlying transaction for tax purposes.

In many countries the separate transactions theory is applied. The gain or loss on the exchange of currency is treated separately from the gain or loss on the underlying transaction. This applies to both exports and imports. The gain on the debt denominated in a foreign currency is not recognized for tax purposes until the transaction is closed by payment. If the debt is unpaid at the accounting year end the profit or loss has no tax effect until payment takes place in the following period.[1] The separate transactions theory also applies to payment for fixed assets, even if payment is by instalment. If the foreign currency is devalued, the foreign exchange gain is taxed on each future instalment.[2]

Generally US tax legislation states that foreign exchange gains or losses on trading transactions, whether current or fixed, have a tax effect only when the transaction is closed by payment. A problem will only arise when a credit transaction in one period is paid up in the following period and the exchange rate changes between these points in time. The gain or loss will have a tax effect in the latter period. There may be an exception to this rule in the case of royalties.

FOREIGN CURRENCY LOANS

Many countries treat a gain or loss on exchange on repayment of a loan in a foreign currency as taxable or allowable against tax. If a loan is denominated in a foreign currency the repayment value of the loan in the home currency is affected by an adjustment in exchange rates between the two currencies. The exchange value of the interest payment is also affected.

The tax treatment of these exchange rate gains and losses varies a great deal between countries. In some countries the gain or loss on both capital and interest is treated as ordinary income for tax purposes. Gains are taxed, losses are allowable against tax. However, in many countries the gain or loss has no tax effect until the payment is made, i.e. the loss on revaluation of foreign currency is not allowed until the loan is repaid or interest payment is transferred. In other countries gains are not taxed until realized but losses are allowed on the revalued foreign loan.

In the case of the United States the gain or loss is usually not recognized for tax purposes until the deal is closed by repayment of the loan. The separate transactions theory clearly applies to these cases.[3] The profit on the deal and the profit or loss on the foreign exchange transaction are treated for tax purposes as separate entities. This appears to be the current tax situation in the United States, but some older legal cases took a different view. In the B.F. Goodrich case[4] in 1943, the currency gain on a loan in French francs was held not to be taxable.

In the US, the tax situation regarding foreign exchange gains or losses on loans denominated in foreign currencies is not certain. For example, in the KVP Sutherland Paper Co. case[5] the purpose of the underlying transaction appeared to affect the tax decision. If the foreign currency gain is treated as capital in nature, the gain is likely to be assumed to be sourced domestically, unless foreign tax of at least 10% has been paid on the deal.

The tax situation in the United Kingdom is unusual in that great stress is laid on the *length* of the loan. If it is a long-term loan beyond, say, one year, then exchange losses on capital are not allowable against income and exchange gains are not taxable, a fact which caused much distress to UK companies funded via Swiss franc loans during the period 1974−1978 when sterling depreciated by 50% against the Swiss franc!

If exchange losses on foreign loans are not allowable, great care must be taken to avoid the subtantial cash flow loss resulting from the removal of the tax cushion on losses. For example, if a capital asset is financed using Swiss francs and sold in the UK a month later at 10% profit, the UK corporation would be taxed on the profit at its marginal rate of tax, say, 30%. If sterling had fallen in value by 15% during this period the exchange loss in repaying the debt from devalued sterling would not be allowed against tax. The UK corporation would be taxed on the 'profit' despite the fact that the transaction resulted in a real loss in cash flow terms.

In particular, as Chown and Finney (1977) point out, parent corporations borrow foreign currency to finance deals in that same currency in the fond belief that the venture is self-hedging. This is not so if exchange losses on the foreign loan are not allowable against tax by the revenue authority, while the profits from the venture are taxed. A considerable exposure to exchange risk may exist.

Finney and Meade (1978) recommend that the treasurer calculates the 'break-even exchange rate' on borrowing. This is the exchange rate at the termination of the loan which equates the foreign borrowing rate to the home borrowing rate, both net of tax. The treasurer can then judge whether this rate is likely to be exceeded by the termination date.

The Canadian tax authorities differentiate between loans supporting transactions of a capital nature and loans supporting income transactions, i.e. the purchase of machinery versus the purchase of inventory. One half of the exchange gain, if of a capital nature, is subject to tax. If the gain or loss is treated as income then it is taxed as ordinary income. The exchange gain or loss is usually taxed or allowed only when realized.

FORWARD EXCHANGE TRANSACTIONS

When a corporation enters into a forward foreign exchange contract, using the separate transactions approach, it usually happens that the forward rate differs from the future spot rate at the time the contract matures. This results in a loss or gain on the contract. In most countries this loss or gain is treated as ordinary income for tax purposes. Gains are taxable, losses deductible. But a number of variations occur. These are:

1. The tax effect may not occur unless the gain/loss is actually realized. No effect will occur if it is carried forward. For example in the Netherlands an unrealized gain can be carried forward and the tax postponed until the gain is realized. Note that unrealized losses are allowed even if not realized. In Italy unrealized gains are taxable but unrealized losses may not be deductible.

2. Occasionally the use to which the funds are put affects the tax position. For example in the United Kingdom a gain or loss on a forward contract covering a capital transaction may have no tax effect.

3. The length of the forward contract may affect the position. A long-term contract[6] gain or loss may have no tax effect or may be taxed at a capital gains rate.

In the United States the tax effect of the hedging gain or loss depends upon the nature of the underlying transaction. If the transaction is income in nature, the gain or loss is treated for tax purposes like ordinary income, see Corn Products Refining case.[7] If the transaction is capital in nature the gain is treated as a capital gain, see International Flavors and Fragrances case.[8]

The situation for the sourcing of income is the same as for foreign currency loans.

In April 1979 a US tax court handed down a decision which could have important implications for hedging translation losses. The decision in Hoover v. the Commissioner was as follows. Exchange gains or losses on translation hedges must be treated as capital gains or losses for tax assessment. Translation losses will be allowed at the lower capital tax rate rather than the higher ordinary rate. This case may persuade US multinationals to do their translation hedging in offshore locations.

Where balance sheet translation exposure hedging is attempted by the parent corporation care must be taken to gross up the forward hedge if a profit on forward hedging is liable to tax. A hedge by a Swiss multinational to cover its US subsidiary net assets of $1 million would need to be grossed up at the effective tax rate to be charged on the profit on the forward contract to be fully effective as a hedge.

BALANCE SHEET TRANSLATION

When a multinational company consolidates its accounts into the single currency of the parent country a gain or loss on translation will arise. This gain or loss on currency translation may have a tax effect. Some countries tax an unrealized translation gain and allow an unrealized loss to be set off against profits from other sources. The key questions here appear to be:

1. Does the unrealized translation gain or loss have a tax effect?
2. Can this tax effect be avoided if the gain or loss is omitted from the consolidated accounts?

The most common treatment seems to be that unrealized losses *must* be deducted for tax purposes but unrealized gains may be deferred. There are many variations on this theme. The variety of treatment can be gauged from the following examples.

In Belgium unrealized gains and losses are taxable and allowable. In Denmark and Italy gains are taxable but losses are not allowable. In Germany unrealized gains may be ignored but losses must be brought into the tax computation. In the Netherlands unrealized profits can be deferred until the profit is actually realized. In the United Kingdom unrealized translation gains and losses are generally ignored for tax purposes, even when brought into the consolidated accounts. In the USA an unrealized exchange profit would increase profits liable to tax and also decrease the effective foreign tax rate and so decrease the foreign tax credit. An unrealized loss would have the opposite effect. It is possible that a US corporation may be permitted to elect to ignore unrealized gains and losses so long as the election is applied to *all* the corporation's foreign operations.

THE MULTICURRENCY MANAGEMENT CENTER

Some multinational companies have set up currency handling centers to centralize the control of the many currencies used by a multinational company. It is likely that the cost of such a center will outweigh the benefits unless the value of currency handled is substantial. There may also be problems in persuading the various tax authorities to accept the center as a legitimate business venture and not simply a vehicle for tax avoidance. However, once a multicurrency management center (MMC) has been set up, it can provide possibilities for minimizing a corporation's tax bill, although this is unlikely to be the prime objective for setting up the center.

Since the MMC is likely to be used to centralize the processing of invoices in various currencies, it can be arranged that the MMC carries the foreign exchange risk for the entire corporation. However, the tax implications of such a move need to be studied carefully. The problem is that an offshore tax haven may eliminate or reduce the tax charge on foreign exchange gains, but not provide any relief for foreign exchange losses or the cost of administering the MMC itself. The MMC should also be set up in a location which has tax treaties with other countries which are beneficial to the multinational involved. For example, tax on interest or dividend withheld at source should be amenable to reduction and foreign tax credits should be capable of being offset against local taxes. The location will be chosen after a careful assessment of the worldwide tax burden of the company in the context of the tax legislation in each operating location.

If a multinational wishes to charge the foreign exchange losses and the administration cost of the MMC between its various subsidiaries it will require to prove the need for the MMC other than as a tax avoidance device. This is best effected by charging a fee for the use of the MMC to subsidiaries, perhaps 0.5% of the value of each deal. This charge would be in line with a fee charged by an independent agency. Tax authorities tend to view fees paid to offshore MMCs with great suspicion, particularly where the local corporation rate is very low. A scheme for pooling foreign exchange gains or losses plus MMC costs is likely to meet a more favorable response from the tax authorities.

DEVISING A FOREIGN EXCHANGE TAX STRATEGY

The multiplicity of rules imposed on foreign exchange gains and losses by the tax authorities makes it difficult to see the wood for the trees. The treasurer, or his tax adviser, tends to be overwhelmed by the sheer volume of rules, controls, and exceptions. The problem is compounded by the frequent changes in the rules of the game. Ring (1976) an experienced tax adviser in this area, writes that 'the tax effect of foreign exchange profits and losses is, unfortunately, one of the most volatile and obscure aspects of international taxation'.

The first step in devising a tax strategy must be to decide on an objective. This is to maximize profit net of tax, not, be it noted, to minimize the tax bill. This objective, however, must be placed in a proper perspective. Tax planning is a subsidiary activity within the general business strategy. The tax strategy is subject to more important business goals. For example, if a multinational decides to maximize the autonomy of its foreign subsidiaries it is not likely to allow a tax tactic of repaying loans to obtain tax credits to compromise this key policy objective. Low profits in certain foreign subsidiaries, manipulated for tax reasons, could demoralize the key staff of the foreign subsidiary and damage the image of the corporation.

Tax planning must be integrated into the corporation's overall business policy. This said, the variation of the tax treatment of exchange gains and losses provides considerable scope for the ingenuity of the corporation treasurer. Particular attention should be paid to the lack of symmetry in the tax laws.

The second step in devising a tax strategy is to set out a table of the tax rules, exchange controls and tax rates in each country where the multinational operates. This is the frame within which the tax strategy is built. The third step is to set down the expected cash flows in each currency and the assets and liabilities held in each currency. This table should already have been prepared as one of the stages in conventional exposure management. The fourth step is to examine the possible tax effects of future transactions, in particular loans in foreign currencies, forward cover and translation gains or losses. The possible benefits and costs of channeling transactions through an offshore tax haven should also be considered at this stage. The treatment of individual transactions will depend upon the tax laws and exchange control extant at that particular time. The flavor of what is possible can perhaps be gauged from the following examples.

Financial assets can be shifted between subsidiaries so that translation gains will occur in countries where the tax on such gains is low or non-existant (UK). Intercompany debt repayment can be accelerated to avoid expected exchange gains on a loan if the tax on this gain is significant. One subsidiary can borrow from another in a weak foreign currency if the exchange gain on the loan devaluation is not taxed, and borrow in a strong currency if the loss on the loan revaluation is allowable. In both cases the tax effect may be the key factor in the decision as to which currency one should borrow. If the unrealized loss on a foreign loan is not allowed against tax until the loan is repaid, repay it and refinance funding. Ensure that allowable exchange losses occur in those countries where tax rates are highest. Exchange rate gains may be concealed by off-balance sheet financing such as leasing in a weak currency country. A subsidiary in a weak currency country can be funded by a foreign loan. The exchange loss can be set off against local profits. If additional depreciation is not allowed on the assets held in a devaluing country, sell the assets and re-equip the corporation, perhaps with second-hand assets from abroad. Finance a venture with a series of short-term roll-over loans which are exchange loss allowable against tax rather than with a long-term loan which is only allowable on termination of the loan. Make all currency contracts assignable, i.e. saleable. A gain may be taxed at the lower capital gains rate or be free of tax. All of these schemes must conform to the local exchange control regulations, but within the framework of the regulations much can be done to alleviate the tax burden.

CONCLUSION

The tax law regarding gains or losses on foreign exchange transactions is complicated and subject to frequent change. The treasurer of a multinational company has no option but to take expert advice on each case. We have attempted to direct the reader's attention to the principles involved in devising a tax strategy and set out some of the currency tax legislation on the subject of foreign exchange gains and losses. The tax strategy must always be directed to maximizing income *net of tax*. Particular attention should be paid to any lack of symmetry in the tax treatment of foreign exchange gains and losses.

REVIEW QUESTIONS

1. Provide an example of the profit on foreign exchange arising from the sale of 10,000 widgets from a Californian corporation to a British company. Assume a rise in sterling against the US dollar.

2. Why do you think foreign exchange gains on capital transactions are often exempt from tax, or suffer a lower rate of tax compared to profits on revenue transactions?

3. 'Two basic approaches are discernible in the tax treatment of foreign exchange gains and losses.' Describe these two basic approaches.

4. Define: (a) ordinary income, (b) open transaction, (c) realized transaction, (d) source of income.

5. What is the usual treatment of foreign exchange gains on normal import/export transactions outside the United States?

6. What is the separate transactions theory as applied in the United States?

7. Describe the tax treatment of a foreign currency gain on a French franc loan taken out by a company resident in the United States.

8. Why is the UK treatment of exchange rate losses on foreign currency loans unusual?

9. A US corporation hedges a possible foreign exchange loss in Italian lira by taking out a forward contract. A 'profit' is realized on this forward transaction. Discuss the tax implications.

10. Do you consider it fair to tax unrealized foreign exchange translation gains?

11. What tactics are available to persuade the tax authorities that an offshore multicurrency management center is not simply a tax avoidance device?

12. Describe the possible tax advantages of setting up an MMC.

13. Do you consider that translation exposure should be hedged up to the limit of the possible tax liability?

14. 'The balance sheet method reflects foreign exchange tax effects more quickly.' Explain.

15. A subsidiary of Cosmic International operating in Arcadia is very profitable. However, it expects a devaluation of the Arcadian lyre within the next six months against the US dollar. The treasurer of CI in Chicago thinks it might be a good idea to raise a local loan in lyres and send a substantial 20% dividend to the USA with the cash so raised. What factors must the treasurer take into account before making this decision? Would a tax haven subsidiary in Jamuda, a holiday island in the West Indies, help?

NOTES

1. See case GCM 4954 VII–2 CB 293 (1928) and Church's English Shoes Ltd. 24 TC 56 (1955).
2. See US revenue ruling 78/281 (7/24/78) re foreign loan to purchase machine for rental.
3. See Anderson, Clayton and Co. v. US 562 F 2d 972 (5th Cir. 1977).
4. See B.F. Goodrich Co. (ITC 1098 (1943)); also W.H. Coverdale (4 TCM 713 (1945)).
5. KVP Sutherland Paper Co. 344 F 2d 377 (Ct. Cl. 1965).
6. Usually in excess of six months (UK) or one year (USA).
7. See Corn Products Refining Company 350 US 46 (1955).
8. See International Flavors and Fragrances Inc. 62 TC 232 (1974) and later revisions (1975) and (1977).

BIBLIOGRAPHY

Chown J. and Finney M. (1977), *Foreign Currency Debt Management*. London, J.F. Chown and Co Ltd.

Consultative Committee of Accountancy Bodies (1976), *Borrowings in Foreign Currency*. December.

Curtis D.W. (1975), 'Hedging balance sheet exposure after tax', *Euromoney*, April.

Edwardes-Ker M. (1975), *International Tax Strategy*. In Depth Publishing Ltd.

Finney M. and Meade N. (1978), 'A practical approach to corporate borrowing and exchange risk', *Euromoney*, October, p.191.

Hammer R.M. and Burge M. (1978), *Taxation of Foreign Exchange Gains and Losses*. Price Waterhouse.

Inland Revenue (1976), 'Borrowings in foreign currency', Discussion Paper, 6 October.

International Fiscal Association (1973), Papers 1972 Conference.

Ring A. (1976), 'The impact of taxation on foreign exchange exposure', *Euromoney*, January, p.82.

APPENDIX   11A

Tax Treatment of Foreign Exchange Gains and Losses in Various Countries (1980)

The tax treatment of foreign exchange gains and losses is subject to frequent change in most countries. The following table should only be taken as a rough guide. Expert advice should be sought in particular cases.

1. Foreign exchange gains on imports and exports.

	Countries
1.1 Gains treated as ordinary income. Losses treated as allowable deductions.	USA, Belgium, Denmark, France, Germany, Italy, Holland, Norway, Sweden.
1.2 Long-term transactions and capital transaction *may* be treated as subject to capital taxes.	United Kingdom.

2. Foreign currency loans.

2.1 FE gains and losses treated as ordinary income.	USA, Belgium, France, Holland, Norway, Sweden.
2.2 FE realized gains and losses taxable or allowed against tax.	Germany, Italy, Denmark, Switzerland.
2.3 Usually FE gains and losses have no tax effect.	United Kingdom.

3. Forward exchange contracts.

3.1 Gains or losses on forward contract less actual spot treated as ordinary income.	France, Belgium, Denmark, Norway, Switzerland, UK (revenue items only). USA (transaction must be closed).
3.2 As above but gain must be realized.	Germany.
3.3 All gains, realized or unrealized, taxable. Unrealized losses not deductible.	Italy.

3.4 All losses. realized or unrea-   Holland.
     lized, allowable but unrealized
     gains may be deferred.

4. Balance sheet translation.

   4.1 Unrealized gains and losses   Belgium, France.
      taxed like ordinary income
      (if recorded).

   4.2 Unrealized gains taxable but   Sweden, Norway, Holland.
      tax may be deferred until
      gain realized.
      Unrealized losses deductible.

   4.3 Unrealized gains taxable but   Italy, Denmark.
      unrealized losses not deduc-
      tible.

   4.4 Unrealized losses must be   Germany, Switzerland.
      brought into tax computation
      immediately. Treatment of
      gains optional.

   4.5 Unrealized gain or loss   United States.
      carried to profit and loss
      account for tax purposes.
      May be treated as ordinary
      income, capital gain or
      ignored depending on
      circumstances.

   4.6 Gain or loss usually ignored   United Kingdom.
      until realized.

CHAPTER 12

A Review of Exchange Control Regulations

Caution

Exchange controls are in an almost continuous state of change. The rules set out in the following chapter should only be taken as a rough guide to a complex legal jungle. In all cases an expert on exchange controls should be consulted before any decision on exchange controls is made.

The value of a currency at a given point in time depends upon the demand for and supply of that currency on the foreign exchange market. A free market in a currency will always find an equilibrium value which balances supply and demand. Unfortunately throughout most of recorded history goverments have been unwilling to accept this 'equilibrium' value and have attempted to alter the free market value in some way and control the exchange rate of their currency. The control procedures are particularly severe in developing countries which are attempting to 'take off' into a period of self-sustaining growth. Countries such as Brazil or Nigeria need to import large quantities of capital goods and this usually results in a heavy demand for foreign currencies, allied to an attempt to maintain the value of the home currency at an artificially high level to reduce the cost of imports. This combination of circumstances often results in the imposition of a set of exchange control regulations which are Draconian in their severity.

A few countries, such as the United States, the UK, and West Germany, employ a concise and simple set of exchange control regulations, but the exchange control regulations applied to most of the world's currencies are both complex and subject to frequent change. Appendix 12B to this chapter sets out the principal features of exchange control in a wide range of countries. In many cases it is not easy to discover the exact exchange control procedures ruling at a given point in time in a given country.

The range and complexity of exchange control procedures are such that it is not possible to review them in a single book, let alone a single chapter. In this chapter we will attempt to provide a general introduction to exchange control procedures.

We will first review the mechanism of control; second, we will discuss those factors which are regulated; third, we will review some tactical approaches to exchange control management, with particular emphasis on developing countries; and, finally, some advice will be provided on how to find out about exchange control regulations in specific situations.

THE ORGANIZATION OF EXCHANGE CONTROL

The ultimate responsibility for exchange control usually lies with the Treasury function of the government of the given country. The Treasury decides the general strategy to be adopted but the tactics and general implementation of exchange control is invariably delegated to the central bank. The central bank, in its turn, may delegate a great deal of the day-to-day working of exchange control to commercial banks and other authorized dealers in foreign currency.

The extent of the delegation from central bank to authorized dealers depends upon the shortage of foreign exchange and the degree of corruption extant in the given country. Where foreign exchange is scarce, a condition unfortunately all too common in developing countries, the central bank usually keeps the issue of foreign exchange under its own direct control. This centralization of foreign exchange control can cause considerable delays in negotiating exports into developing countries. In one African country known to the author, the bureaucratic delay in releasing foreign currency has delayed payment for several years.

Where the central bank is prepared to delegate the day-to-day running of the system to authorized dealers, the release of foreign currency is much expedited. The United Kingdom apparatus of exchange control, before 23 October 1979, used to operate on this principle. The central bank, the Bank of England, delegated a good part of the day-to-day vetting of foreign exchange transactions and the exchange of currency, to 250 authorized commercial banks. A second group called authorized depositories were permitted to hold foreign securities on deposit and to carry out certain transactions involving foreign currency. The authorized depositories were mainly banks and legal firms although some stockbrokers and accountants were involved. These organizations were told how they must vet the authenticity of the deal underlying the foreign exchange transaction and the rules governing the exchange of currency. A considerable degree of trust is involved in delegating these powers and duties.

The authorized banks and depositories were informed of the rapidly changing rules of supplying foreign exchange via a series of *administration notices*. These were sent to the authorized organizations when published. They were frequently updated.

For almost all types of foreign exchange transactions a specific form is available. The applicant collects this form from his bank and returns the completed form to the authorized organization with documentary proof of the underlying deal. The authorized organization vets the authenticity of the deal and checks that this deal is of a type approved for the release of foreign exchange. It then releases the foreign currency. Occasionally the exchange control department must be informed to obtain permission to release foreign currency for a specific deal.

The above comments describe how foreign exchange control operated in the UK before October 1979 but the system in other countries which delegate the release of currency is very similar. The apparatus of exchange control can be best understood by examining the proposition, 'Who can do what with which currency where?' The 'who' refers to the *residence* of the applicant for currency. The 'what' refers to the type of transaction — importing, exporting, investing, holiday, etc. The 'which' refers to the type of currency used, i.e. official currency, investment currency, etc. The 'where' refers to the zone where the transaction will take place — the world can be divided into several zones such as dollar area, sterling area, Comecon area and so on and differing rules may be applied to trading or investing in each area. Since each category of control can itself be broken down into several further categories the number of combinations applied to any specific case is very large. This combinatorial factor is responsible for the well publicized complexity of the exchange regulations in many countries.

Residence

Almost all companies operating in a given country are treated as resident in that country for exchange control purposes. The fact that the head office or controlling staff reside in another country does not usually affect the fact of residence. In the case of financial institutions which import and export large amounts of foreign currency a special set of rules often applies. In some tax havens, such as Luxembourg and Nassau, the rules regarding residence for companies not trading in the country are such as to convey special privileges. Note that residence for exchange control purposes is usually determined by a different set of rules from that which determines residence for taxation assessment.

Currency zones

The world economy is divided up into various currency zones. The countries within each zone tie their own currency to a dominant currency within the zone. The US dollar, French franc, Soviet rouble, and UK sterling are used to fix the value of other currencies within their zone. Another zonal system is based on trading areas such as the EEC.

The exchange control regulations between residents in the same zone are usually much less rigorous than between residents in different zones. For example, the United Kingdom, before October 1979, differentiated between countries in the *scheduled territories* and the rest of the world. The former, comprising the UK and a few small islands like Gibraltar, could transmit currency between themselves with almost no restrictions. The remainder of the world was further divided into the Overseas Sterling Area, the EEC and the rest. Different regulations applied to these three zones, but in all cases they were more restrictive than those applying to the scheduled territories.

The French franc zone applies very liberal regulations for the transmission of currency between France and its old colonial territories, and the Comecon countries in Eastern Europe operate a currency zone based on the Soviet rouble which encourages trade in that area.

There are situations where it pays to set up a subsidiary in a given country simply to gain access to the exchange control privileges of being resident in that country.

Type of transaction

Exchange control regulations vary according to the type of transaction involved. As illustrated in Figure 12.1, the initial classification is between current transactions and investments. By current transactions we mean the import or export of goods and services. Note that exchange control regulations frequently differentiate between 'visible' transactions, i.e. goods, and 'invisible' transactions, i.e. services. The classification of foreign investment is often quite complex. The major classification is between direct investment and portfolio investment (p. 241) but direct investment is usually classified further into several categories which are subject to different treatment. The borrowing of money is a further category.

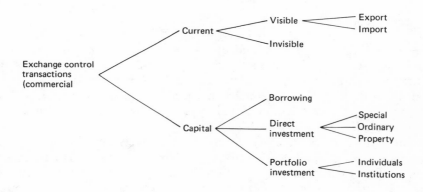

Figure 12.1 A Classification of Exchange Control Transactions

CURRENT TRANSACTIONS – IMPORTS

Most countries of the world require that a license or certificate must be obtained from an authorized bank or government department before goods can be imported. The license may be either a specific license or certificate to cover a specific contract or a general license to import goods of a specific category. Examples of import authorizing agencies are PERNAS in Malaysia, CACEX in Brazil and IBLC in Belgium.

Once the license is obtained the importing company must usually provide documentary proof of the underlying import transaction, such as shipping documents, to an authorized bank to obtain the requisite amount of foreign currency. In such countries as Spain and Belgium this is a simple process but in certain developing countries a number of additional obstacles must be surmounted. An import deposit may have to be lodged with the authorized bank some time in advance of payment. For example, in 1976 in Brazil an advance deposit at zero interest equal to 100% of the value of the transaction was required to be made up to one year before release of the currency. Italy at one time required a deposit equal to 50% of the value of the transaction to be lodged 90 days before release of currency. Argentina required the purchase of special government import bonds and Chile at one time demanded an extraordinary 10,000% advance deposit!

The exchange control board may insist that the transaction be denominated in a specific currency. For example, Brazil in 1977 insisted that all non-bilateral deals be denominated in US dollars if not in Brazilian cruzeiros.

The *value* of the import transaction may have to be validated by a government agency. Kenya, for example, insists that all imports exceeding KSh 20,000 be subject to preshipment check as to quality and value by the General Superintendence Company. A Swiss agency carries out the evaluation in Europe.

The official exchange rate for imports may differ from that for exports. Brazil operates a complicated exchange rate system by classifying goods into several categories and applying a different exchange rate to each.

Dealing on the forward exchange market may be permitted on some but not on all types of transaction, and only after documentary proof of the deal has been obtained. Certain imports may only be bought through a national trading organization as in Tanzania and Nigeria. Imports may be permitted only from certain countries with which bilateral trading deals have been made. This situation, for example, applied to Polish importing organizations in 1978. It may be required that the exporting country finances the deal before an import licence is obtained or, alternatively, financing may only be permitted in the local currency.

The above examples are sufficient to provide the reader with the flavor of the complex sets of rules which can surround exchange control regulations for imports. The exporter is advised to familiarize himself with the particular regulations and customs of the importing country.

CURRENT TRANSACTIONS — EXPORTS

The regulations controlling exports are normally much less restrictive than those controlling imports. The government usually tries to encourage exports by reducing the paperwork involved in exporting. Except in rather unusual circumstances a general license to export is all that is required to permit an exporter to ship goods or sell services abroad. An export certificate may be required to ensure compliance with exchange control regulations. The export of certain agricultural products is sometimes prohibited or controlled; for example, the export of coffee from Brazil is subject to authorization by the Brazilian Coffee Institute. The export of petroleum products requires a specific export license in Nigeria.

The timing of the payment for export is usually controlled. Payment is rarely allowed to be delayed much beyond six months of shipment (India, France) except in the case of capital equipment where special payment arrangements may be negotiated. The foreign exchange proceeds of an export deal must normally be offered to an authorized bank within a short period of being received (France — one month). Conversion is usually at the free market rate but some developing countries state the official rate for conversion which may differ widely from the free market rate. In Sri Lanka, for example, export proceeds are converted into export certificates with a face value in Sri Lanka rupees equal to the FOB value of the export. These can be used for buying imports for up to six months.

Many countries provide open or concealed subsidies on exports by remitting sales taxes or manipulating the exchange rate to provide a higher rate on export proceeds.

Invisibles

Insurance, consultancy fees, royalties, foreign travel, and other non-tangible items are called 'invisible' exports and imports. The rules regarding invisibles, particularly invisible imports are usually stricter than for tangible exports and imports. Insuring abroad is usually forbidden and in developing countries the rules for releasing foreign currency for invisible imports such as consultancy are exceedingly tight.

CAPITAL TRANSACTIONS — INVESTMENT ABROAD

Capital transactions are generally classified as direct or portfolio investment. Direct investment is defined as investment with the purpose of controlling the operations of a foreign firm. Portfolio investment is defined as investment whose primary purpose is the receipt of future income. The classification as direct or portfolio is a question of fact; does the investment give the investor an effective controlling interest in the foreign firm?

Some countries, such as the United States, allow a relatively free flow of capital into and out of the country either in the form of direct or portfolio investment, but this is rare. Most countries impose strict limitations on the outflow of capital, particularly for portfolio investment and carefully scrutinize direct investment. On inflows the situation is reversed. Portfolio investment inwards is encouraged but inward direct investment is carefully vetted. Even when inward investment is encouraged, as in many African countries, strict rules as to repatriation of profits are set down.

Takeovers in Canada are scrutinized by the Foreign Investment Review Agency, in Australia by the Foreign Investment Review Board. Often external participation in local firms is limited to certain sectors (Nigeria) or to a certain percentage (50% Australia, in natural resources). In Brazil inward portfolio investment is permitted through a Brazilian investment company and must remain in the country for three years.

One of the most complex set of regulations on foreign investment was operated by the United Kingdom before April 1979 and since the principles involved are interesting, we will examine the UK regulations in some detail even though they are now (temporarily?) suspended.

Investment Abroad by UK Residents

The former UK exchange control regulations differentiated between two types of investment, *direct investment,* by which is meant investment in an operating company abroad which allows the investor to participate in the management of that company, and *portfolio investment,* investment for income in foreign securities. Direct investment is expected to improve the trading position of a UK company abroad by expanding sales or consolidating a company's position in the foreign market. In particular, it must be demonstrated that the investment will benefit the UK balance of payments.

The exchange control regulations applied to all direct investment outside the scheduled territories by companies operating in the UK. Application for currency to effect direct investment had to be made to the Bank of England together with a detailed proposal supporting the case, including projected cash flows.

Super-Criterion Investments

The former UK regulations divided direct investments into two categories, *super-criterion* investments and other direct investments. Super-criterion investments enjoyed the considerable advantage that they could be financed with foreign currency bought at the official free market rate with sterling, whereas other direct investments abroad had to be financed indirectly by more circuitous means. A super-criterion investment could be financed by foreign currency purchased at the official market rate up to the value of £250,000 or 50% of the cost whichever was greater. This provided a considerable financial advantage over other methods of financing foreign investments. Foreign loans can be expensive in terms of a depreciating home currency and the cost of purchasing investment currency (see ahead) could be high.

However the conditions required to qualify a direct investment for the super-criterion category were very stringent. The investment had to (a) *directly* encourage UK exports and (b) it had to be proved beyond reasonable doubt that the investment would generate an improvement in the UK balance of payments at least equal to the cost of the foreign investment *within three years*. In addition it had to be demonstrated that the benefits listed under (b) were a direct result of the investment and would continue after the three year period was ended.

These were very stringent conditions indeed. A payback period as short as three years is not often found among large-scale capital investments. Super-criterion investments were therefore mainly service improvement investments. Fortunately, these rules were changed by the incoming Conservative government in July 1979.

Other Direct Investments

Few foreign investments fell into the super-criterion category, and so few foreign investments could be financed by purchasing foreign exchange with sterling at the official market rate. Some other method of financing had to be devised. A few of these methods are discussed below.

(a) Free export of equipment and inventory. This method of setting up a foreign investment is highly recommended if it is feasible since it avoids currency risk and loan cost. The equipment or inventory must, of course, be manufactured in the home country.

(b) Foreign loans. A company can arrange a foreign loan to cover its foreign direct investment. The loan capital will be repaid out of the proceeds of the investment. The *interest* can be paid by purchasing foreign currency with sterling at the official market rate.

Note that capital may also be repaid by purchasing foreign currency at the official market rate if, and only if, it can be demonstrated that foreign exchange benefits of equivalent amount have accrued to the home country balance of payments.

(c) Back to back loan. A UK company could make an arrangement with a foreign company such that each can lend the other money in their own currency of an equivalent amount at the official exchange rate. A UK company could make a loan to the subsidiary of a United States company in sterling in the UK and the US company would, at the same time, make a loan in dollars to a subsidiary of the UK company in the USA. The premium on investment currency was avoided and the interest rate paid was probably rather lower than on an 'arm's length' loan. However, if the interest rate on the sterling loan was too low compared to the current market rate, the Bank of England might have intervened.

(d) Using the investment currency market. The investment currency market is described on p. 246. It is unlikely that a UK company would have used the investment currency market to make a direct foreign investment, although it could theoretically have done so. To acquire investment currency the UK company would have to have paid the substantial investment currency premium, but it was not permitted to recoup the premium when it liquidated its foreign currency investment at a later date. Foreign direct investment (when liquidated into foreign currency) must be converted into sterling at the official market rate.

Only if a UK company was desperate to make a foreign direct investment and all other means were blocked would it have considered using this method.

(e) Share issue. If a UK multinational makes a direct investment abroad it may provide equity shares in its UK operation rather than cash as compensation to the previous owners of the foreign assets. This procedure is permitted but very carefully vetted by the Bank of England since the shares could be transferred at an artificial value or the transaction could breach the inward investment rules. The following regulations were strictly applied by the Bank of England:

1. The shares issued to the non-UK resident must be held by an authorized depository until sold.
2. The value placed on the shares must be proved to the satisfaction of the Bank of England.
3. If, when sold, the shares fetch a value below that of the benefit received by the UK balance of payments, then the difference between the original selling price and the benefit to the UK must be made up by the UK investor. He could for example borrow foreign currency or buy investment currency.

Share issue can provide a cheap form of foreign direct investment as long as the strict regulations applied do not prove unduly onerous.

The above section describes the UK regulations before July 1979 which were strict for a developed country. Other developed countries such as France, Sweden and Belgium had much less strict regulations controlling the outflow of capital but developing countries tend to follow the former UK approach.

On 18 July 1979 the UK government introduced a new exchange control package which considerably reduced the severity of exchange control procedures. The more important provisions of the package were as follows:

1. Currency would be made available for outward *direct* investment by UK companies without limit. Foreign currency borrowing to finance this type of investment can now be repaid at the official rate. The two-thirds repatriation of overseas profits rule was abolished.

2. UK residents can buy currency at the official rate (i.e. not including investment currency premium) to obtain EEC securities (excluding unit and investment trusts).

3. The same rules apply to securities issued by international organizations of which the UK is a member.

4. The sale proceeds of existing securities in the EEC can no longer be disposed of in the investment currency markets. (This imposed a loss on holders who had bought through the investment currency market.)

This easing of restrictions on the UK market caused a dramatic fall in the value of the investment currency premium but otherwise had no noticeable effect on the sterling exchange rate. A fact which might cast doubt on the value of exchange control regulations.

UK exchange control regulations were abolished in October 1979.

ABOLITION OF THE UK EXCHANGE CONTROLS

On 23 October 1979 the Conservative government in the UK announced the abolition of almost all exchange controls. The decision was opposed by the opposition Labour Party.

The main consequences of the abolition of exchange controls in the UK on corporations were as follows.

1. The rules concerning the remittance of overseas profit by subsidiaries are very much eased. Foreign subsidiaries of UK corporations can retain profit abroad and so defer UK corporation tax; but note that UK profit must still be reported in terms of sterling and so the conversion and the translation problems still arise.

2. The investment currency concept is abolished, thus the investment currency premium is abolished. Currency for investments from UK to overseas, or vice versa, is freely available at the free market rate. There is now no bias against investment overseas by UK corporations or between different kinds of investment overseas. The authorized depository concept is abolished. However, it should be noted that permission must still be obtained from various government departments to invest overseas. For example, under ICTA 1970 Section 482, Treasury consent is needed if a UK corporation is sold to a non-resident corporation or becomes non-resident by other means. Also a UK resident corporation must obtain permission to allow its overseas subsidiary to issue shares or obtain loans (except bank loans).

3. Extended credit on exports and prepayment of imports are now permitted without limitation so far as exchange control is concerned.

4. UK resident companies are now permitted to grant guarantees to non-residents, and the rules regarding payment of service charges overseas are relaxed.

5. Foreign currency bank accounts can be maintained in the UK or abroad without permission, and operating restrictions on the spot or forward markets are abolished.

6. Loans in foreign currency can be negotiated freely and existing foreign loans repaid as the parties to the loan so wish.

Although exchange control has been abolished (or temporarily suspended?) by the UK it is important to note that certain regulations on overseas financial transactions are based on tax rather than currency regulations. For example, we noted above the continuing restrictions on the ownership of UK corporations and the limitation regarding the issue of shares or debentures abroad. Restrictions continue to be placed on transactions with foreign associated companies which are not at 'arms length' and on long-term leasing to non-resident corporations.

We suspect that the existing situation regarding exchange controls may only last a few years. Corporations resident in the UK are advised to take full advantage of this 'freedom window' to organize their worldwide asset base to their long-term advantage. The choice may not come again. By 1990 the UK may no longer enjoy the advantages of trading in a petro-currency!

MULTIPLE CURRENCIES

In 1977 no less than thirty of the 130 countries who are members of the International Monetary Fund operated some kind of multiple currency. By a multiple currency is meant a currency which has at least two values at any one time, usually an official value and a free market value.

Investment Currency

Before October 1979 if a UK resident wished to buy foreign shares outside the scheduled territories or the EEC he bought, or rather he authorized his banker to buy, a sufficient amount of investment currency to purchase the foreign shares. The investment currency was usually denominated in US dollars, although shares in any foreign currency could be bought with it. The potential investment currency was a fund which represented 75% of the total value of all foreign securities held by UK residents which were not direct investments. At any one time only a very small part of this fund was liquid in the form of investment currency held by an authorized bank or dealer.

Since investment currency tends to be scarce relative to demand, it is invariably sold at a premium over the official exchange rate. The premium ranged as high as 80% over the official market rate, which made foreign shares more expensive in sterling and might be expected to discourage their acquisition by UK residents. When the foreign share was liquidated, 75% of the proceeds were sold through the investment currency market (thus recovering some of the premium). The remainder were sold at the (lower) official market rate.

Since the investment (dollar) premium varied through time, it added an additional speculative element to foreign investment by UK residents. However investment currency dollars could be bought and sold forward like official currency. The three-month forward market was the deepest but a six-month market did exist. The investment premium rate was quoted as a percentage based on a fixed parity of $2.60 to the pound. Since the actual parity was usually well below this figure, the nominal parity had to be adjusted downward to find the true 'effective' premium. For example, if the nominal premium was quoted as 50% (on $2.60) and the official parity is £1 = $1.90, the effective premium is found by using the formula:

$$\left(\frac{50 + 100}{1} \times \frac{1.90}{2.60}\right) - 100 = 10\% \text{ (approx.)}$$

A substantial difference on 50%!

Overseas securities quoted on the London Stock Exchange had to include the investment premium (if appropriate) in their quoted price. A non-UK resident could find the value minus the premium by multiplying the quoted price by the *conversion factor* provided daily in *The Financial Times*.

It is unlikely that a UK company would have used investment currency for foreign investment unless no other route was available. But in certain circumstances it may have had no other option. Other countries, such as Belgium and South Africa, operate parallel markets for investment currency, although the reasons for doing so in the case of South African security rands are quite different from those applying in the UK. In Belgium most current transactions are settled in the official market and most capital transactions in the free market. When a direct foreign investment is liquidated there are usually strict controls on the reinvestment of the funds if there were strict controls over the initial investment.

BORROWING ABROAD

The rules for borrowing in foreign currencies are subject to frequent change depending upon whether or not the government wishes to encourage or restrict the inflow of foreign currency. In 1976, for example, the UK government encouraged UK firms to borrow abroad to reduce the balance of payments deficit. Conversely the West German Bundesbank discouraged, although did not prohibit, borrowing abroad in the same year.

Many developed countries such as United States, Canada, West Germany, the Netherlands and currently the UK, place almost no restrictions on non-residents borrowing in their capital markets. This attitude is, however, the exception: most countries including the vast majority of developing countries prohibit borrowing by non-residents. In Australia, for example, apart from export financing Australian dollars, lending to non-residents is usually restricted. Developing nations are particularly averse to allowing foreign subsidiaries, resident in their countries, to raise local loans to finance profitable enterprises which subsequently repatriate substantial profits. This activity is usually controlled, as in Kenya, by requiring non-resident controlled companies to obtain specific approval from the central bank before they raise a loan.

REPATRIATION OF PROFITS

Profits made in a foreign country are of no value if they cannot be repatriated, in some form or other, to the home country. The repatriation of profit is one of the most complex aspects of both foreign exchange management and exchange control.

A few developed countries allow the free repatriation of all profits and capital at any time, but this is rare. The usual rule is that capital injected into a country can be repatriated (the initial value not being adjusted for subsequent inflation) but the repatriation of profits is subject to strict limits. Since many countries demand a quick repatriation of profits on foreign investment by their own nationals, there is, in this case, a clear clash of interest between the governments of the investing and the receiving states.

In place of the word 'profit' it is more accurate to use the word 'value'. Value can be transmitted in the form of dividends paid out of profit, but it can also be transmitted in the form of royalties, R and D contribution, adjusted transfer payment for goods exported to a subsidiary and so forth. The exchange control agencies of developing countries are now very knowledgeable about these alternative channels of transmitting value, and will normally cover them in the profit expatriation agreement.

Many countries limit profit expatriation by taxing the profit earned and allowing the balance to be expatriated abroad. Some countries limit the amount to be expatriated to a given percentage of gross or net profit, thus forcing reinvestment of the profit. Another scheme is to allow 'blocked' profits to be invested in government bonds for say, five years and then allowing the proceeds to be sent abroad when the bond matures (Argentina). This is a poor option if a low interest rate on the bond is allied to a high local rate of inflation. Occasionally these bonds can be traded and the proceeds repatriated. In Israel foreign investors in approved projects can transfer all the profits, free of tax, in the same currency at the official rate. Investments in developing countries are frequently segregated into approved and ordinary status, a privileged repatriation position being awarded to the approved status. Perhaps the most important concession is the right to convert profits at the official rate of exchange which may be well above the free market rate.

The rules on profit transfer are so varied and complex and subject to such frequent change that one can do little more than advise companies contemplating foreign investment to invest in a careful scrutiny of the regulations and ensure that a legally watertight agreement is drawn up on capital and profit repatriation. Even this may not be enough. A new government could renounce all previous agreements. In this case the compensation guarantees of one's own government is the last resort, i.e., in the UK, the Exports Credit Guarantee Department: in the USA ExImbank.

BANK ACCOUNTS OF NON–RESIDENTS AND FOREIGN CURRENCY ACCOUNTS

Special permission is often required if a non-resident wishes to open a bank account in a foreign country. The bank accounts of non-residents are usually segregated from those of residents. Different regulations are then applied to the movement of funds into and out of these accounts.

In the United Kingdom the sterling accounts of non-residents are called external accounts. The transfer of funds into those accounts by residents was, before October 1979, only permitted for authorized payments. Transfer to and from other external accounts is freely permitted. The USA imposes almost no limitations on foreign currency accounts and non-resident accounts.

In Nigeria bank accounts are allocated to three categories — external, non-resident and blocked. The external account regulations are the same as in the UK. The non-resident accounts are fed with funds from local sources (with no authorization needed). The blocked accounts are made up of funds which are blocked by a direction from the Nigerian Exchange Control Act.

Belgium differentiates between convertible accounts available to all non-residents, financial accounts, only available to non-residents in convertible area countries, and bilateral accounts. The convertible accounts generally operate through the official market, the financial accounts through the free market, and the bilateral accounts operate with those countries with which Belgium has drawn up bilateral trading agreements.

These examples cover most of the types of bank accounts available to non-residents. The proceeds of blocked accounts can often be invested in designated government securities and repatriated on maturity of these securities. Table 12.1 sets out the position regarding permission to open a foreign currency account at home or abroad for 12 major countries as at January 1980.

Table 12.1 Exchange Control Regulations regarding Permission to open a Foreign Currency Account (1980) either at Home or Abroad.

Country	Domestic	Abroad
USA	NPR	NPR
UK	NPR	NPR
Australia	PR	PR
Brazil	NO	NO
Canada	NO	NO
France	NO	NO
Germany	NPR	NPR
Italy	PR(D)	NO
Japan	NPR	NO
Holland	NPR	PR
South Africa	PR(D)	PR(D)
Switzerland	NPR	NPR

NPR No permission required
PR Permission required
D Difficult to obtain
NO Not permitted

Rare exceptions are permitted in almost every case.

EXPOSURE MANAGEMENT TECHNIQUES

In Chapter 7 we described some internal exposure management techniques which are helpful to the corporate treasurer. The exchange control regulations of certain countries prohibit the use of some of these techniques. The following section will discuss the limitations imposed on the use of exposure hedging techniques.

Netting

By netting we mean offsetting a projected currency flow in one direction by a currency flow in the other direction. We must differentiate bilateral netting from multilateral netting. Bilateral netting offsets currency A against currency B. Multilateral netting is more complex. Currency A is offset against currency B, B against C and finally C against A. More complex nets are possible. The Netherlands allow bilateral netting to be employed without permission, but exchange control permission needs to be obtained before one can employ multilateral netting. Table 12.2 sets out the exchange control rules for certain countries in 1980.

Forward Exchange

Many countries allow residents to cover foreign exchange transactions only with regard to resident banks, but the USA, Canada, Germany, the UK, and Switzerland, among the major trading nations, allow residents to freely use foreign forward exchange markets. The

Table 12.2. Exchange Control Netting Regulations for 13 Countries (1980)

	Netting regulations		
	Bilateral	Multilateral	Forward Trading
USA	NPR	NPR	NR
UK	NPR	NPR	NR
Australia	PR	PR	PT
Brazil	NO	NO	6m
Canada	NPR	NPR	NR
France	NPR	PR	12m (exports) 2m (imports)
Germany	NPR	NPR	NR
Italy	PR (D)	lPR	6m
Japan	NO	NO	PT
Holland	NPR	PR	NR
South Africa	PR	PR (D)	6m
Switzerland	NPR	NPR	NR
Sweden	NPR	PR	24m

NPR	No permission required	NR	No regulations
PR	Permission required	D	Difficult to get permission
NO	Not permitted	PT	Period of transaction

time period of the forward cover on the home market is often restricted, usually to up to six months ahead for normal trading. Table 12.2 sets out the rules on forward exchange trading for several major trading countries.

Leading and Lagging

Since leading and lagging are the classic techniques for hedging or speculating on exchange adjustments, many countries have laid down careful regulations to limit their use. Different sets of rules may be applied to imports and exports, and minimum and maximum leading or lagging times prescribed. The key dates which set minimum limits to leading and lagging are:

> shipment date
> custom's clearance or entry
> invoice due date or preparation date

The maximum variation permitted from these dates normally extends from three months to one year. Most industries have standard pay-

Table 12.3 Exchange Control Regulations on Leading and Lagging (1980) for 12 Countries

| | Leading | | | | Lagging | | | |
| | Imports | | Exports | | Imports | | Exports | |
	min.	max.	min.	max.	min.	max.	min.	max.
USA	—	—	—	—	—	—	—	—
Canada	—	—	—	—	—	—	—	—
Germany	—	—	—	—	—	—	—	—
Switzerland	—	—	S	—	S	—	—	—
UK	—	—	—	—	—	—	—	—
Australia	S	30	S	30	S	180	S	180
Brazil	I	I	—	—	I	180	CC	180
France	CC	CC	—	—	—	—	I	180
Italy	I	60	I	360	I	360	I	120
Japan	S	S	S	360	S	120	S	180
Holland	S	360	S	S	S	360	S	360
South Africa	S	S	S	—	S	360	S	180

S	=	shipment date
CC	=	custom's clearance
I	=	invoice date
180	=	180 days, etc.
—	=	no limit

ment terms and the exchange control authority will usually require to know the reason why these have not been adhered to in a particular case.

Again we find a few major trading nations who place virtually no restrictions on leading and lagging. These are the United States, Canada and Germany and, currently, the UK. Table 12.3 presents the rules applying to several countries in 1980. These rules are subject to frequent changes. The journal *Business International Money Report* provides a list of exchange control limits on leading, lagging and netting.

EXCHANGE CONTROL AND EXPORT CONTRACTS

The terms of payment are set out in the export contract. The exporter should verify that these terms do not break the exchange control regulations of the government at either end. The terms which may be affected by exchange control regulations concern such things as currency denomination of contract, timing of payments, the right to place an amount at credit for a non-resident, the use of the proceeds from the contract, validation of value, financing contract, licensing procedure and so on. The rules of payment for export and import are usually available from the commercial section of the foreign consulate (see questionnaire in Appendix 12A to this chapter).

Exchange Control Strategy on Foreign Investment

If a corporation is contemplating an investment in a foreign country, an important preliminary step must be to study the exchange control regulations of that country. The rules regarding the transfer of value out of the foreign country are as relevant to the project's implementation as the analysis of its economic viability. Local commercial banks or the commercial section of the country's consulate will normally provide information on this topic, but other sources of information are suggested in the section on p. 254.

Once the current regulations are studied and digested the next step is to examine the trade record of the country concerned with regard to keeping exchange control agreements. If the country is politically unstable, or if strong feeling against 'foreign exploitation' exists, the agreement, unless guaranteed by assets held outside the foreign country, may prove of little value. If the profitability of the project is thought to justify the risk involved the next step is to negotiate an agreement on repatriation of dividends, capital, and any other likely transfers such as technical and R and D costs with the foreign government. The regulations regarding price evaluation of exports and imports should also be carefully negotiated. The rules regarding currency denomination of contracts and swap agreements should be set down.

The company negotiating the agreement would be well advised to have the amounts involved expressed in explicit figures, i.e. '10% of initial capital invested', or 'an amount equal to initial investment denominated in current US dollars'. Vague terms such as 'the government will be sympathetic to higher dividends being paid out if the project is very successful' should be avoided if possible.

An explicit agreement having been drawn up, the final step should be to study the options available to hedge losses if the agreement is abrogated unilaterally. A wide range of guarantees are available to cover foreign blocking or expropriation of assets. Apart from conventional insurance, many governments have set up export and investment guarantee agencies, i.e. ECGD (UK), ExImbank (USA). These guarantees, if available, in effect absorb a good part of the exchange transfer risk. Finally it may be well worthwhile examining alternative local outlets for blocked dividend income. The foreign government may be sympathetic to repatriating income in the form of increased exports which do not damage the balance of payments and provide local employment. Alternatively, it may be permitted to invest blocked currency in specified government bonds the value of which can be repatriated when they mature.

Finding out about Exchange Control Regulations

Exchange control regulations are changed so frequently that the enquirer should first attempt to grasp the general principles of exchange control such as those outlined in this chapter and then proceed to more detailed expositions depending on the degree of detail required. The official exchange control regulations are usually embodied in a legislative act but legal presentations of this nature are usually too broad to be helpful.

The Annual Report on Exchange Restrictions published by the International Monetary Fund provides a useful overall scan of exchange controls on a global basis. The publication covers 130 of the 158 sovereign states of the world, the main exceptions being certain Communist states, in particular the Soviet Union. For a more detailed description of exchange control restrictions, one needs to gain access to the current list of exchange control regulation pamphlets from the relevant central bank.

Before October 1979, in the UK the Bank of England provided an Exchange Control Manual and sent current updates to authorized banks and depositories. The library of the various accounting institutes keeps an updated record of current regulations in the UK. Naturally, the foreign departments of the commercial banks keep updated files on current regulations and will provide advice to clients on everyday matters regarding exchange control. Everett (1976) was a useful text on UK exchange control regulations at that time and Anthony Parker's *Exchange Control* published annually provides a current update on the UK situation. Several legal firms and professional accountants provide specialist advice on exchange control tactics. This applies to most countries outside the communist block.

In many developing countries it is not at all easy to keep up to date on current exchange control regulations. There is inconsistency of treatment between cases and dubious ethical practices can affect decisions. But these strictures apply to a much wider area than exchange control. It will usually pay to employ the somewhat expensive services of an expert on these matters in the country concerned.

REVIEW QUESTIONS

1. Why do governments impose exchange control regulations to impede the operation of the free market? What benefits do they expect to gain?

2. Who has ultimate responsibility for exchange control in most countries? What is the chain of command between this point and the commercial banks?

3. What is an authorized depository for the purposes of exchange control?

4. What are the four aspects of foreign exchange transactions which are controlled by the exchange control regulations?

5. What is a currency zone for the purposes of exchange control? Give two examples.

6. Describe the usual rules for obtaining foreign currency to pay for the import of a trading good by a corporation trading in that good.

7. Explain what is meant by denomination, validation and differential rates with regard to imports.

8. Why are the exchange control rules regarding exports so much less restrictive than those regarding imports?

9. Explain the difference between direct and portfolio investment.

10. What advantages did super-criterion investment enjoy in the UK before July 1979?

11. Describe alternative methods of investing in direct investment abroad (rather than buying investment currency) if a multicurrency system is operating.

12. What is a back-to-back loan?

13. What were the more important provisions of the package which relaxed exchange control restrictions in the UK in July 1979?

14. What is a multiple currency? Give two examples.

15. How did the investment currency market work in the UK? If the quoted premium is 40% what is the effective premium if the rate of exchange is £1 for $2.20?

16. Describe three methods by which a subsidiary can transmit value out of a country which prohibits sending the value in the form of dividend payment.

17. Suppose you are given the job of negotiating a profit expatriation agreement with the government department in a developing country. List the most important points for negotiation.

18. Who is likely to be the guarantor of last resort in the UK and USA with regard to foreign contracts?

19. If your foreign bank account is blocked what actions can you take to retrieve the money?

20. To avoid exchange control regulations you decide to raise a $100 million loan through a subsidiary in a tax haven. What problems might arise?

21. How can you find out about the exchange control regulations for a given country?

BIBLIOGRAPHY

Bank of England,* *Exchange Control Manual,* Annually.

Bank of England (1967), 'The UK exchange control. A short history,' *Quarterly Bulletin,* Vol. 7, September.

Everett A.C. (1976), 'A Guide to UK Exchange Control.' *Accounts Digest No. 37,* London, Institute of Chartered Accountants in England and Wales.

Evitt H.E. (1945), * *Exchange and Trade Control.* London, Pitman.

International Monetary Fund (1978), *Annual Report on Exchange Restrictions. Washington,* IMF, 520 pp. Annually.

McRae T.W. (1978),* 'Exchange control restrictions on UK resident companies'. *Managerial Finance,* Vol. 4, No. 2.

Parker A. *Exchange Control* (Update Service). London, Jordans, Annually.

Sibley A. (1977),* 'The investment currency premium', *The Accounting Magazine,* October, p. 424.

Swidrowski J. (1975), *Exchange and Trade Controls.* London, Gower Press.

Wooley P.K. (1977),* 'The UK Investment Currency Market.' *IMF Staff Papers,* Vol. 24, No. 3, November.

*A good part of these publications became obsolete when the UK abolished almost all exchange controls on 23 October 1979. However they are of historical interest and controls may be reintroduced at some time in the future.

APPENDIX 12A

Questionnaire on Exchange Control

1. Administration of exchange control.
   1.1. What is the address of the authority who administers exchange control regulations for:
      1.1.1. Exports and imports.
      1.1.2. Capital transactions.
      1.1.3. Property.
   1.2. What documentation is required to acquire foreign currency for:
      1.2.1. Exports and imports.
      1.2.2. Capital transactions.
   1.3. Is exchange control delegated from the central bank? If so to whom? On what transactions?
      1.3.1. Current transactions.
      1.3.2. Capital transactions.

2. Currency zones.
   2.1. Is the world divided up into different currency zones for exchange control purposes?
   2.2. Define these zones and the rules applying to each.

3. Residence.
   3.1. Set down the precise rules which define residence and non-residence for the purpose of exchange control.
   3.2. What are the advantages/disadvantages of residence?
   3.3. What are the advantages/disadvantages of non-residence?
   3.4. How does tax definition of residence differ from exchange control definition of residence?
   3.5. What permission is needed to open an account for a non-resident in your companies' books?

4. Currency markets.
   4.1. What is the procedure for dealing in the spot market? What permissions are needed?
   4.2. Does a forward market exist in this currency? What are the rules for operating in this market?
   4.3. Must profits on forward trading be declared? Given up? Are they taxed?

4.4. Are bilateral currency agreements in existence? What are the rules regarding dealing in bilateral currencies?

4.5. Does a multiple currency market exist? What are the names of each type of currency (official, free market, investment, financial)? What rules govern the buying and selling of each type of currency?

5. Bank accounts.

5.1. What are the rules regarding opening a bank account?

5.2. What various types of bank account exist for exchange control purposes (resident, non-resident, external, blocked)?

5.3. What are the rules regarding the movement of funds into and out of these accounts?

5.4. What are the rules regarding convertibility of currencies?

5.5. What interest rates are allowed on non-resident accounts?

6. Imports.

6.1. Is an import licence needed?

6.2. Is a general import licence obtainable or must specific import licences be obtained for each transaction?

6.3. How does the import authority differentiate between a visible and invisible import?

6.4. What documentation is needed to support a claim for foreign currency from a bank?

6.5. Can the import contract be denominated in any currency or is the currency restricted (i.e. to a bilateral deal currency)?

6.6. Must the value of the import be validated? What is the procedure for this?

6.7. What are the rules regarding the timing of payments for imports? Advance deposits can be paid how many months before delivery and to what percentage of value? Payments can be delayed for how long after delivery?

6.8. What is the waiting time before currency is released by bank after transaction validated?

6.9. What are the rules, if any, regarding the financing of the import transaction?

6.10. Are there any hidden charges on imports (i.e. prior interest from deposits, differential exchange rates) apart from normal import duties?

6.11. Is there a list of prohibited imports, or import countries?

7. Exports.

7.1. Is a general or specific export licence needed for this transaction?

7.2. Do the exchange control regulations differentiate between a visible and invisible export?

7.3. Can the export contract be denominated in any currency?

7.4. What are the rules regarding timing of payment in the exporting and importing country?

7.5. What are the arrangements regarding method of payment? Are these in accord with exchange control regulations?

7.6. Are hidden subsidies available on exports (i.e. differential exchange rates, equivalent import value licences)?

7.7. Is the exporter permitted to open a credit account for the importer without permission? How is permission granted?

7.8. Can the proceeds from the export deal be sent directly to the exporter or must it be sent via the central bank?

7.9. Are limitations placed on the uses to which the proceeds from export can be put?

7.10. Is there a list of prohibited exports or countries to which exports are prohibited?

8. Capital.

8.1. Foreign investment is classified into how many categories? How is each category defined?

8.2. What exchange control limitations, if any, are applied to each category?

8.3. The cash to finance foreign investment may be raised from what sources?

8.4. What are the rules regarding repatriation of dividends and capital?

8.5. Re direct investment:

8.5.1. Is direct investment permitted? In this industry?

8.5.2. What are the rules regarding the percentage of foreign control of local companies?

8.5.3. Are certain foreign investments given privileged treatment? What are these privileges?

8.6. Re portfolio investment:

8.6.1. Is this type of investment permitted?

8.6.2. Is investment limited to certain shares?

8.6.3. Can such securities be treated in the foreign country?

8.6.4. At what percentage control does portfolio investment become direct investment?

8.6.5. Must portfolio investment be conducted through a local investment company?

8.6.6. Do special rules apply to tax haven investment?

8.7. Re borrowing abroad:

8.7.1. What are the rules regarding borrowing by non-residents?

8.7.2. What rules apply if foreign investment income is unable to service debt or repay loan?

8.7.3. Are limitations placed on rate of interest paid?

8.7.4. How is repatriation of loans guaranteed?

8.7.5. Are minimum and maximum periods placed on length of loan?

8.7.6. What controls are placed on intercompany indebtedness across frontiers?

8.7.7. What are the tax deduction rules concerning payment of interest to non-residents?

APPENDIX 12B

Exchange Control Restrictions by Country 31 Dec 78 (in most cases)

Key and Footnotes

- ● indicates that practice exists.
- — indicates that practice does not exist.
- ⊕ indicates that position is undetermined.
- ▫ indicates that the composite is the SDR

[1] Practices indicated as existing do not necessarily apply to all transactions.

[2] In most cases, December 31, 1978. Where the date is a different one, this is indicated in a footnote.

[3] Country had not yet opted for Article VIII or Article XIV by December 31, 1978.

[4] Margins of approximately 2.25 per cent either side of parity.

[5] Restrictions on payments to member countries in the form of quantitative limits or undue delay, other than restrictions imposed for security reasons.

[6] Resident-owned funds.

[7] The import surcharges do not affect any items bound under the GATT nor any items negotiated with LAFTA countries.

[8] Position on January 1, 1979.

	Afghanistan	Algeria	Argentina	Australia	Austria	Bahamas	Bahrain	Bangladesh	Barbados	Belgium & Luxembourg	Benin	Bolivia	Botswana	Brazil[7]	Burma	Burundi
1 Article VIII status	−	−	●	●	●	●	●	−	−	●	−	●	−	−	−	−
2 Article XIV status	●	●	−	−	−	−	−	●	●	−	●	−	●	●	●	●
3 Exchange rate maintained within relatively narrow margins[4] in terms of:																
(a) U.S. dollar	−	−	−	−	−	●	−	−	●	●	−	●	●	−	−	●
(b) sterling	−	−	−	−	−	−	●	−	−	−	−	−	−	−	−	−
(c) French franc	−	−	−	−	−	−	−	−	−	−	●	−	−	−	−	−
(d) Australian dollar, Portuguese escudo, South African rand, or Spanish peseta	−	−	−	−	−	−	−	−	−	−	−	−	−	−	−	−
(e) a group of currencies (under mutual intervention arrangements)	−	−	−	−	−	−	−	−	−	●	−	−	−	−	−	−
(f) a composite of currencies	−	●	−	−	●	−	−	−	−	−	−	−	−	□ ●	−	−
(g) a set of indicators	−	−	●	−	−	−	−	−	−	−	−	−	−	●	−	−
4 Exchange rate not maintained within relatively narrow margins as in (a)–(g) above	●	−	−	●	−	●	−	−	−	−	−	−	−	−	−	−
5 Special exchange rate regime for some or all capital transactions and/or some or all invisibles	●	●	−	−	−	●	−	●	−	●	−	●	−	−	●	−
6 Import rate(s) different from export rate(s)	●	−	−	−	−	−	−	●	−	−	−	−	−	●	−	−
7 More than one rate for imports	●	−	−	−	−	−	−	●	−	●	−	−	−	−	−	−
8 More than one rate for exports	●	−	−	−	−	−	−	−	−	●	−	−	−	●	−	−
9 Restrictions exist on payments in respect of current transactions[5]	●	●	−	−	−	−	−	●	●	−	−	−	−	●	●	●
10 Restrictions exist on payments in respect of capital transactions[5,6]	●	●	●	●	●	●	−	●	●	−	●	−	⊕	●	●	●
11 Prescription of currency	●	●	●	●	−	−	−	●	●	●	●	−	●	●	●	●
12 Bilateral payments arrangements with members	−	●	−	−	−	−	●	−	−	−	−	−	−	●	−	●
13 Bilateral payments arrangements with non members	●	●	−	−	−	−	●	−	−	−	−	●	−	●	−	−
14 Import surcharges	●	−	●	−	−	●	−	−	−	−	−	−	●	●	−	●
15 Advance import deposits	●	−	−	−	−	−	−	−	−	−	−	●	−	●	−	−
16 Surrender of export proceeds required.	●	●	●	●	−	−	−	●	●	●	●	●	●	●	●	●

	Cameroon	Canada	Cape Verde[3]	Central African Empire	Chad	Chile	China, Republic of	Colombia	Comoros[3]	Congo	Costa Rica	Cyprus	Denmark	Djibouti[3]	Dominica[3]	Dominican Republic
1 Article VIII status	—	•	—	—	—	•	—	—	—	—	•	—	•	•	—	•
2 Article XIV status	•	—	—	•	•	—	•	•	—	•	—	•	—	—	—	—
3 Exchange rate maintained within relatively narrow margins[4] in terms of:																
(a) U.S. dollar	—	—	—	—	—	—	•	—	—	—	—	—	—	•	•	•
(b) sterling	—	—	—	—	—	—	—	—	—	—	—	—	—	—	—	—
(c) French franc	•	—	—	•	•	—	—	—	•	•	—	—	—	—	—	—
(d) Australian dollar, Portuguese escudo, South African rand, or Spanish peseta	—	—	—	—	—	—	—	—	—	—	—	—	—	—	—	—
(e) a group of currencies (under mutual intervention arrangements)	—	—	—	—	—	—	—	—	—	—	—	—	•	—	—	—
(f) a composite of currencies	—	—	•	—	—	—	—	—	—	—	•	•	—	—	—	—
(g) a set of indicators	—	—	—	—	—	•	—	•	—	—	—	—	—	—	—	—
4 Exchange rate not maintained within relatively narrow margins as in (a)—(g) above	—	•	—	—	—	—	—	—	—	—	—	—	—	—	—	—
5 Special exchange rate regime for some or all capital transactions and/or some or all invisibles	—	—	—	—	—	—	—	—	—	—	•	—	—	—	•	•
6 Import rate(s) different from export rate(s)	—	—	—	—	—	—	•	—	—	—	—	—	—	—	•	•
7 More than one rate for imports	—	—	—	—	—	—	•	—	—	—	—	—	—	—	•	•
8 More than one rate for exports	—	—	—	—	—	—	•	—	—	—	—	—	—	—	—	—
9 Restrictions exist on payments in respect of current transactions[5]	—	—	•	—	—	—	•	•	•	•	—	•	—	—	•	•
10 Restrictions exist on payments in respect of capital transactions[5,6]	•	—	•	•	•	•	•	•	•	•	•	•	•	—	•	•
11 Prescription of currency	•	—	•	•	•	•	•	•	•	•	•	•	•	—	•	—
12 Bilateral payments arrangements with members	—	—	•	—	—	—	•	—	—	—	•	—	—	—	—	—
13 Bilateral payments arrangements with non members	—	—	•	—	—	—	—	•	—	•	•	•	—	—	—	—
14 Import surcharges	—	—	—	—	—	—	—	•	—	—	°	•	•	—	—	•
15 Advance import deposits	—	—	—	—	—	•	•	—	—	—	—	—	—	—	—	•
16 Surrender of export proceeds required,	•	—	•	•	•	•	•	•	•	•	•	•	•	•	—	•

Ecuador	Egypt[8]	El Salvador	Equatorial Guinea	Ethiopia	Fiji	Finland	France	Gabon	The Gambia	Germany, Fed. Rep. of	Ghana	Greece	Grenada	Guatemala	Guinea	Guinea-Bissau	Guyana	Haiti	Honduras	Hong Kong	Iceland	India	Indonesia	Iran	Iraq	Ireland
●	–	●	–	–	●	–	●	–	–	●	–	–	–	●	–	–	●	●	●	●	–	–	–	–	–	●
–	●	–	●	●	–	●	–	●	●	–	●	●	●	–	●	●	●	–	–	–	–	●	●	●	●	–
●	●	●	–	●	–	–	–	–	–	●	●	●	–	●	●	●	–	●	●	●	–	–	–	–	●	–
–	–	–	–	–	–	–	–	–	●	–	–	–	–	–	–	–	–	–	–	–	–	–	–	–	–	●
–	–	–	–	–	–	–	–	●	–	–	–	–	–	–	–	–	–	–	–	–	–	–	–	–	–	–
–	–	–	–	–	–	–	–	–	–	●	–	–	–	–	–	–	–	–	–	–	–	–	–	–	–	–
–	–	–	●	–	●	●	–	–	–	–	–	–	–	–	□	□	–	–	–	–	●	–	–	–	–	–
–	–	–	●	–	●	●	–	–	–	–	–	–	–	–	●	●	–	–	–	–	●	–	–	–	–	–
–	–	–	–	–	–	–	●	–	–	●	–	●	●	–	–	–	–	●	●	–	●	●	–	–	–	–
●	●	–	●	–	●	–	–	–	●	–	–	●	–	–	–	–	–	–	–	–	●	–	–	●	–	–
–	●	–	–	●	–	–	–	–	●	–	–	●	–	●	–	–	–	–	–	–	–	–	–	–	–	–
–	●	–	–	●	–	–	–	–	●	–	–	●	–	–	–	–	–	–	–	–	–	–	–	●	–	–
–	●	–	–	–	–	–	–	–	●	–	–	–	–	–	–	–	–	–	–	–	–	–	–	●	–	–
–	●	●	–	●	●	–	–	–	–	–	●	●	●	–	●	●	●	–	●	●	–	●	●	–	●	–
–	●	●	●	●	●	●	●	●	●	–	●	●	●	–	●	●	●	⊕	–	–	●	●	–	●	●	●
●	●	●	–	●	–	●	–	–	–	–	●	–	–	–	–	–	–	–	–	–	●	●	–	●	–	●
●	●	–	●	–	–	–	●	–	–	–	–	–	–	–	●	–	–	–	–	–	–	–	●	–	●	–
●	●	–	–	●	–	●	–	–	–	–	–	–	●	–	–	–	–	–	●	●	–	●	–	●	–	–
●	●	●	–	–	–	–	–	●	–	–	●	–	●	●	–	–	●	●	–	●	●	–	●	●	●	–
●	–	●	–	–	–	–	●	●	–	–	–	–	–	–	●	–	–	●	–	–	●	–	–	●	–	–
●	●	●	●	●	●	–	●	●	●	–	●	●	–	–	●	●	●	–	●	–	●	–	●	●	–	●

	Israel	Italy	Ivory Coast	Jamaica	Japan	Jordan	Kenya	Korea	Kuwait	Laos People's Dem. Rep.	Lebanon	Lesotho	Liberia	Libyan Arab Jamahiriya	Madagascar	Malawi
1 Article VIII status	—	•	—	•	•	—	—	—	•	—	—	—	—	—	—	—
2 Article XIV status	•	—	•	—	—	•	•	•	—	•	•	•	•	•	•	•
3 Exchange rate maintained within relatively narrow margins[4] in terms of:																
(a) U.S. dollar	—	—	—	—	—	—	—	—	•	—	•	—	•	•	—	—
(b) sterling	—	—	—	—	—	—	—	—	—	—	—	—	—	—	—	—
(c) French franc	—	—	•	—	—	—	—	—	—	—	—	—	—	—	•	—
(d) Australian dollar, Portuguese escudo, South African rand, or Spanish peseta	—	—	—	—	—	—	—	—	—	—	—	•	—	—	—	—
(e) a group of currencies (under mutual intervention arrangements)	—	—	—	—	—	—	—	—	—	—	—	—	—	—	—	—
(f) a composite of currencies	—	—	—	—	—	□•	□•	—	•	—	—	—	—	—	—	□•
(g) a set of indicators	—	—	—	—	—	—	—	—	—	—	—	—	—	—	—	—
4 Exchange rate not maintained within relatively narrow margins as in (a)–(g) above	•	•	—	•	•	—	—	—	—	•	—	—	—	—	—	—
5 Special exchange rate regime for some or all capital transactions and/or some or all invisibles	—	•	—	•	—	—	—	—	—	—	—	—	—	—	—	—
6 Import rate(s) different from export rate(s)	—	—	—	•	—	—	—	—	—	—	—	—	—	—	—	—
7 More than one rate for imports	—	—	—	•	—	—	—	—	—	—	—	—	—	—	—	—
8 More than one rate for exports	—	—	—	—	—	—	—	—	—	—	—	—	—	—	—	—
9 Restrictions exist on payments in respect of current transactions[5]	—	•	—	•	—	•	•	—	—	•	—	—	—	—	•	•
10 Restrictions exist on payments in respect of capital transactions[5,6]	•	•	•	•	•	•	•	•	—	•	—	•	—	•	•	•
11 Prescription of currency	•	•	•	—	—	•	—	•	—	•	—	•	—	—	•	—
12 Bilateral payments arrangements with members	—	—	—	—	—	•	—	—	—	—	•	—	—	—	—	—
13 Bilateral payments arrangements with non members	—	—	—	—	—	—	—	—	—	•	•	—	—	—	—	—
14 Import surcharges	—	—	—	—	—	•	—	•	—	—	•	•	—	•	—	•
15 Advance import deposits	—	—	—	—	—	—	•	•	—	—	—	—	—	•	—	—
16 Surrender of export proceeds required.	•	•	•	•	—	•	•	•	—	•	—	•	—	•	•	•

Malaysia	Maldives[3]	Mali	Malta	Mauritania	Mauritius	Mexico	Morocco	Nepal	Netherlands	Netherlands Antilles	New Zealand	Nicaragua	Niger	Nigeria	Norway[8]	Oman	Pakistan	Panama	Papua New Guinea	Paraguay	Peru[8]	Philippines	Portugal	Qatar	Romania
•	–	–	–	–	–	•	–	–	•	•	–	•	–	–	•	•	–	•	•	–	•	–	–	•	–
–	–	•	•	•	•	–	•	•	–	–	•	–	•	•	–	–	•	–	–	•	–	•	•	–	•
–	•	–	–	–	–	•	–	•	–	•	–	•	–	–	•	•	•	–	•	–	–	–	–	–	•
–	–	–	–	–	–	–	–	–	–	–	–	–	–	–	–	–	–	–	–	–	–	–	–	–	–
–	–	•	–	–	–	–	–	–	–	•	–	•	–	–	–	–	–	–	–	–	–	–	–	–	–
–	–	–	–	–	–	–	–	–	–	–	–	–	–	–	–	–	–	–	–	–	–	–	–	–	–
–	–	–	–	–	•	–	–	–	–	–	–	–	–	–	–	–	–	–	–	–	–	–	–	–	–
•	–	–	•	•	□	–	•	–	–	–	–	•	–	–	–	•	–	–	•	–	–	–	–	–	–
–	–	–	–	–	–	–	–	–	–	–	–	–	–	–	–	–	–	–	–	–	•	–	•	–	–
–	–	–	–	–	•	–	–	–	–	–	–	•	–	–	–	–	–	–	–	–	•	–	•	–	–
–	•	–	–	–	•	–	–	–	•	–	–	–	–	–	–	–	–	•	•	–	–	–	–	–	•
•	–	–	–	–	•	–	–	–	•	–	–	–	–	–	–	–	–	•	•	–	–	–	–	–	–
–	–	–	–	–	•	–	–	–	•	–	–	–	–	–	–	–	–	•	–	–	–	–	–	–	•
–	–	•	•	•	•	–	•	•	–	–	•	•	•	•	–	•	–	–	–	–	–	•	•	–	•
–	–	•	•	•	–	–	•	•	–	•	–	•	•	•	–	•	–	•	–	•	–	•	•	–	•
•	–	•	–	•	•	–	•	•	–	•	–	–	–	•	•	–	–	•	•	–	•	•	•	–	•
–	–	•	–	–	–	•	–	–	–	–	–	–	–	•	–	–	–	–	–	–	–	–	–	–	•
–	–	•	–	–	–	•	•	–	–	–	–	–	–	•	–	–	–	–	•	–	–	–	–	–	•
•	–	–	–	•	•	–	•	•	–	•	–	–	–	–	•	•	–	•	•	–	•	•	–	•	–
–	–	–	–	–	•	–	–	–	–	–	–	–	•	–	–	–	•	–	•	–	–	•	–	–
•	–	•	•	•	•	–	•	•	–	•	•	•	•	•	•	–	•	–	•	•	•	•	•	–	•

	Rwanda	Sao Tomé & Principe	Saudi Arabia	Senegal	Seychelles	Sierra Leone	Singapore	Solomon Islands[3]	Somalia	South Africa	Spain	Sri Lanka	Sudan	Surinam	Swaziland
1 Article VIII status	−	−	●	−	●	−	●	−	−	●	−	−	−	●	−
2 Article XIV status	●	●	−	●	−	●	−	−	●	−	●	●	●	−	●
3 Exchange rate maintained within relatively narrow margins[4] in terms of: (a) U.S. dollar	●	−	−	−	−	−	−	−	●	●	−	−	●	●	−
(b) sterling	−	−	−	−	●	−	−	−	−	−	−	−	−	−	−
(c) French franc	−	−	−	●	−	−	−	−	−	−	−	−	−	−	−
(d) Australian dollar, Portuguese escudo, South African rand, or Spanish peseta	−	−	−	−	−	−	−	●	−	−	−	−	−	−	●
(e) a group of currencies (under mutual intervention arrangements)	−	−	−	−	−	−	−	−	−	−	−	−	−	−	−
(f) a composite of currencies	−	□●	−	−	−	□●	●	−	−	−	−	−	−	−	−
(g) a set of indicators	−	−	−	−	−	−	−	−	−	−	−	−	−	−	−
4 Exchange rate not maintained within relatively narrow margins as in (a)−(g) above	−	−	●	−	−	−	−	−	−	●	●	−	−	−	−
5 Special exchange rate regime for some or all capital transactions and/or some or all invisibles	−	−	−	−	−	−	−	−	−	●	−	−	●	−	−
6 Import rate(s) different from export rate(s)	−	−	−	−	−	−	−	−	●	●	−	−	−	−	−
7 More than one rate for imports	−	−	−	−	−	−	−	−	●	−	−	−	−	−	−
8 More than one rate for exports	−	−	−	−	−	−	−	−	●	●	−	−	●	−	−
9 Restrictions exist on payments in respect of current transactions[5]	●	●	−	−	−	●	−	−	●	●	−	−	●	−	−
10 Restrictions exist on payments in respect of capital transactions[5,6]	●	●	−	●	−	●	−	−	●	●	●	●	●	●	●
11 Prescription of currency	●	●	−	●	−	●	−	−	●	●	●	●	●	●	●
12 Bilateral payments arrangements with members	●	●	−	−	−	−	−	−	−	−	●	●	●	−	−
13 Bilateral payments arrangements with non members	−	●	−	−	−	●	−	−	●	−	−	●	−	−	−
14 Import surcharges	−	−	−	−	−	●	●	−	−	●	−	−	●	●	●
15 Advance import deposits	−	−	−	−	−	−	−	−	−	−	−	−	●	−	−
16 Surrender of export proceeds required.	●	●	−	●	−	●	−	●	●	●	●	●	●	●	●

Sweden	Syrian Arab Rep.	Tanzania	Thailand	Togo	Trinidad & Tobago	Tunisia	Turkey[8]	Uganda	United Arab Emirates	United Kingdom (1978)	United States	Upper Volta	Uruguay	Venezuela	Viet Nam	Western Samoa	Yemen Arab Rep.	Yemen, Peop. Dem. Rep.	Yugoslavia	Zaire	Zambia
●	—	—	—	—	—	—	—	—	●	●	●	—	—	●	—	—	—	—	—	—	—
—	●	●	●	●	●	●	●	●	—	—	—	●	●	—	●	●	●	●	●	●	●
—	●	—	—	—	●	—	—	—	—	—	—	—	●	—	—	●	●	—	—	—	—
—	—	—	—	—	—	—	—	—	—	—	—	—	—	—	—	—	—	—	—	—	—
—	—	—	●	—	—	—	—	—	—	—	—	●	—	—	—	—	—	—	—	—	—
—	—	—	—	—	—	—	—	—	—	—	—	—	—	—	—	—	—	—	—	—	—
—	—	—	—	—	—	—	—	—	—	—	—	—	—	—	—	—	—	—	—	—	—
●	—	□	●	—	—	●	—	□	□	—	—	—	—	□	●	—	—	—	□	□	—
—	—	—	—	—	—	—	—	—	—	—	—	●	—	—	—	—	—	—	—	—	—
—	—	—	—	—	—	—	●	—	—	●	●	—	—	—	—	—	—	●	—	—	—
—	—	—	—	—	—	—	●	—	—	●	—	—	●	●	●	—	—	—	—	—	—
—	—	—	—	—	—	—	●	—	—	—	—	●	—	—	●	—	—	—	●	—	—
—	—	—	—	—	—	—	●	—	—	—	—	●	—	—	—	—	—	—	●	—	—
—	●	●	—	—	●	●	●	—	—	—	—	—	●	●	—	●	—	●	●	●	●
●	●	●	●	●	●	●	●	—	●	—	●	●	—	●	●	—	●	●	●	●	●
—	●	●	—	●	●	●	●	—	●	—	●	●	—	●	●	—	—	●	●	●	●
—	●	—	—	—	●	—	—	—	—	—	—	●	—	—	—	—	—	—	●	●	—
—	●	—	—	—	●	—	—	—	—	—	—	●	—	—	—	—	—	—	●	—	—
—	●	●	—	—	●	●	—	—	—	●	●	—	●	—	●	—	●	●	●	●	—
—	—	—	—	—	—	—	●	—	—	—	—	—	—	—	—	—	—	●	—	—	—
—	●	●	●	●	●	●	●	—	●	—	●	●	—	●	●	—	●	—	●	—	●

Glossary

Accounting (or Translation) Exposure
This arises from the process of consolidating foreign currency items into the parent-currency-denominated group financial statements. It consists essentially of those foreign currency assets, liabilities, revenues and expenses which are consolidated at current exchange rates.

All-Current (Closing Rate) Method
A foreign currency translation method: all foreign currency items are translated at current exchange rates.

Arbitrage
When a product is traded in several different markets it must trade at the same price (allowing for transport costs) in each market if free trading between the markets is permitted. Arbitrage is that activity which eliminates temporary rate discrepancies between different foreign exchange markets. *Arbitrageurs* buy in the low cost market and sell in the high cost — thus spot and forward rates in different markets are forced towards a common price.

Authorized Dealer
A dealer who is authorized by the monetary authority of the country concerned to engage in certain specified foreign exchange activities. The activities are mainly concerned with exchange control.

271

Balance Sheet Exposure

This arises from the process of translating foreign currency balance sheet items into the parent-currency-denominated group financial statements. This is one of the two components of Accounting Exposure — the other is Income Statement Exposure.

Best Order

An order to an agent or dealer to buy or sell an amount of foreign currency at the best price available. No rate limit is stipulated.

Bid Rate

The rate of exchange at which a foreign exchange dealer will buy a currency.

Bilateral Netting

A pair of affiliated companies regularly offset their receipts and payments with each other, so that a single net intercompany receipt or payment is made between the pair in each period. *See* Netting and Multilateral Netting.

Blocked Account

The bank account of a non-resident of a country, where the amount of currency in the account cannot be transferred to another country or currency without special permission.

Broker

A broker *arranges* the buying or selling of currencies between third parties, usually banks. He does not buy or sell currency on his own account.

Brokerage

Commission charged by a broker for his services.

Business Day (also Banking Day, Clear Day, Market Day and Open Day)

Any day on which a foreign exchange contract can be settled, i.e. the banks at both ends of the deal must be open for business that day.

Buyer's Option

The owner of a buyer's option can take delivery of the currency contract at any time between the dates specified in the option. *See* Optional Date Forward Contract.

Cash Flow (or Economic) Exposure
This is concerned with the effect of currency changes on the parent currency value of the future cash flows generated by a company's foreign operations.

Closing Exchange Rate
The exchange rate prevailing at a financial reporting date.

Confirmation
This is the written document confirming the verbal foreign exchange contract agreed by telephone between dealer and dealer or dealer and client.

Convertible Currency
A currency which can be converted into another currency without special permission of exchange control authority.

Covered Interest Arbitrage
Borrowing one currency, converting the proceeds into another currency where it is invested, and simultaneously selling this other currency forward against the initial currency. Covered interest arbitrage takes advantage of — and in practice quickly eliminates — any temporary discrepancies between the forward rate and the interest rate differential of two currencies.

Covering
Protecting the value of the future proceeds of an international trade transaction, usually by buying or selling the proceeds in the forward market.

Cross Rate
The rate of exchange between two foreign currencies. For example, when a dealer in New York buys (or sells) Italian lira for French francs, he uses a cross rate.

Current Exchange Rate
The exchange rate ruling at the balance sheet date or during the income statement period.

Current/Non-Current Method
A foreign currency translation method: current balance sheet items denominated in foreign currencies are translated at current exchange rates and long-term items at historical rates.

Dealer (or Trader)   Specialist in a bank or corporation who is authorized to effect exchange transactions. He usually attempts to keep his book in balance but may be allowed to take a position.

Direct Quotation   A rate of exchange quoted as n units of foreign currency per one unit of the home currency (*see* Indirect Quotation).

Discounting   Where a sale is to be settled by bill of exchange, the seller can 'discount' with a financial institution and receive payment before the receivable settlement date.

Economic Exposure   *See* Cash Flow Exposure.

Euro-currency   Currency held by non-residents and placed on deposit with banks outside the country of the currency, e.g. US dollars owned by a Middle East country and deposited in London.

Euro-dollars   US dollars held by anyone who is not a resident of the United States and deposited outside the United States. These are mostly deposited in Western Europe.

Exchange Contract   A contract to exchange one foreign currency for a given amount of another on a given date.

Export Finance Vehicle   A vehicle company set up to buy the export receivables of affiliated companies. Export finance companies perform exposure and/ or liquidity management functions. *See* Intermediary Company.

External Exposure Management Techniques   Specific contractual arrangements, 'external' to the firm, which are designed to reduce or eliminate an existing exposure. Examples of external techniques are forward exchange contracts, foreign currency borrowing, discounting, factoring and government exchange risk guarantees.

Factoring   A financing method where the borrower assigns his customer receivables as collateral.

Fisher Effect   *See* the Interest Rate Theory of Exchange Rate Expectations.

Fixed Exchange Rate The monetary authority of a country agrees to keep the value of their currency within a given percentage of the fixed value of certain other currencies.

Floating Exchange Rate The exchange rate of a currency is allowed to find its own level depending on the demand and supply for the currency.

Forward Contract   A contract to exchange a given amount of one currency for another at some future date. Usually at one, three, or six months ahead.

Forward Discount   Under the direct quotation system, if the forward value of a foreign currency is at a discount to the home currency, it is weaker than the home currency.

Forward/Forward Swap (or Forward Swap) A pair of forward exchange deals involving a forward purchase and a forward sale of a currency, simultaneously entered into, but of different maturities.

Forward Margin   The difference between the forward rate and the spot rate of a currency. The forward margin is either at a discount or a premium to the spot rate.

Forward Market   The future market in foreign exchange.

Forward Option Contract *See* Optional Date Forward Contract.

Forward Premium   The excess of the forward rate above the spot rate (*see* Forward discount).

Forward Swap   *See* Forward/Forward Swap.

Hedging	The protection of the accounting value of foreign currency assets and liabilities against unrealized foreign exchange (translation) losses — by, for example, forward sales or purchases.
Histogramming	A decision making technique which can be applied to interest rate and exchange rate forecasting.
Historical Exchange Rate	The exchange rate ruling at the date an asset or liability was aquired, or at the date of a subsequent change in the accounting valuation of the asset or liability.
Home Currency	*See* Parent Currency.
Host Country	The country in which a foreign subsidiary is located.
Hot Money	Speculative bank deposits which are moved around the international money markets to take advantage of currency and interest rate movements.
Income Statement Exposure	This arises essentially from the process of translating foreign currency income-statement items into the parent-currency-denominated group financial statements. This is one of the two components of Accounting Exposure — the other is Balance Sheet Exposure.
Inconvertible Currency	A currency which cannot be converted into another currency, usually, but not exclusively, because of exchange control regulations.
Indication Rate	This rate tells the enquirer the going exchange rate, but the dealer is not necessarily prepared to deal at exactly this rate.
Indirect Quotation	A rate of exchange quoted as n units of home currency per one unit of foreign currency (*see* Direct Quotation).

Intercompany Trade Trade flows between units (parent, subsidiaries) of the same corporate group.

Interest Parity The process which ensures that forward margins equate the interest rate differentials on equivalent securities in the two financial centers involved (*see* Covered Interest Arbitrage).

Interest Rate Theory of Exchange Rate Expectations (or the Fisher Effect) The difference between the interest rates of two currencies should equal the expected rate of change of the exchange rate during the appropriate maturity period.

Intermediary Company The intermediary acts as a conduit for the transfer of funds between the parent company, its subsidiaries and/or third parties. For exposure management purposes, the two most common types of intermediary company are the export finance vehicle and the re-invoicing vehicle.

Internal Exposure Management Techniques Business-related tactics, 'internal' to the company, which are generally aimed at reducing or preventing an exposed position from arising. Examples include matching, leading and lagging, pricing policies and asset and liability management.

Internal Forward Cover System A system in which central treasury offers operating units guaranteed internal or 'paper' forward rates, and these 'paper' rates are used to evaluate operating management performance. Treasury is left with the decision of whether the company should actually take the market's forward rate or stay uncovered — and is evaluated on this decision.

Leading and Lagging The adjustment of intercompany credit terms, 'leading' meaning a prepayment of a trade obligation and 'lagging' a delayed payment.

Local Currency (LC)	The local currency of a foreign subsidiary.
'Long' Exposure Position	A net asset, net revenue and/or net cash inflow position in a currency. If the currency appreciates a foreign exchange gain is generated; if it depreciates a loss is incurred. The opposite is true of a 'short' position.
Matching (or 'Natural' Matching)	A process whereby a company matches its long positions in a given currency (assets, revenues or cash inflows) with its offsetting short positions in that currency (liabilities, expenses, or cash outflows). The remaining unmatched position is the net exposure in the currency (*see* Parallel Matching).
Maturity (or Settlement) Date	The date on which a foreign exchange contract is due to be settled.
Monetary/Non-Monetary Method	A foreign currency translation method: non-monetary assets and liabilities are translated at their historical exchange rates and monetary items are translated at current exchange rates.
Multilateral Netting	Each member of a corporate group offsets its receipts and payments with the rest of the group as a whole, so that a single net intercompany receipt or payment is made each period (*see* Netting and Bilateral Netting).
Netting	A procedure by which members of a corporate group which has two-way intercompany trade or financial flows pay only the net (rather than the gross) receipt or payment (*see* Bilateral and Multilateral Netting).
Odd Date	Most contracts on the forward market are settled one, three, or six months ahead. Dates outside these standard periods (e.g. 35 days) are called 'odd' dates.

Open (or Net) Position	The difference between the long and short positions in a given currency.
Optional Date Forward Contract (or Forward Option Contract)	A forward exchange contract where the rate is fixed but the maturity is left for the company to decide subsequently, within a specified range of dates (*see* Buyer's Option).
'Parallel' Matching	A long (or short) position in one currency is matched against a short (or long) position in a different currency, since movements in the two currencies are expected to run closely parallel (*see* Matching).
Parent Country	The country in which the parent company is located.
Parent (or Home) Currency	The currency of the parent company.
Parity	The official rate of exchange between two currencies.
Pip	Usually the most junior digit in a currency quotation, i.e. £1 = $2.10365. The fifth place after the decimal point is '5 pips' (*see* Point).
Point	The second most junior digit in currency quotations, i.e. £1 = $2.10365. The fourth place after the decimal point is 6 points (*see* Pip).
Price Adjustment Period	The period taken by a subsidiary to raise its local selling prices in order to offset the adverse effects of an exchange rate change on the parent currency value of the subsidiary's net income or net cash flow.
Purchasing Power Parity (PPP) Theory	This states that, over time, the difference between the inflation rates of two countries tends to equal the rate of change of the exchange rate between their two currencies.

Reinvoicing Vehicle A vehicle company which performs group exposure and/or liquidity management functions. Goods exported from (or imported to) an affiliate company are shipped direct to third-party or affiliate customers but invoicing is performed in the name of the reinvoicing vehicle. Hence title to the goods and payment are channeled through the vehicle.

Roll-Over When a forward exchange contract is about to mature a new forward 'contract' is created to extend the date when payment is due.

'Short' Exposure Position A net liability, net expense or net cash outflow position in a currency. If the currency depreciates a gain is generated; if it appreciates a loss is incurred. The opposite is true of a 'long' position.

Spot/Forward Swaps The simultaneous spot purchase or sale of a currency and an offsetting sale or purchase of the same currency in the forward market.

Spot Market The currency market for 'immediate' delivery. Delivery is usually two working days after transaction date, though in some markets spot transactions may be executed for next day value (*see* Forward Market).

Spot Rate The current rate of exchange quoted between two currencies. The spot rate is usually quoted as a bid rate and an offer rate.

Spread The difference between the buying and selling rate for a currency.

Stop-Loss Order Instruction by a client to a dealer to cover an exposed position if a given currency changes in value by a specified amount. 'Realize Profit Orders' are less common.

Swap	The simultaneous buying and selling of a currency for different maturities. The two types of swap deals are forward/forward swaps and spot/forward swaps.
Temporal Method	A foreign currency translation method, under which the translation rate adopted must preserve the accounting principles used to value assets and liabilities in the original financial statements. Items stated at historical cost are translated at historical exchange rates; the current exchange rate is used for items stated at replacement cost, market value or expected future value.
Third-Party Trade	Trade between companies which are not part of the same corporate group.
Transaction Date	In the foreign exchange market, the date on which a foreign exchange contract is agreed.
Transactions Exposure	The exposure inherent in a foreign currency transaction, both commercial (trade receivables and payables) and financial (dividend and loan payments).
Translation Exposure	*See* Accounting Exposure.
Valeur Compensée	Principle governing foreign exchange transactions: on the contract settlement date payment is made in the two markets on the same day.
Xeno Currency	A new name for Euro-currency. The 'Euro' element is less important now that such deposit markets have been established elsewhere (e.g. the Asian currency market).

Index